In a Guardsman's Boots

In memory of Marjorie

In a Guardsman's Boots

A Boy Soldier's Adventures from
the Streets of 1920s Dublin to
Buckingham Palace, WWII and
the Egyptian Revolution

Paddy & Caroline Rochford

Pen & Sword
MILITARY

First published in Great Britain in 2016 by
Pen & Sword Military
an imprint of
Pen & Sword Books Ltd
47 Church Street
Barnsley
South Yorkshire
S70 2AS

Copyright © Caroline Rochford 2016

ISBN 978 1 47386 391 0

The right of Caroline Rochford to be identified as the Author of this
Work has been asserted by her in accordance with the Copyright,
Designs and Patents Act 1988.

A CIP catalogue record for this book is available from the British
Library

Typeset in Ehrhardt by
Mac Style Ltd, Bridlington, East Yorkshire
Printed and bound in the UK by CPI Group (UK) Ltd,
Croydon, CRO 4YY

Pen & Sword Books Ltd incorporates the imprints of Pen & Sword
Archaeology, Atlas, Aviation, Battleground, Discovery, Family
History, History, Maritime, Military, Naval, Politics, Railways, Select,
Transport, True Crime, Fiction, Frontline Books, Leo Cooper,
Praetorian Press, Seaforth Publishing and Wharncliffe.

For a complete list of Pen & Sword titles please contact
PEN & SWORD BOOKS LIMITED
47 Church Street, Barnsley, South Yorkshire, S70 2AS, England
E-mail: enquiries@pen-and-sword.co.uk
Website: www.pen-and-sword.co.uk

Contents

Acknowledgements

Firstly, special thanks should go to Paddy's late widow, Marjorie, who gave his notes, letters, ephemera and draft manuscript to my husband and me. I'm sorry she never got to see the finished story in print.

To Michael, my husband: what can I say? Your genealogical skills and knowledge of history know no bounds. What would I do without you?

To Phyllis and our extended Irish family: thank you for your hospitality, and for sharing your family tales and photographs with a quartet of strangers who turned up on your doorstep. Also, thank you to Charlie for your thoroughly enjoyable whistle-stop tours of Dublin. You've all helped me to bring Joey's story to life.

To Linne at Pen and Sword: thank you for seeing the potential I could see, when others couldn't.

To Steven Spielberg (in advance!): I'm looking forward to the Hollywood premiere …

Chapter 1

The Royal Hibernian Military School

The sound of marching boots has echoed in my ears since before I can remember. My childhood wish was to follow in my father's footsteps and become a brave soldier; but little did I know back then just how many years I'd march, sweat and fight side by side with the tallest of Guardsmen, in their big boots, whilst I'd always remain small in my little boots. Yet those boots were destined to take me to faraway lands, leading me further and further from my loved ones and the provincial village of Chapelizod, near Dublin, I used to call home so long ago.

The only life my father ever knew was the life of a soldier, spending his days marching across bloody battlefields under many a foreign sun. He survived countless front line combats, from the Second Boer War all the way through to the First World War, until he was discharged and forgotten. Many were the times when hope was failing, but with a strong heart and a love of God, king and country, he marched on until his own last post.

An old, and probably false, family legend tells that we Rochfords are descended from the great eighteenth-century earls of Belvedere. Somewhere along the line our branch of the family tree must have become fractured, for it began to grow along a completely different path. My grandfather, Patrick Rochford, was just a lowly chimney sweep from the mean streets of Dublin. Orphaned in his teens, he survived on the edge of society, stealing a crust of bread whenever he could. Living conditions were bleak for those who had no money, and Patrick died when Father was just two years of age, leaving his widow, Mary, with a young child to feed. The burden of parenthood weighed heavily on her shoulders, and unable to cope, my grandmother left Dad on the doorstep of St Brigid's Orphanage on Eccles Street, never to see him again.

It was a cold winter's morning in 1889 when the scrawny little youth left the home of his adoptive mother, Mrs Glynn, to join the British Army and take the King's shilling, as enlistment was called in those days. Before Father was even strong enough to pick up a rifle, he was placed in a pair of oversized army boots and in a few short years was shipped off to fight in India, where he and his comrades found themselves caught up in the mountains and the Relief

Chapelizod, 17 August 1902: Paddy's parents, Joseph and Annie Rochford, on their wedding day.

Joseph Rochford in his army uniform during the First World War while serving as a sapper with the Royal Engineers. In peacetime he worked for Ordnance Survey in Phoenix Park, Dublin.

of Chitral. For just a shilling a day, he battled through war and campaign for many a long year, before finally leaving behind the friends he'd made in the East Lancashire Regiment to settle down to what he hoped would be a normal, civilian life.

On 17 August 1902 he married my mother, little Annie Gaffney, who stood barely over 4½ feet tall. Laying down roots on Park Lane in the village of Chapelizod, life was bearable for the growing family. Though they were poor, the vast, sprawling expanse of the beautiful Phoenix Park was their own back garden. Father took a job at the Ordnance Survey, whose headquarters were in the park, and Mother was able to feed and clothe her young children in relative comfort.

There were four surviving daughters born before my arrival on 1 April 1912, just days before the world's most infamous ship embarked on her maiden, and only, voyage. The *Titanic* was said to have been unsinkable. The nation's hearts almost stopped when the news came through that this floating bastion of wealth was doomed to an afterlife on the seabed, along with scores of men, women and children from every walk of life.

So, here I arrived, little Joseph Patrick Rochford, after my father and grandfather. I was Mother's April Fools' joke; that was what she thought, anyway, when the doctor told her, 'It's a boy!' after so many girls.

Just a babe in arms, I was blissfully unaware that trouble was brewing far away on the horizon; and when the year 1914 came it brought with it the news that Britain was at war with Germany. Without hesitation my father picked up his rifle and pack once again, leaving his wife and children to land with the first troops in France. Here, often buried to the waist in mud, he moved backwards and forwards amid shot and shell, and in the midst of the grey dawns he'd charge across no-man's-land on the front line during bayonet attacks. Life was hard. During the Retreat from Mons he sucked the leather tongue of his boot to save his sanity. He used to keep stones in his pocket to suck on whenever he was thirsty or hungry, which was most days.

As Father struggled through the trenches, so my mother battled to raise a family by herself. The dreaded telegrams: 'your husband is missing', and later: 'he has reported back to his lines', did nothing to help.

In 1916 bombs and bullets began thudding and flying through the streets of Dublin, though this time the Germans weren't to blame. The Emerald Isle was under attack from its own people, as the Irish rose to fight for freedom. In those days Ireland was under British rule; it had been this way for more than seven centuries. The wearing of the 'Green' signified that you were on the side of the Irish, whilst the wearing of the 'Red, White and Blue' showed you sympathized with the English. The wearing of either could mean instant death. 'Down with the English!' posters and other such slogans began to appear. Sons took opposite sides to their fathers; brothers were shooting brothers.

Though I was only young, I can still recall the wooden turf carts winding their way along the Dublin Road. Asleep amongst the straw could be spied khaki-clad figures returning home on leave from France. Many a jeer and shout would be directed at them from the rising Irish if they were spotted, and this filled me with anger. My father was doing his bit to help, and to me he was a hero, as was every other uniformed man.

I began proudly announcing to everyone I came across that I was going to become a soldier just like my father.

'You'll have to grow first, little Joey!' they'd tell me with a smile.

I was always so small, just like Dad. Though he was a tough, capable soldier, he stood just 5 feet 5 inches tall. He had flame-red hair and a moustache to match, and the kindest, twinkling blue eyes one could ever wish to gaze into.

One day, with my 'gun' over my shoulder, I set off for France to help him win the war. Halfway along the road to Dublin, my feet became tired and my heart faint when I realized I didn't know the way. The village policeman, Sergeant Kelly, found me sitting and crying by the wayside some while later. With a kind word and a pat on the head he perched me jauntily on his crossbar and set off for home. We arrived back in Chapelizod just in time to meet a search party of about twenty women, led by my mother. She was furious with me. Her face set and white, she led me into our little house on St Laurence's Road and sent me straight to bed with a sore bottom.

My great joy as a young child was to roam the lovely Phoenix Park with my four older sisters, Josie, Louie, Nellie and Maggie. This vast stretch of luscious parkland bordered my village, where the flowers and trees were scattered amongst the greenest of grass that grew from the softest turf. My sisters and I would while away our days watching the cattle browse and the deer speed on their way. We'd spot the squirrels gathering nuts, and hear the cries of the rooks and jackdaws flying over our heads. To watch the baby rabbits run for cover and the birds teach their young to fly was the greatest pleasure of all. There was peace and tranquility here, even though a short distance away over on the great '15 acres', khaki-clad soldiers from England marched and countermarched behind military bands. Across the park I'd march with my troopers and my fantasies to sit on the grass and listen, spellbound, to the stories of the real life soldiers who'd just returned from the trenches. They were friendly and softly spoken. One story I can still remember concerned the exchange of a valuable Hunter watch, made from pure gold, for a single slice of bread.

Day after day I returned to visit the soldiers in their camp. I was laughing along with one of them as he gave me a piggyback ride around the tents, when his shoulder badge accidentally grazed my bare leg. As the tears spilled from my eyes, the soldier took out a handkerchief, spat on it, and wiped away the blood that seeped from my battle wound.

'Ah now, you'll have to learn to be brave, little Joey,' he said, with much kindness in his voice. 'Soldiers don't cry.'

Later that evening, just before sunset, I was watching the troops marching around their camp on the last parade of the day. I suddenly noticed an officer with an angry red face approach one of the soldiers. He began shouting and waving his marching stick inches from the soldier's face. I was scared he was about to strike the soldier, and vowed to do something to stop him; but what could I do?

I kept my eyes on the stick throughout the rest of the parade. I watched closely as the officer paused to mop his perspiring brow, placing the stick on the ground beside him. This was my chance. Like a young gazelle I leapt across to where the officer was standing, seized his stick and ran away with it as fast as my tiny legs would go.

'You, boy! Halt!'

A cacophony of surprised voices called out as I fled, but with my head tucked into my chin and the stick grasped in my sweaty palm, I raced through the gates of the park and along by the little stone chapel. I was in such a hurry I even forgot the old custom of making the sign of the cross as I passed. Before I knew it, I was in through my front door and bounding up the stairs into my bed. I pulled the covers tightly over my head and clung on to the stick. My heart pounded, and with sweat running down my neck, I waited, though I didn't know what for.

From downstairs I heard the familiar voices of my sisters talking to Mother, followed by the sound of heavy footsteps marching up the wooden stairs. In silence, I was yanked from my bed, returned straight to the park and brought face to face with the owner of the stick. I looked up into the officer's face and my knees began to tremble. I knew I was in big trouble.

'Why did you take my stick, young fellow?'

I swallowed hard, dreading what this man was going to do to me. 'S... so that you would n... not hit the s... soldier with it.'

Hearty laughter greeted my feeble words. 'I'd never strike a soldier, son. Whatever gave you that idea?'

'You were waving it in a soldier's face. I saw you.'

The officer chuckled. 'You're alright, sonny, but you'll never make a sergeant major.'

With a pat on my head and a sparkling new shilling placed in my hand, I was marched back home again. Mother was so amused she laughed long and loud as we walked home, but she made me share my shilling with my sisters.

My best friend during those carefree days was a boy called John. He lived just down the road from me and we often used to play together in the street.

One summer's day, John was hanging around the horse-drawn carriages that brought their rich passengers to Phoenix Park to stroll in the sunshine and listen to the playing of the military band. John was entertaining himself by drawing pictures in the dirt with a stick, when he suddenly spied a ten-shilling note on the ground. Not wanting anyone else to see it, he put his bare foot over the money. Looking around to make sure he wasn't being watched, he stooped down and lifted it into his trouser pocket, before scurrying away from the scene of the crime; but it was too late. He'd been spotted by a group of men who were also hanging around in the hope of a copper or two flung to them by the rich. Poor John had no hope of escape. The gang dived on top of him, bringing him to the ground. He was punched, kicked and bitten, but still he valiantly clung on to his newfound fortune.

'Hey, leave that boy alone!'

Providence was clearly on John's side that day, for a passing member of the Royal Irish Constabulary witnessed the scuffle.

John seized this opportunity. In the confusion he managed to free himself and race off into the depths of the park, where he clambered up a tree out of harm's way. He was so frightened he hid up there all day until darkness fell, and only when he was certain the coast was clear did he scamper back to his home. He arrived late in the evening, covered in blood, and feared he'd be in big trouble for what he'd done. Bracing himself for another beating, he decided to come clean and told his father everything. To the young boy's surprise, his father grinned at him.

'Have you still got the money, son?'

John took the crumpled bit of paper from his pocket and showed it to his father, wondering if it was destined to go straight into the family purse that fed them. However, to John's amazement, his father smiled and patted him on the head.

'First thing in the morning, take yourself away to Dublin and buy yourself a pair of boots.'

A pair of boots; his very own pair of boots. John was so excited he hardly slept that night. He'd be the only child in the village to be blessed with such a luxury.

At the first light of dawn he was up and away, and straight into the first boot store in Dublin he could find. Booted and proud, the little boy began making his way back to Chapelizod to show his mother and father. Not being used to footwear, they nipped and pinched his feet but he tightened his lips, braced his shoulders and hobbled on. He'd hoped to save the penny fare for the horse tram home, but he'd spent every bit of his money and had to walk all the way. Feeling like a king, he proudly showed the shining footwear to all his friends and family, and he cleaned them twice a day, every day. He was one of the lucky ones, and vowed never to go anywhere barefoot again.

Times were tough during my childhood, and I once saw a chap standing on a wooden soapbox, loudly addressing his fellow workers as they came out of a factory in Dublin.

'Vote for me, and I'll put boots on all the barefoot children in the city!' he bellowed.

I'm happy to say that when Ireland gained its independence, the *Dublin Herald* started a boot fund for the barefoot children, and thousands of pairs of boots were given to the half-starved yet cheerful urchins from the crowded slums.

My early childhood flew by, and before I knew it I was packed off to school. I can look back with fond thoughts to my time at the Mount Sackville Convent School on the fringe of Castleknock, just a stone's throw from the country house of the Guinness family. Mother Patrick was my teacher, and though she was as strict as she was devout, we all loved her. She kept our noses to the blackboard and always made us sit up with shoulders straight. The stories she told and her fine sense of humour had a great effect on me; and though I was only a child, she gave me the determination to apply myself. This led me to reveal, during a conversation in class about what we'd like to be when we grew up, what my greatest ambition was.

'I'm going to be a sergeant major in the army,' I squeaked.

I gave the school its greatest laugh that day, but Mother Patrick came over and put a comforting arm around my tiny shoulders.

'Good for you, Joey,' she enthused. 'But you'll have to put on plenty of inches first.'

The days sped by, and I soon settled in with my new classmates. We were cocooned in an environment filled with learning and prayers, yet outside the walls, trouble was brewing. How vividly I can still recall that frightful morning when Mother Patrick burst into the classroom, her face as white as a sheet.

'Kneel down with me, children,' she commanded as she got down on the floor. 'Kneel down and pray very hard with me.'

We all did as she instructed but we didn't know what we were praying for. It later transpired that a gunman had murdered a senior British Army officer by shooting him in the back, just yards from the school gate.

This, however, was nothing new, and we'd hear this same story many times over.

'SOLDIER KILLED IN PHOENIX PARK', the newspaper headlines declared.

'BRITISH OFFICER SHOT IN THE ROAD'.

The violence escalated on Easter Monday, 1916, when hundreds of Irish civilians, dressed in green uniforms, marched through the streets with guns at the ready. They gave battle against the small British force and set up headquarters in the post office on Sackville Street. I couldn't understand why these terrible things were happening, but I wondered where my father was and why he hadn't come home to sort all the mess out.

Rumour had it that over in France, in the shell-ridden trenches, a bond of friendship had grown between an English officer and his Irish batman. One day, the batman returned to Ireland on leave and saw with anger how the English were treating his fellow countrymen. Seething with rage, he was persuaded by his lovely Irish girlfriend, Colleen, to join the IRA. He deserted from the English forces and was soon given command of a squad of gunmen. Before long, the batman was out on the country roads leading to and from the city of Dublin, laying siege to British convoys, blowing up bridges and generally causing mayhem.

The Fates have often been known to play queer tricks on us, and this was one of those occasions. The English officer whom the ex-batman had once served was posted to Ireland. On his first raid he captured his former companion, killing his entire squad in the process. Confronted by his ex-master, the deserter was overcome with guilt and was persuaded to act as an informer. 'Escape' was arranged and the ex-batman reported back to his pals in Dublin, telling them that he'd been captured but had managed to get away. They accepted his story and he was sent back on duty with a fresh squad.

Plans soon began to go wrong for the IRA and many attempted ambushes failed with heavy losses. They quickly realized somebody must have been informing. The brains of the outfit decided everyone should be closely watched and they soon became suspicious of the ex-batman. One day he was spotted entering a police billet, so he was seized on his way out and court-martialled in a basement cellar, where he was sentenced to death.

Early one Sunday morning, the church bells of Dublin called the faithful to worship. On their way to Mass, the congregants came across the body of a man nailed to a cross inside the grounds of the churchyard, with the word 'traitor' etched across his skin. At his feet, sobbing and stripped to the waist, was Colleen. Her hair had been shorn and pinned to the breast of the dead man. Her crime had been introducing an unreliable soldier to the movement.

'The war is over!'

In 1918 everybody had this cry on their lips, and the streets were filled with joy. Posters of Lord Kitchener, which had once stared down from the walls of buildings and told us 'You are wanted!', were now hanging in ribbons.

At home, Mother was full of tears. We were all kissed and made to sing. We could hear people cheering in the street outside, though others were booing. Some were singing *Land of Hope and Glory*, and others, *Wrap the Green Flag Around Me, Boys*. In our parlour we had a horn-o-gram, and even though Mother disliked the British with a passion, she played the 24-inch record of the English national anthem. The music must have sounded for miles away.

My mother was a fearless lady and she hadn't a care for what anybody thought of her. Though she was only tiny, she'd once whipped a soiled dishcloth across the face of a gunman who happened to take refuge near our home from the Black and Tans, a dreaded force of men that had been sent over from England to put down the Irish revolt. This makeshift army had many names in Ireland: jail birds, murderers; but whatever their name, they were brutal, and despised throughout the land. Mother's action was nothing to do with a love of the Tans, however. She hated the merest utterance of their name and would insist on everybody making the sign of the cross at such a mention. Her disapproval was roused when the gunman woke her sleeping children, and that was enough to incur the wrath of any mother in Ireland. Perhaps she'd failed to notice the man was armed to his teeth.

Though the Great War was finally over, the war in Ireland was just hotting up. People spoke in whispers, never daring to trust each other, and the returning heroes were looked upon as traitors because they'd fought side by side with the accursed English.

In a desperate attempt to quash the rebels, the prime minister, Lloyd George, vowed to strengthen the Irish Constabulary. An advertisement appeared in English newspapers asking for applicants to join the Black and Tans for the princely wage of ten shillings per day. Seven thousand violent men, many of whom had just been released from jail and were looking to start a new life, were selected and sent across the sea to Ireland.

Soldiers began being demobilized in their hundreds. They were no longer required now the war was over, but they had little chance of finding civilian work, their previous positions having been filled long ago. This led to mass unemployment and poverty in many households. The little work there was paid meagre wages. Families were large and houses were small. The streets were swarming with barefoot children who'd lift their grimy faces and beg with a prayer.

'A penny for a crust of bread,' was their constant plea.

Dublin had a strange smell lingering in the air. The floors of public houses were covered with horse droppings, rotting fruit and vegetables, and damp sawdust. Sanitation was unheard of, and visitors from overseas nicknamed the capital 'Dirty Dublin'. It wasn't the townsfolk who were to blame, though. If they didn't empty the garbage in the streets, there was no other place for their rubbish apart from the muddy waters of the river Liffey. Refuse was piled high; flies, rats and mice were breeding in the damp dwelling houses. It was here where the poor people of the land eked out an existence and many died at an early age. Consumption was sapping the strength of the Irish people and there was misery everywhere, except, of course, in the grand houses of the rich, where 'poverty' was a dirty word in their drawing rooms. The scent of port and Havana cigars disguised the foul smell of destitution outside. These members of the privileged classes couldn't have cared less about the plight of the poor, and their attitude was causing the common people to react with fury. In the troubles that were to follow, the rich were the first to have their homes burnt to the ground.

In the wider world, the victorious and vanquished countries alike were plunged into desperate straits. American troops were called out to put down their former servicemen who were demonstrating in the streets. In Germany, Nationalism was beginning to turn the country into an isolated state. France, too, was experiencing her own troubles. Disturbances, police baton charges, unemployment and bitterness filled the once cosmopolitan streets. England, too, was on her knees.

None of this concerned little me, however, for my father had come home at long last, healthy but pale. My sisters and I cheered as we saw him coming round the corner of our street, and we all swarmed over him, laughing and crying at the same time. His khaki uniform was spotlessly clean, and his boots and buttons polished, but Mother directed him straight through to the back room and made him strip off and bathe. She burnt his uniform, and this, we were told, was for no other reason than to make sure the lice from the trenches didn't settle in our home.

Our newfound happiness was shattered on many occasions, as gunfire tore holes into the brickwork of our house. Many were the times when the seven of us would find ourselves lying face down on the floor underneath the rickety old kitchen table, scared out of our wits and ashen faced, waiting for the shooting to end. This went on day after day, night after night, sometimes lasting well into the early hours as the fight against the English rulers intensified.

I was by that time coming up to eight years of age and old enough, Father thought, for my career choice to be decided upon. Sitting me down one morning after breakfast, he placed his hand on my shoulder and looked at me with a serene expression on his face, though there was no twinkle left in his eyes anymore. I used to imagine he'd lost his sparkle in the mud somewhere in a foreign field, which was probably closer to the truth than I'd realized.

'Do you still want to be a brave soldier, Joey,' he asked, 'despite everything you've witnessed for yourself? Are you prepared to spend a lifetime facing the horrors that war brings?'

'Yes,' I insisted. I wondered why he was asking me this and assumed he was going to try to talk me out of it, but looking back I think that was the last thing he ever intended to do. 'I want to be a hero, like you.'

'Good lad,' he said, squeezing my shoulder. 'Then you'll be pleased to hear I've secured you a place at the Royal Hibernian Military School, over in the park, where you'll learn how to become a real British soldier.'

All too soon my days at the Mount Sackville Convent School came to an end, and as Mother Patrick kissed me goodbye, I could feel her warm tear on my cheek.

'So, my little child will be a soldier after all,' she sighed. 'Your road will be long and hard, young Joey, but always remember that God will be with you.'

Those few words stayed with me for a long time.

As I walked by my father's side towards the great military school, looming like a dark castle out of the luscious greenery, I could feel my heart beating faster and faster against my ribs. I took one last look over my shoulder towards the road that led to my home. I couldn't understand why Mother had wept so bitterly as she kissed me goodbye. I'd be seeing her again soon, wouldn't I?

The Royal Hibernian stood at the top of a hill in Phoenix Park overlooking the beautiful Liffey Valley, the shadow of the Wicklow Mountains just visible in the distance. The school had been formed way back in the 1760s and incorporated by royal charter as an industrial home for the sons of British soldiers, many of whom had been orphaned. Passing through the wrought-iron gates of this famous institution, I felt as if the ghosts of its past were swirling around me. My stomach began to flutter. Finding it hard to catch my breath, I didn't see where I was putting my feet and I fell down into an open coalhole. I must have looked a frightful sight being fished out my by father, covered from head to toe in coal dust. I'd quite literally put my first foot wrong as I took my first steps into military life.

Washed and clean after my mishap, Father and I went to announce my arrival. I could see lots of boys about my age dressed in scarlet tunics with shining buttons. They were marching through the grounds with backs straight and arms swinging, every so often making a smart salute and turning their eyes towards a tall, white cross that had a dagger-like knife in its centre, and words written upon it that I couldn't see clearly.

'That's the school memorial cross,' Father told me, his voice full of pride. 'It was set up there in honour of soldiers who've given their lives over the centuries for king, queen and country.'

This worried me a little; I hoped I wasn't expected to die as well.

After being led into the cavernous Great Hall, where I was told I'd be spending my meal times, an enormous quartermaster with rows of coloured ribbons on his chest began handing me item after item of kit; and it soon dawned on me I wasn't going to be returning home any time soon.

When I was all kitted out and ready to go, I followed my father back outside into the courtyard. With the least amount of fuss or affection he bade me farewell, closed the iron gates behind him and started marching back towards the road without even a backwards glance. My little eyes watched him go, and as he disappeared from view I put my head in my hands and sobbed. For the first time in my life I was completely alone. What was I going to do without Mother and my sisters? When would I see them again? I looked up again, hoping Father was going to reappear and take me home. How I willed for him to come back, but he never did.

'What's the matter, boy?' came a deep voice from behind me. 'Soldiers don't cry.'

Soldiers don't cry. Those words sounded familiar. I remembered hearing them before when talking to a soldier in Phoenix Park.

Looking up I saw a man in uniform, very much like the quartermaster, except this face was kindly. I stood up as straight as I could, wiped my tears from my eyes and received a warm handshake from the man, who introduced himself as Company Sergeant Major Malone MM. I later learned this friendly officer was to be my housemaster, and in some ways, my new father in this strange new world I'd been catapulted into.

With my kitbag slung over my shoulder, I was marched away to begin my new life. The first day passed by in a blur, and the following morning I was woken abruptly. For a split second I'd forgotten where I was. It wasn't long until I remembered I was in my extremely hard bed, where the previous night I'd silently cried myself to sleep. The dormitory was small and cold; and though it was still dark, a bugle was sounding from somewhere and a voice at the door was shouting at me.

'Come on, show a leg!'

I wondered if I was expected to hold my legs up in the air for him to inspect, but the boy in the next bed told me I'd merely heard the 'army alarm clock', which meant we all had to get up, wash, dress and go to breakfast as swiftly as possible. I found myself dashing about with all the others on that first chilly morning.

Clean and presentable, I 'fell in' with the others and marched to the Great Hall. The head prefect said grace, and then we all sat down at our tables. I was surprised at the amount of noise that took place. Everybody chatted to each other as they tucked in to the wholesome food that was put before us. We were given porridge with milk, kippers, bread, butter and marmalade, and a china mug of tea.

I glanced nervously around the room. I was surrounded by hundreds of fine-looking boys who were to be my new companions. Some of them looked a few years older than me, but many seemed to be about my age. On the oak-panelled walls around the hall were large oil paintings depicting various battles from long ago. Some of the pictures had gold plaques beneath them that bore their names. I also spotted flags, pennants, swords and guns mounted on display stands, which were dotted about the room. They'd all been put there for one purpose: to make one feel like a true soldier.

After breakfast, my comrades and I were on parade. To begin with I had difficulty marching as smartly as the others, but I was doing my best and trying hard to enjoy myself.

'Shun.'

'Quick march.'

'Left, right, left, right.'

'Halt.'

'Left turn.'

So many instructions were ringing in my ears that it made me dizzy, until at last I heard something familiar.

'Boy Rochford.'

Before I had time to think, I was marched in front of the school commandant, Colonel Bent OBE, the master of ceremonies. Even though he was sitting behind a desk, I could tell he was only a small man, but he had an authoritative face, and a monocle held to his right eye. One thing that struck me was that all these men wore lots of coloured ribbons, and this man was no exception. I felt tremendously out of place among these decorated warriors, but I was put at ease by the man's soothing words of welcome and the explanation of what this fine school stood for, and what it hoped to instill into boys like me. When he'd finished, I was marched out again with sentences ringing in my ears such as, 'to fear God and honour the king', this being the school motto.

There were about 500 boys at the school and they were mostly Irish. The few English boys who were with us had fathers serving in Ireland, and some whose parents were on the staff. The general purpose of the school was to train the boys to become full-time soldiers in the regular army. Sports were played at an exceptionally high level, and education formed a primary part of our lives. The schoolmasters were the best in the land, having been drawn from the ranks of the Army Education Corps, and what these men couldn't teach us about the military wasn't worth worrying about.

Meanwhile, outside the school gates, the violence on the streets of Dublin prevailed. Bombs and bullets were flying around most days now, and innocent blood ran down the walls and streets, as some poor woman's husband or son – or both – was shot dead or blown to kingdom come. Each day the crisis worsened, but inside the walls of the school, life continued as normal.

The weeks passed, each one the same as the last, and after several months I was considered to be a reasonable soldier for my age. I was even allowed to go home at weekends but had to return to sleep at the school. It was a proud day for me when I passed through the school gates for the first time, dressed as a soldier. Down towards Chapelizod I marched, my scarlet tunic contrasting against the greenest of grass that only grows in Ireland, and my golden buttons glinting in the sun. My parents and sisters were thrilled to see me, but Father seemed concerned. I think it was because he had a fair idea about what I was going through, and more importantly, what lay ahead.

One Saturday afternoon he sat me down with a look of sympathy in his eyes. It made me uneasy.

'What is it like, son?' he asked.

'It's alright,' I shrugged, feeling it was best to be honest, 'but very lonely. I miss you all, dreadfully.'

He slipped a half-crown into my hand and patted me on the head without another word.

It was 1921 and I'd turned the grand old age of nine. A whole year had passed since I'd enrolled and I felt much more settled. During free periods I enjoyed exploring the school grounds and would regularly wander down to the chapel in the graveyard whenever I was feeling low, as it was such a peaceful place. There were hundreds of little stone crosses marking the graves of all the boys from the school who'd died from various diseases over the years, and I used to read their names and imagine what they were like. I'd watch the birds, the squirrels and the deer passing by, just as I'd done back in the carefree days with my sisters whenever we visited the park.

I acquired my first black eye following a skirmish with another student. It had been worth it, though, for it helped me find my place among the hundreds of other boys. Feeling fed up one day, I'd been sitting in a corner on my own and for no reason at all, other than to show off in front of the others, somebody came up and pasted me. It was a big brawny lad called Ginger, one of the most notorious bullies at the school. His father had been a member of the Royal Irish Constabulary, and was thus a marked man. Poor Ginger had witnessed the brutal murder of his father on the doorstep of his own house as the family was setting out for church one Sunday morning. This had affected Ginger to such an extent that he began venting his anger towards all the other boys.

Sitting with my face held between my hands, trying hard not to cry, the school boxing instructor, Sergeant Pat Hastings, approached me.

'What's the matter, boy?' he barked. 'What's happened?'

'I didn't do anything, sergeant,' I snivelled, leaping to my feet and standing to attention. 'I was just sitting here when a boy came up and gave me a good hiding for no reason at all.'

Sergeant Hastings suggested I should spend my evenings with him at the school gymnasium where he'd teach me the art of self-defence. Our meetings went well and I soon felt so confident that I agreed to have a bout against Ginger in the school boxing competition that was taking place. I trained hard every night until the big day finally arrived.

With a quivering sensation in the pit of my stomach, I climbed into the ring. Hundreds of eyes were upon me, but that was the least of my worries. Across in the other corner sat Ginger, looking extremely cool. No doubt it was all just a joke to him, the big, tough boy who was going to knock pathetic little Joey straight through the roof in front of the whole school; but I was able to draw confidence from the fact that my father had come to watch, and he'd given me a few words of encouragement before the bout.

The shouting from the crowd died down as the bell sounded, and Ginger came out of his corner like a bullet. In no time at all he was belting and slogging into me, but caution was my defence and I let him do all the work in the hope he'd soon tire.

Except for a red mark on my cheek, I weathered the first round; and as the bell sounded I went over to my corner and sat down, feeling happier than I had done in a long time. There was something about boxing that sent a wave of exhilaration throughout my body and I knew, at last, I'd found something I excelled in.

The bell sounded again and we both got up and walked towards each other. This time Ginger was using caution but his right hand was strong, and when he swung for me I didn't duck in time. He landed a stinging blow on my cheek. Thankfully, I'd been taught a two-fisted attack against a stronger opponent, so I let him have it, and was pleased to see Ginger screw up his face. I knew I was hurting him. I gritted my teeth, dug my feet into the ground and punched as straight and hard as I was able. Before I knew it, Ginger was on his back and was counted out.

Amid the cheers must have been gasps of surprise, but I didn't care. I'd beaten him in front of the whole school, and my father. He was delighted with me, of course, and as he left to go home he slipped a silver coin into my hand.

From that moment on, all the bullies left me alone. Life took a new and interesting turn. Over time I became quite a handy boxer and fought many times in the ring. My housemaster was pleased with my progress, even though

I was useless as a 'shine' – a cleaner of boots and other such items – but like everything else this eventually came to me after many sound rebukes.

In the outside world the rule of the gun was now a part of daily life. The British Government invited an Irish delegation over to Westminster to discuss the ever-worsening situation. An agreement, which became known as the Anglo-Irish Treaty, was ultimately signed, dividing Ireland into thirty-two counties. Of these, twenty-six were given to the Irish and this nation became known as the 'Irish Free State' under its own government. The other six counties remained under the control of Britain and would become Northern Ireland. Some factions of Sinn Fein, however, didn't agree with this, believing the whole of the country should belong to them. Consequently the party split into two. The new head of government of the Free State was the politician William Thomas Cosgrave, and the fine soldier, Michael Collins, was commander-in-chief of the National Army. The republicans were led by Eamon de Valera, and bitter fighting broke out between these two political groups. It certainly seemed to us like a case of divide and conquer, even if that hadn't been England's intention.

One night, just as we boys had retired to our beds, bursts of machine-gun fire were heard coming from outside. We rushed to the small dormitory windows to see that the Dublin skies were alight. Great red and white bursts were flashing in the darkness above, as 'crump' after 'crump' resonated all around. The Four Courts and the Public Records Office were engulfed in flames. All we could do was watch, helplessly, as a thousand years of Irish history burned to the ground. In the flickering light we could make out silhouettes armed with rifles, running around the streets and on the flat-topped roofs. Now and again some of these figures would throw up their arms and topple into the streets, dead.

Morning told the full story. The Free State Army had attacked the positions held by the republicans in the Four Courts with cannons and machine guns. General Michael Collins had given them the chance to come out with their hands up but they'd refused, hence the battle. Many Irish lives were lost that night and it was five years or more before the Four Courts was rebuilt.

That was not the end of the carnage. People hardly dared speak to their neighbours any more. House searches went on day and night by both sides, looking for arms and the enemy. Many innocent men and women were cut down in the streets and even in their own homes. Day after day, night after night, murder and rape was committed. Catholic Ireland was incensed, and many people who hadn't even taken part in the revolt now carried guns wherever they went.

Strict curfews made the city of Dublin appear dead after nightfall. To walk in the streets after curfew meant instant death. Nobody was ever challenged;

the trigger was squeezed and there was blood on the streets once more. Behind closed doors and curtains, prayers would be offered up for the dead and the dying.

One day while on leave from school, I went with my mother on a shopping trip into Dublin. The old steam tram we were travelling on was brought to a halt halfway along the road, where several police lorries were drawn up and Tans with drawn pistols were standing in line. They'd been ordered to search all the men for arms, and just before they boarded the tram, I saw guns being passed in front of my eyes to the female passengers. In a flash the weapons vanished underneath skirts or behind shawls, for the women weren't searched in those days.

The search completed, we were allowed on our way; and as we passed by Kilmainham Gaol, which was filled to bursting with soldiers of the IRA, we heard shouting drifting from their cell windows.

'Up the rebels!'

'Death to the Black and Tans!'

The streets below the gaol were packed with mothers, fathers, wives and sisters with tears streaming down their faces as they sobbed words of encouragement up to their loved ones. It was a harrowing sight. Some of the prisoners were under sentence of death and would eventually be taken to the bleak Mountjoy Prison for the early morning drop. This was the building where hundreds of freedom fighters were lodged. Among the Irishmen who were hanged for what was deemed treason was a young boy, Kevin Barry, just eighteen years old. He was taken to the gallows early one morning as the grey skies were clearing. His crime was blowing up a lorry-load of Black and Tans. The explosion had knocked Kevin unconscious and he was arrested before he came round. One of the rebel songs that was being sung by the Irish was dedicated to Kevin, and it was against the law to be heard singing it, though I still recall the lyrics.

> *Just a lad of eighteen summers,*
> *And for that, no man knows why,*
> *For as he walked into the scaffold,*
> *He held his young head high.*
> *'Shoot me like a soldier; do not hang me like a dog,*
> *For I fought for Ireland's freedom,*
> *And for that I was to die.'*

There were many sad songs dedicated to the struggle. Another haunting melody I remember well used to drift up and down the streets of Dublin like a whisper in the wind.

Oh, I wish I had a penny,
I'd buy myself a gun,
I'd fill it full of powder,
And make those English run.

Oh then, Paddy dear, and did you hear,
The news that's going around?
For they're hanging men and women,
For the 'Wearing of the Green'.

Perhaps the pages of history would have been written differently if the murderous Black and Tans hadn't been formed and sent to this tragic land.

Many hearts in Ireland, and even in England, fell heavy when the news came in late August 1922 that General Michael Collins had been murdered, though by whose hand nobody knew for sure. Speeding towards Dublin in his staff car, he turned a bend in the road and a volley of shots stopped his vehicle. One well-aimed bullet caught him at the back of the ear.

The whole of Ireland mourned this great patriot. Much good work had been expected of him; he could have been the man to lead Ireland to greatness. Along with my father and countless other mourners, I remember filing past the coffin to pay our last respects to this distinguished man who lay in his green uniform with the Irish flag above his head. Mick Collins was loved and respected by all. He was a brave man, a fine soldier, leader and a gentleman.

For me and all the other boys, the troubles had only just started. One chilly morning, before the sun had risen, our commandant stood in front of the whole school and broke the news to us that we were to leave Ireland for good and set up a permanent home far across the sea in England. This came as a crushing blow to all the young boys, many of whom had never even ventured beyond Dublin's streets. He explained to us that one of the things that the Anglo–Irish Treaty introduced was the withdrawal of the Black and Tans, and all the English soldiers, from Irish soil. As the Royal Hibernian was British-controlled, we boys had to be evacuated too.

The evening before we left, a party of green-clad soldiers from the Irish Free State Army marched into the school grounds and lowered the Union Flag that had proudly fluttered over the school for 150 years. In its place was run up the green, white and gold flag of the Irish Free State.

Ireland was truly free.

Everybody had much hope that things would finally get better. I, however, felt torn. I didn't know what to think. My heart was full of joy and sorrow as the last post sounded and I made my way to bed. Tomorrow promised to be a momentous day in my young life. The thought of leaving Ireland had broken my heart. Some of the other boys' parents had taken their sons out of school upon hearing the news, but there was nothing I could do to convince my father to do the same. He wanted me to have a good career with the British Army rather than an uncertain future in Ireland.

It was a dull, grey morning in 1922. The band of the Royal Berkshire Regiment played as we said our brief goodbyes to our families on the school parade ground before being marched away to the waiting Crossley lorries. Though my parents were silent as we parted, I could hear one of my sisters sobbing. It took all my determination to stop myself from from shedding any of

Dublin, 1922: the boys of the Royal Hibernian Military School on parade for the final time prior to leaving for England.

my own tears, and I kept bringing to mind the words that were so often drilled into me: 'soldiers don't cry'.

The cobbled streets of Dublin seemed strangely quiet as the lorries snaked along them. Many of us raised our hands in salute as we passed the sad ruins of the Four Courts. I could smell the yeast and rye from the distillery at St James' Gate and from the barges on the river Liffey carrying stout out to the big ships in Dublin Bay. I saw barefoot men, women and children spitting on the pavements, as they knew no better. I saw boys with dirty faces picking up crusts of bread and even fighting the rats for morsels. I thanked God that at least my own family was in a better position.

As we swung in through the gates of the docks, the enormous vessel that was to carry us across the endless sea came into view. She was called TSS *Menevia*. The docks were filled with noise and activity when we arrived, and crowds of people, mostly friends and relatives, were waiting to see us off. Many were kneeling on the wet ground, hands clasped, praying that we wouldn't go. The Dublin fruit sellers, whom we'd fondly nicknamed 'the Biddy Girls', were handing out their wares to all and sundry.

'Me darlin' bhoys!' they were crying. 'May the blessed Virgin watch and pray over yeh.'

We tore ourselves away from the hugs and kisses and walked up the gangplanks, the salty sea air filling our nostrils with every step we took. The Number One Army Band of the Irish Free State began playing *A Soldier's Farewell*; and as the *Menevia* moved out to sea, the mournful *Auld Lang Syne* drifted across the wind towards us. I stood in silent contemplation as the shores of Ireland faded into the mist. Dear, wretched Ireland. It was the only home I knew; the only one I yearned for. Little did I think, as I sailed away from the unsettled shores of that battered and bruised land, that I'd live to experience the same troubles over and over again in many a foreign clime; but first I was to learn to become a soldier in England.

Chapter 2

The Shores of a New Land

The sea air was filled with the singing voices of some 350 people who'd made what was called 'The Great Trek from Dublin'. Standing to attention on the decks of the *Menevia*, the school song rang out:

> *We're proud of our Alma Mater,*
> *Proud of the dear old Hib,*
> *Proud of past records of its sons,*
> *Proud to be one of its present ones.*
>
> *We'll always do our duty,*
> *And to our motto cling;*
> *'Be proud to strive and proud to try,*
> *To fear God, honour the king.'*

As we approached the shores of England we could see crowds of dockworkers watching us and shouting words of welcome. We disembarked and set off by steam train towards Shorncliffe, near Folkestone, the place that was to be our new home for the next couple of years. As we settled down in our seats to enjoy the long journey, our thoughts strayed back over the Irish Sea to the homes and families we'd left behind.

We watched the unfamiliar landscape passing by through our rain-splattered window. Somehow England looked much different to Ireland, but I found it difficult to put my finger on what it was. The people outside all seemed friendly though, smiling and waving to us as we chugged by.

The hours ticked slowly along as we zigzagged across the countryside, from one side of England to the other. It felt as if we'd been travelling forever; but finally, tired and aching, we found ourselves on a long march behind the school band towards Somerset Barracks. Many of the townspeople stood silently watching us with curious eyes, and I suppose feeling a little bit sorry for us too.

Shorncliffe, 1922: the remnants of the boys of the Royal Hibernian shortly after their arrival in England.

As we approached the barracks I was surprised by how pleasant the place looked, even though it was behind barbed wire. If it hadn't been for the fortifications it would have reminded me more of a country residence, with its large windows and countless chimneys, than a military base; yet life for us was far from aristocratic. Our days still followed the same old usual pattern. When we didn't have our noses in books we held parades on the nearby Sir John Moore Plain and gave the locals a chance to see the boy soldiers at work. We marched around the coastal town of Folkestone with the band and Corps of Drums and Pipes, and became a popular local attraction.

News from home came regularly, and on mail day we'd all troop down to the library to receive our letters. I received a half-crown postal order every week, and I suppose, like all boys, I was more interested in that than the letter inside.

Though our military camp comprised more than 230 acres of land, there was little free time for us to spend exploring it. Drills, parades, training and schooling were the order of the day. When our duties were done, we were marched off to bed to get a few hours of much needed rest before we were up again the next morning to do it all over again.

I woke one day feeling particularly under the weather, but like a good soldier I held my head high, gritted my teeth and battled on through the pain. I tried hard to concentrate but it all got a bit too much for me that morning; I collapsed while on parade and was dashed across to the school hospital. The doctor, uncertain in his diagnosis, decided to send me to the much larger and better equipped military hospital at Folkestone as my temperature was running high. Feeling drowsy and scared, I was carried on a stretcher to the waiting horse-drawn ambulance that had no doubt seen service during the war years in France.

The great brick military hospital appeared to rise out of the ground like a grove of knarred oak trees, and it was here, in this foreboding institution, where I witnessed the first real consequences of war. The wards were full to bursting with soldiers who were still suffering from terrible wounds. Some had been blinded from mustard gas in Flanders. Others had no limbs and those who were spared a leg hopped around on crutches.

I had to stay in hospital for quite some time, and I later learned that daily letters passed between the school and Chapelizod. Major Harris, the adjutant at the Royal Hibernian, wrote to my parents to inform them I wasn't suffering from appendicitis, as originally thought, but from a form of pleurisy, explaining that I was seriously ill but responding well to treatment and would be confined to the hospital ward for some time further.

Those bedridden days seemed to slow down to an unbearable tempo, though the other patients were friendly and easy to get along with. I think they felt sorry for little me, all alone and out of place in a world full of Goliaths.

One day during my stay, a tall Coldstream Guardsman was brought into the ward. He was gravely ill when he first arrived, and was given a bed beside mine. It became clear, as I got to know him, that he loved his regiment with a passion. As his health recovered, stories of the black bearskin and scarlet tunic could soon be heard drifting through the ward, and tales of Guard Mounting at the royal palaces and the Trooping of the Colour filled me with awe. I decided there and then that this was the life for me. Though I was small and Guardsmen were traditionally tall, this didn't put me off. My determination was renewed, and I vowed to get myself better again so I could return to school and continue my military education.

Illness was notoriously hard to cure in those days, and I was in hospital for almost eight months. Just as I was discharged, I learned the sad news that the Royal Hibernian Military School was to be disbanded after one and a half centuries of history. I wondered what my fate would be and if I'd be returning home to Ireland, but I didn't have to ponder for long. My father sent me a letter advising it would be in my best interests to carry on with my training. He told me I was to transfer with the other boys to the Duke of York's Royal Military School at Dover.

Despite my sadness at seeing this school closed, I'm proud to say I was among the last of the boys ever to attend the Royal Hibernian, and was present at the final roll call at Somerset Barracks.

It was now the summer of 1924 and I'd started yet another new chapter in life amongst the lovely green fields atop Lone Tree Hill that looked down onto the town of Dover. The Duke of York's School was a most imposing place, spread out over a large area that was bordered by walls and iron gates. When we arrived I could see the enormous school halls interspersed between lots of other brick buildings. Standing in the centre of the yard was a huge clock tower, which reminded me of pictures of Big Ben I'd seen in my textbooks. Flying high over the school was the familiar Union Flag, and I felt like I was back in Phoenix Park again. It was a welcome sight.

The 'Dukie' boys were smart chaps, and, like me, were the sons of British soldiers. I was posted to Wellington House, home to many fine English boys, though the remnants of the 'Hib' school who'd moved here with me were sorted into another house, so I felt really lonely at first. Settling in was a bit of a challenge. There were constant fights between the ex-Hibs and the Dukies in 'England versus Ireland' contests. The battles always took place after lights out but after a while the school commandant, Colonel Poyntz, told us it would be better if we confined our battles to the sports ground, and this we did. Many a competitive game took place between the two groups, and it was all rather evenly matched.

I soon became unpopular with the other boys from the Hibernian School. I was looked upon as a spy simply because I'd been posted to Wellington House – a Dukie house – and refused to reveal information to the Irish about the English, nor would I join in the many Irish raids that took place after lights out. Consequently, a raid on Wellington House was planned with the sole purpose of taking me by force and giving me a good beating. It was supposed to have been a surprise attack but we got word of their plot and laid traps for them. As the raiders stormed our dormitory, we were waiting. We poured boiling hot water over the invaders' heads, and with cloth coshes, knocked some sense into them. We'd also set a trap for the leader of the raiders, Mad Mick, and successfully captured him along with two companions in the shoe cleaning room. After tying them up we covered them from head to foot with boot polish and made Mad

Mick eat the piece of paper that had the words 'Death Sentence' written on it, which had been intended for me. From then on my popularity was assured with the Irish, who were no doubt scared of what might happen next if their hostility continued.

It was 1925. I was thirteen years of age and the proud wearer of four good conduct stripes. I was considered to be a smart soldier and was even promoted to acting lance corporal. I was the champion boxer for my weight and a decent hockey player. In fact, I had a fair knowledge of all the sports that were played at our school, thanks to the excellent sports master. I loved drill and became quite an expert under the school's regimental sergeant major.

I'd been informed that I was allowed home on leave for a few days. As I stepped off the ship and set foot in the great city of Dublin again, I was conscious that this was probably the first time since the evacuation of British soldiers in 1922 that the khaki uniform had been spotted in the streets, which were much cleaner than the last time I'd seen them. The new Irish Government had done a great deal of work to improve the sanitation and general quality of life, but there was still a long way to go.

The ever-usual transport strike was on, so Father, who'd come to meet me at the docks, hailed a jaunting car for us both. With a flick of the whip, the driver got the horses moving and off we went, back to my beloved village. The driver sang cheery songs as the high cart trundled along the Lucan Road, swaying from side to side. Father and I spent the journey catching up with each other's news, and as we turned the corner into Chapelizod, I could see my family waiting to greet me outside the little house that I loved so dearly.

Great was my joy at seeing Mother again. I was surprised to find that her once dark hair was now flecked with silver, and as we embraced I noticed fine lines were spreading around her smiling Irish eyes. She looked tired, but that was probably down to the fact she now had three more children to raise.

The daily bombings and shootings were still taking place over divided loyalties, and hatred had become deeply etched in people's hearts. The slow trickle of families from Ireland's shores in search of work overseas was growing, as thousands began departing this sad isle, leaving behind the old, the hungry and the bitter. The streets of Dublin were home to too many beggars, and it angered me to see so many former heroes sitting in the gutter, many of whom had their medals pinned to their chests. During my stay I always made sure I put my hand in my pocket and placed a few coppers in their outstretched palms.

Though it was strange, given recent events, I received many a friendly pat on my shoulder as I walked through the streets in my dreaded English uniform. It seemed that there were still many who felt sorry that the English soldiers had gone. The soldiers had been good and fair, and had done nothing but their duty; but the brutal Black and Tans were still despised, and the Irish never ceased in their quest to hunt them down in every corner and crevice of Dublin City. One was even followed to Australia and shot dead by a 70-year-old widowed mother to avenge her dead husband and son.

My holiday finished all too soon and before I knew it I was on the ocean waves once more, on my long way back to Dover. My time at the Duke of York's Royal Military School was nearing an end, and on my return from Dublin I applied to the school commandant for permission to join the Coldstream Guards, much to the amusement of the schoolmasters. Even my Dukie pals found the idea comical.

'You'd better start growing, Paddy!' they'd snigger.

Parading on the final morning was an emotional experience. I'd first entered the school gates as a nervous child, with little idea of where I was heading; and now I was walking out of them as a well-trained and disciplined soldier with a promising career ahead of me. With ten shillings in my pocket, I boarded the train at Dover with detailed instructions on where to get off and to whom I should speak on the way.

It was a cold, wet day as the train rattled to a halt amid clouds of smoke and steam. I saw the word 'Farnborough' out of my window and I knew I alighted here. Standing in the entrance to the station was the tallest man I'd ever seen. He must have been nearly 7 feet tall, and his shoulders were almost as broad. He was dressed in a grey field overcoat with a row of shining brass buttons. On his head was a peaked cap, and on his feet were boots so highly polished they could have doubled up as a mirror. A neat moustache that the former German Kaiser would have been proud of completed the figure. The man lowered his gaze and his eyes fell on me as I approached.

'Lance Corporal Gee to escort you, boy,' he roared.

I have to admit I was rather scared. I held out my hand expecting a shake, thinking I was being polite, but I quickly learnt that this was not the done thing. Setting off in quick time we marched out of the station and down the long road to Aldershot. I expected the man to make small talk on the way but he remained impassive and stared straight ahead the whole time. We passed several officers on our brisk march and they all smiled at me. I expect they were amused at the contrast in our sizes.

After a while I began to tire as I struggled to keep up with my escort's gigantic strides. Just as I was wondering how much further we had to go he suddenly spoke, startling me.

'You are small but appear well trained.'

Those words of encouragement gave me the strength to finish the march, and before I knew it we'd arrived at Albuhera Barracks at Aldershot, where more giants stood proudly at the gate. These fine men, who were to be my comrades, were all 6-footers, and their uniforms were smart beyond words. Many had served in the First World War and a rainbow of ribbons decorated their chests.

Colonel George Monck, the first commander of the Coldstream Guards, formed the regiment in 1648 and set up his headquarters in the town of Coldstream on the Scottish Borders by the banks of the river Tweed. Over the centuries the Guardsmen held their association with the Duke of Wellington with pride. The Iron Duke had a high regard for his Brigade of Guards; and it was on his recommendation that all privates in the Guards Regiment should be termed Guardsmen, to put them one foot above other regiments of the line. Queen Victoria took just as much pride in her ceremonial Guardsmen. They were the Household Brigade of Guards, and very close to the Crown.

It was on a windy and rainy day in 1927 that I had the honour of enlisting in this historic regiment of Foot Guards that was *Nulli Secundus* – the regiment's motto, which means 'second to none'. I offered all 5 feet and 3 inches of myself to march, fight and grumble side by side with these giants of men in the service of God, king and country.

When I arrived at the camp the 3rd Battalion of the Coldstream Guards was away on manoeuvres somewhere, training to fight and march across long distances, carrying full kit over their shoulders. Here in the empty barracks I found only a rear party who took me into their care and showed me around. They made me feel welcome and I began to look forward to the work ahead.

The next day I was called into the drum major's office, and to my astonishment I found myself face to face with the man who'd inspired me to join this great regiment in the first place. I was pleased to see he'd made a full recovery and had returned to duty fit and well after his stay in hospital. He smiled at me and invited me to sit down with him at his desk. He was extremely kind and gave me a pep talk, warning me to be careful with any money I might have, for there was the odd thief lurking in the army.

'There are one or two crooks in every unit,' he told me. 'Anything you have of value, you are to place under your blankets when you go to bed at night.'

Aldershot, 1927: Paddy (left) and a friend, having just joined the 3rd Battalion of the Coldstream Guards.

Meal times were also explained to me. I was told that up until recently the last meal of the day had been served at 4.30 pm but a lot of the young boys were becoming hungry between dinner and breakfast the following morning at 6.30 am. As a result, a supper was laid on nightly, and though only a bowl of soup and a slice of bread with a mug of hot cocoa, it was most welcome.

With the pep talk over, I left the drum major's office but was startled by an almighty roar from an open window.

'Swing your arms up, you idle man!'

As I was the only one in sight, I knew the shout must have been directed at me. There was always a non-commissioned officer about, though more often than not you'd never see him. Even when you went to the WC there always seemed to be a voice shouting out at you.

Everything was done in double time here. One never walked anywhere but marched, at all times wearing your headdress properly, with your eyes to the front and your arms swinging in the correct military manner. Nothing else would do; even the sick and lame had to report to the orderly sergeant to be inspected and then had to march quick time to the sick room. I was warned it was a bad idea for a soldier to report sick, and unless a chap was half dead, it was best for him to think twice about such a notion. They used to tell us that whenever we felt under the weather, we were to roll up our sleeve and look at the back of our elbow joint to find the stream of gold-coloured 'elbow grease'. This was our extra store of energy to call upon in such times. After inspection the medical officer would mark a sick soldier either 'fit for duty' or 'medicine and duty'. This tonic, known as 'Black Jack', was a shocker, and was supposedly good for the stomach. However, all it did was send the poor man running to the loo in the shortest possible time. He'd later emerge white faced, but surprisingly enough almost recovered. If you were marked fit for duty then you were placed on a charge, and this could mean seven to fourteen days confined to barracks, or seven days in the clink. The charge was for malingering, which was nearly as bad as stealing a comrade's rations or appearing dirty on parade. Guardsmen, therefore, tried as hard as possible never to report sick, and consequently one chap died from continued pains in the stomach that went untreated.

Just before turning in on a night, we enlisted boys had to 'fall in' by our beds, dressed in nightshirts and in our bare feet. The orderly sergeant would walk past the beds and call out: 'Hands!' These were held straight out with the palms turned to the floor, and after the inspection the boys would turn smartly to the right, count a pause and then jump into bed. We had to be in bed, lying on our right side away from the heart, by 9.00 pm every night without fail.

A Guardsman was kept moving from the reveille bugle call at 6.00 am right up until lights out at 10.15 pm, and there was little time to rest one's feet. After reveille the door to our dormitory would burst open. The sound of boots on concrete floor would follow, and we were greeted with a variety of phrases.

'Wakey, wakey.'

'Show a leg.'

'Rise and shine.'

And, most menacingly: 'Move, or you'll find yourself in the mush.'

This was the name for the Guardroom cell, which was as frightening as a condemned cell but not so well furnished.

Without faltering we were up and dashing to the ablutions. With beds made, breakfast eaten and kits clean and tidy, we'd march off to the barrack square for an hour's drill. After that there'd be music practice, stirring marches, fatigues, lectures and a welcome break in the NAAFI – which stood for the Navy, Army and Air Force Institutes – but as we had little or no money, we just sat looking hopefully at the NAAFI girls, hoping that one day they might take pity on us and offer us a free snack or a drink. They never did.

We had to do the most peculiar things in the Guards, but all things had a purpose. Standing on the outer flank of the barrack square we'd wait for the order 'Get on parade', and then off we'd step in quick time and fall in on the markers. Grown men could be seen at this 3.30 pm parade holding up a pair of properly darned socks, a perfectly groomed bearskin or a towel correctly washed. This was known among the recruits as 'dummies' parade' and was necessary for the Guardsmen to prove that various cleaning duties had been performed to the required standard. I was even to see a chap march on parade with the barrack room table under his arm, while under the other he carried the barrack room coal box, glittering as if made of pure gold.

As on all parades, the regimental policeman would be there to ensure that no stray dog trotted across the ground. If it did, it was his duty to see it off and it was always funny to see a huge Guardsman running in regimental time after a scraggy looking stray. The dog always seemed to enjoy itself, with the Guardsman in hot pursuit calling the dog the choicest of names. Most likely the policeman would find himself on report for 'improperly allowing an animal to walk across the barrack square'.

Later in the afternoon there was weapon training, more drill, school for an hour, teatime, music practice, kit cleaning and perhaps an hour in the NAAFI before bedtime. This was the general run of the day.

I was soon kitted out with a full uniform and equipment, and had so many items I wondered where I'd put them all. I took my cue from the others and soon had stacks of neatly folded clothes in the locker above my bed. My uniform included one bearskin, a blue-grey overcoat, a blue cape and a complete set of white buff equipment for ceremonial parades. Kit inspections were frequent, and woe betided the man who was found lacking.

The only difference from one night to another was my second night. I was kneeling at my bedside saying my prayers – a duty we'd been encouraged to perform at military school – when the chattering in the room from the other nineteen boys suddenly ceased, and was replaced by the odd twitter or chuckle.

'Sling a boot at that idiot,' a voice said.

'If you do, I'll bash your face in.'

I recognized the second voice as belonging to a friend of mine, and it dawned on me that the first threat had been directed my way. I opened my eyes and looked up. One of the rougher chaps was striding in my direction with a set look on his face. He was a tough Londoner with a reputation for having a coarse mouth.

'On your feet,' he growled. Even if I'd been standing, this youth would have towered over me. 'You're acting like a Nancy. Soldiers don't pray!'

I was a good Catholic boy and had no intention of behaving in any other way, so I took no notice of him. I tried to continue what I was doing but he kicked me hard in my ribs and I toppled over. That had done it. Seeing red, I rose to my feet. This chap had no idea that I was a talented boxer, and with all the strength I could muster, I let him have it straight on the nose. He clearly hadn't been expecting that, for he staggered backwards and fell down hard onto my bed. I thought he was out cold but after a second or two he stood up again with blood streaming from both nostrils, and a look of fury in his eyes. He launched himself at me like a wild animal. Four fists began flying in all directions and the other lads gathered around to cheer and goad us on.

'Come on, then, you Irish bastard,' the Londoner taunted.

I gritted my teeth, tucked in my jaw and belted him left, right and centre. My army boxing training came in useful that night, and eventually I was on top. He didn't take defeat well.

'I'll get you for this,' he spat as he skulked away, wiping blood and sweat from his ugly face.

When the drum major heard about the fight the following morning he called us both into his office one by one. The other lad went first and then it was my turn. I entered the room expecting a stern reprimand, but to my surprise the officer shook my hand.

'You were very brave to stand up to that boy,' he told me, and I couldn't help but notice a hint of pride in his voice. 'Do you know who he is?'

I shook my head. 'No, drum major.'

'Then let me enlighten you. That chap is the champion heavyweight boxer, and I've warned him there'll be trouble if he ever pulls a stunt like that again. Fighting outside the boxing ring is not tolerated in the army, but as you've done so well, I'll not be punishing you today. Instead, I'm going to enter you into the battalion boxing tournament.'

This was a great honour indeed, and I assured the drum major I'd do my best to make my battalion proud.

The bugle sounded as usual one bright and breezy morning, but I was sure I heard a sense of urgency in its notes. It soon became clear that something important was afoot. We were duly informed, as we gathered for parade, that the battalion on manoeuvres was making a forced march from the village of Dymchurch in Kent all the way back to barracks – a distance of about 100 miles – and was due to arrive later that afternoon. Beds had to be made and fires lit, and various other duties had to be carried out to ensure that everything was in shipshape for their arrival.

That afternoon some of the other boys and I stood with great excitement near the officers' club at the junction of the road leading to Fleet, and received the thrill of our lives. It looked as if the entire British Army was on the march. Unit after unit came marching up the road. I'd never seen men so tall and so smart before. Their brasses were flashing in the sunlight and they looked so immaculate you'd have thought they'd just started the march instead of being at the end of it. They'd been out on the open road for weeks, exposed to the wind, rain and sun, but none of them looked any the worse for wear. The general officer was very smart in his Savile Row-cut uniform. No doubt he'd just stepped out of a nice hot bath and had been dressed under the care and attention of his batman.

At the head of these troops rode an officer on a fine horse. He was Commanding Officer Lieutenant Colonel J.A.C. Whittaker, the head of the battalion; his adjutant, who was also mounted, followed him closely behind.

As company after company swung past, the Corps of Drums and Fifes played a stirring tune that the chaps standing near me began to join in with.

You are marching back to barracks,
So get off your bloody knees …

Yet these men weren't on their knees. Those lyrics didn't make sense to me; but I was to learn the hard way that those lines were often sung by the troops during a long march. Somehow it made us feel less tired, and gave us the strength to carry on and face whatever challenges lay ahead.

Chapter 3

In a Guardsman's Boots

I was now well and truly a soldier with seven years' military service behind me. My pay was a shilling a day until I reached adulthood, when it would rise to two shillings a day. That wasn't much, but what did we soldiers want with money? Bed, board and every daily necessity was provided by the army.

Payday was a parade, much the same as any other. At 5.00 pm on a Friday we would, in answer to a bugle call, double away to the company office, line up in alphabetical order and wait until our names were called. There was a cruel sequence of events after pay parades, as far as we boys were concerned. The bugle would sound its familiar call to signal our march to the NAAFI, where the drum major would read out the items of cleaning kit that we required. It was always the same: two tins of Blanco, one white and one khaki; soap; toothpaste; black shoe polish; a spare pair of leather laces; needles and thread; and, of course, the thing that was required by all Guardsmen – Brasso. I felt that without Brasso there would have been no Guards Regiment. By the time we'd paid for all these items there was virtually nothing left. There were often cases of chaps who dodged the NAAFI parade and got away with their pay, which would most likely be spent on treats. Just across the road from the barracks stood a civilian who was permitted to sell sweets and chocolates, including a favourite milk bar of mine called 'Heavy Weight'.

There were three meals a day for a soldier: breakfast at dawn and then dinner at 1.00 pm followed by tea at 4.30 pm, with a light supper for the enlisted boys at 7.00 pm. They were good, solid meals but not enough for the strong, healthy giants in the Guards. The usual mad dash to the cookhouse would commence as the bugle sang out to us:

> *Come to the cookhouse door, boys,*
> *Come to the cookhouse door.*

Less than five minutes after this, another bugle call resonated:

Come, hurry up, hot potatoes,
Hot potatoes, hurry up.
Hot potatoes, come.

The orderly officer was there to see that the meals were served properly, and also to attend to any complaints about the food. If the chaps were sensible there'd be no complaints; but like most things in life there were exceptions and grievances were sometimes voiced. If a complaint was deemed to be untenable, the complainant would lose his name for making a frivolous grumble, and the cook would make a mental note to get his own back on the soldier later.

I remember several odd happenings in the dining hall at Albuhera Barracks. One of the officers had a large dog, and on hearing a moan from one of the Guardsmen, the officer took the complainant's fork and scraped the offending piece of food onto the floor, which his dog promptly gobbled up.

'If my dog will eat it, then so shall you,' the officer decreed.

'A soldier's life is akin to a dog's life.' I've heard this saying many times over the years and largely agree, except the dog's life was usually the cushier of the two. Punishment was exact and discipline was strict, for how else could you train a man to face death across the trenches or march into battle knowing there was little chance of survival?

If a soldier ever committed a serious offence, he'd find himself in the dreaded mush. This prison cell was approximately 5 yards square with a single barred window and a wooden bed. The poor unfortunate who was placed inside this bleak reformatory wouldn't be able to tell the time of day or even see the stars at night, for the window was too high and too small. Prior to the soldier going inside, he was stripped of all metals and any other possessions, and the laces were removed from his boots in case he thought about hanging himself. The wooden cell door was a solid mass save for an eyehole in the middle. From time to time, an eye would peer through to check the Guardsman wasn't up to anything, which was virtually impossible, anyway.

There were many other forms of punishments for defaulters, including fatigue duty. These jobs made us so hungry we were never against licking clean the dirty plates in the kitchen, cigarette ash and all. Spud peeling, for example, was an awful job. Armed with an eating knife and a mountain of potatoes, the lads would peel and peel as the hours scraped by. After the first few minutes of banter silence would descend as the endless amount of tubers plopped into the bath of water. The spud mountain never appeared to diminish in size, and when the cooks presented us with even more of the wretched things, the flow of choice swear words came thick and fast. I recall we wasted more than we peeled. One particular chap was caught and placed on a charge for 'allowing the potatoes to suffer idle peeling, and in consequence, did waste soldiers' rations'. He was awarded fourteen days' CB, which stood for 'confined to barracks'. Then there was the time when two chaps lost their tempers and pelted each other with spuds. Unfortunately for them a cricket match was in progress at the rear of the hut.

'You stupid, long-haired, knock-kneed sons of doubtful origin!' a quartermaster raged as he stormed in. 'The cricket field is swimming with potatoes!'

We had our laughs.

Drills were the lowest form of punishment and were awarded for minor forms of crime such as having dusty boots for the picquet officer's daily barrack room inspection, or being a few minutes late for meals, or even having untidy blankets on our beds. It was not easy in the Guards to go through life without losing one's name but it was remarkable how many did, and the name for this was 'undiscovered crime'.

Of the many hundreds of men I was to serve alongside, one in particular, whom I will always remember, was Tom. Tom was a rugged sort of chap with dark hair and an olive complexion that could easily have been mistaken for Mediterranean, though he was from the North of England. He was tall and broad-shouldered and had a warm, open heart, but on each cheek was a scar and this made him look quite ferocious. Unfortunately, this poor lad was constantly getting into trouble for appearing on parade with 'dirty flesh'. This was the name used in the event of dried soap being found behind the ears, or a smear of grit on the face. He never looked smart in uniform and it was for this reason he always lost his name. After every parade he attended, he was placed in the 'book' and was awarded weeks and weeks of CB. Our sergeant became so fed up of him that he put us all 'on the gate', which meant none of us were allowed out. This didn't make poor Tom popular with his comrades. We'd grown so sick and tired of being let down by him that we decided to do something about it.

It was one winter's day when a hard frost had covered the ground like a glistening blanket, and in order to get water to refill the fire buckets one had to break the ice that had formed about half an inch thick on top. Poor old Tom was forcefully undressed and dragged to the cold showers. He was soaped and scrubbed, and scoured with a dry brush until his skin was red raw, and he was climbing the wall in desperation. I can still hear his screams of 'ouch!' even now, as the icy water from the fire buckets was thrown over his naked body. This went on until he was shining bright. His unruly hair was groomed to perfection, and even his teeth were cleaned for him. Dressed in his best and turned out fit to see the king, we marched him over to the drum major for his inspection, and to our delight, we were allowed out that day.

There was one time when we were all to be inspected by the Prince of Wales, the future Edward VIII. As we waited for His Royal Highness, poor old Tom was standing in line looking like a beaten cow. His bearskin looked as if it had seen a ghost. His belt was far too loose, and in consequence, his packed grey coat was hanging halfway down his back. To top it all, his nose was running and he had two long candlesticks dribbling down his upper lip. The adjutant began passing down the ranks of the Corps of Drums, looking reasonably happy with everybody's appearance until he reached Tom, at which point he almost fainted.

'Oh, look, drum major!' the adjutant cried. 'What on earth is this?'

With eyes popping and a red face, the drummie marched furiously up to Tom and stood so close to him that their noses almost touched.

'Are you ill, Guardsman?'

'No, drum major,' Tom answered, a single bead of sweat dripping down his forehead.

'You are now!'

With that, the drummie slammed his ceremonial mace into Tom's ribs. Tom collapsed in an unconscious heap and was quickly carted off the parade ground by a couple of officers just as the Prince of Wales rounded the corner.

It was amazing how Guardsmen who were never 'spit and polish' soldiers had plenty of guts when it came to a showdown, when it all really mattered. Tom died in battle in 1942 in the Western Desert, as brave a soldier as ever there was. Germany's Afrika Korps were smashing our forward troops at the frontier of Sallum. In the heat of battle, through bombs, shells, mortars and machine-gun fire, Tom stood fast among the wounded Guardsmen, tending to them in his usual gentle manner until the last. None of us ever saw Tom again.

Training soon began for the annual Aldershot Grand Military Searchlight Tattoo, the greatest show on earth. It was a wonderful week-long musical event, well known to soldiers and civilians alike, and well attended by both. We used to look forward to those springtime days of the tattoo, though a lot of sweat and toil were used up in practice. For many years before the Second World War the display was held on Rushmoor Arena, a large open area just north of Aldershot. One of the main features of this magnificent spectacle was the performance by the massed bands and pipes of the regiments that were stationed locally.

Although the whole display was presented on a grand scale, the tattoo originated from a simple army procedure, observed as far back as the seventeenth century. In those days all active operations ceased in the late autumn and rival forces were billeted together in the towns and villages in and around the battlefields. The social centres for the troops were the local inns. To get them back to their billets on a night, it was necessary for the innkeeper to turn off his beer taps and to cease the sale of liquor. The time for doing so was between 9.30 and 10.00 pm, when a drummer would march through the billeting area beating a call to notify all concerned it was time to return to their beds.

One can almost picture a bright moonlit night in Flanders about two and a half centuries ago. At one end of the main road through the town or village was assembled a young officer, a sergeant and a drummer. At 9.30 pm on the dot the officer would order the drummer to commence beating. As soon as the innkeepers heard the sound of the drumbeats rolling over the quiet countryside they'd call out their command in Old Dutch: '*Doe den tap toe!*'

When translated into English this meant 'turn off the taps', and was the phrase from which the word 'tattoo' derived. The soldiers, after downing their drinks, poured out of the inns and proceed back to their billets.

In later years a flute player joined the drummer on his march along the road, and instead of a monotonous tapping, short tunes were performed. Eventually this led to the whole Corps of Drums, Pipes and Bands playing music for the entertainment of the troops, and eventually, the public.

The great evening finally arrived and the whole army was on parade; and what a parade it was. The massed bands with their 2,000 bandsmen were marching and countermarching up and down the illuminated Rushmoor Arena, where thousands of spectators from all over the world were gathered.

I was considered too young to take part in this, my first tattoo, so I was given a steward's job instead, and very proud I was with my badge of office hanging from my jacket. One job I had that evening was to help three other comrades, Chibby Charles, Alex Mills and Richard Shaw, to move a conductor's rostrum into the centre of the arena during the massed bands' display. This was to be done as the lights went out and the rostrum had to be in position just as the musicians reached the centre of the arena. Split-second timing was the key. Our moment came, and off we went. Everything proceeded as planned until a tyre on the rostrum burst and panic threatened to overwhelm us, but we made it just in time. The lights came back on just as the director of music, Captain Seymour, marched up the stairs of the rostrum; but the burst wheel had made the whole structure unsecure and one side tipped down.

'Hold it up, you silly soldier!' the captain hissed at Chibby.

Poor purple-faced Chibby had to balance the unsafe corner of the rostrum on his shoulder throughout the entire performance of Handel's *Largo*. Every so often his shoulder wilted under the weight and a cold stare would blaze down onto his head from above.

Training for war was in the nature of a game in those days, and field exercises were ever to the fore. One day we were taken out into the countryside and, placed in position by an officer, I was told I was to represent a platoon of infantry. I was handed a green flag that was to symbolize the anti-tank gun that was currently being developed. Standing by myself at a leafy crossroads outside of town, I waited for something to happen, though I didn't know what; the officer had forgotten to tell me.

Some time passed until eventually, in the distance, I heard a heavy rumbling and clanking noise. From around the corner emerged a giant metallic monster, the likes of which I'd never seen before in my life. Sticking out of the top was a gun, the barrel dead set in my direction. Two smaller monsters clunked and clattered into view behind the first, coming to a halt beside the larger one. I stood transfixed, not knowing what was happening or what I was meant to do. Coming to a quick decision, I dashed out into the road and pointed my flag at these things.

'Halt, or I fire!' I bellowed.

A single head appeared out of the turret of the leading machine, and it looked angry. 'Move away, you bloody fool! Can't you see you're in the path of three tanks?'

'Um … that's why I'm here,' I spluttered, trying to sound as brave as I could. 'This green flag represents an anti-tank gun and you are my prisoners. Pull up at the side of the road and come out with your hands up!'

If looks could kill, I'd have been stone dead. The officer in the tank leapt out of the vehicle and came bounding towards me.

'How in the name of sanity do you think you're going to take us prisoner?' he yelled, his eyes popping and spit flying in all directions. He snatched my little green flag from my feeble grasp and hurled it into the hedge.

It was then it dawned on me that this wasn't part of my exercise. Feeling about 2 feet tall, I stood to attention and gave the man a smart salute. I could think of nothing else to do. Thankfully, I was saved by the appearance of an umpire on horseback. He was amused by the tale, and sent me to report to battalion headquarters.

As the officer in the tank was leaving, he cast one last look in my direction and dryly remarked: 'I'll recommend you for the Victoria Cross.'

I walked away feeling an even bigger fool than I had before, and on reaching my lines reported the incident to the company commander. I never received my VC.

I was to drop another clanger several weeks later while on another training exercise. I was pushing my army cycle through the woods when one of the majors, acting as an umpire, stopped me and asked me what I was up to.

'I'm taking a message to battalion headquarters,' I duly informed him.

'I'm a friendly civilian,' he said.

I gulped. Had the officer got a touch of the sun?

'A large formation of enemy tanks is in the area of Woking,' he continued, 'and rumour has it they'll head this way.'

I blinked in surprise.

'Well?' he prompted after a few seconds of silence. 'What are you going to do about it?'

'Um, thank you very much for being on our side,' I said, feeling terribly embarrassed.

The expression of fury on the major's face told me that wasn't the correct answer; and I was once again sent to report to the company commander. I'd decided field exercises weren't my strong point, but they were easy compared to the gruelling task we had ahead of us.

It was said that Guardsmen's sweat was used to wash the ancient road that went up and over the steep hill known as the Hog's Back, situated somewhere in the Surrey countryside. If that was the case then I must have contributed plenty of mine to the cause. Many past and no doubt present Guardsmen of all regiments of the Household Brigade of Guards will well remember the notorious hill that we were so often required to march up and down, like the Grand Old Duke of York, though it's likely that he, at least, would have been on horseback.

With full packs over our shoulders, we set out one warm summer's day to begin this long march. The crunching sound of steel studs and heel tips filled our ears as we marched in almost perfect unison. Clip-clopping behind were the horses and mules employed to pull the grub-car. Dense black smoke was belching into the air as our infamous brown stew – a bland recipe familiar to everyone in the army – bubbled away. Someone along the line began playing a mouth organ to relieve the tedium and a few tired voices started to sing along:

Cheerily goes the dark road, cheerily goes the night,
Cheerily goes the blood to keep the beat.
Half a thousand dead men marching on to fight,
With a little penny whistle to lift their feet.

We used to sing this tune at the old Hibernian School. It was written during the Great War and spoke of an incident that happened during the Retreat from Mons. The story goes that there were some 400 British stragglers, too tired and too dispirited to go on. In an attempt to lift the spirits of the half-dead men and return them home, the commander acquired a tin whistle and a toy drum, giving the former to his trumpeter and the latter to an officer. Miraculously, he got his men onto their feet, and, led by the whistler and drummer, they eventually reached their regiments after an all-night march.

We'd always set off on our marches in good spirits, singing merrily; but after bouts of torrential rain and scorching sun, our backs would ache and our feet would be rubbed to blisters. A few score miles into the march the singing would die down and silence would reign, though perhaps if you accidentally kicked the heels of the chap in front he'd turn and snarl.

I forget how many miles we marched along the Hog's Back that day, but we carried on moving until the long-awaited command came:

'Fall out on the side of the road.'

At once we let our bodies sink into the welcoming soft bank. It was a lovely feeling to relax after such a long march, and we began to prepare for a meal of brown stew, complete with the bits of grass and twigs that would always find their way into a soldier's mess tin.

We slept rough that night and for many a night after, feeling like kings if we were lucky enough to nap in some farmer's barn, with hay for our mattress and rats for bedfellows. Onwards we trudged the following morning, not caring or knowing where we were heading, though it always seemed to be uphill. The rain continued to lash down on us, and following one particularly nasty thunderstorm one of our chaps took ill. He died from pneumonia some days later.

After weeks and weeks of hard work I was assigned to the Corps of Drums, the pride of the regiment, and was considered good enough to carry a drum with the other Guardsmen.

My newfound pride came to an abrupt end when I received some alarming news from home. Mother was not well. On 2 July 1927 she'd given birth to my youngest sister, Phyllis, and wasn't recovering as quickly as the doctor had hoped. Luckily, my army leave was drawing near so I resolved to go home for a few days to spend time with my family; but there was a problem. I'd been informed that the British Army uniform was no longer permitted in the Irish Free State, and if a soldier was spotted wearing it, he'd be shot on sight. Not being able to afford a civilian suit, I wondered what on earth I should do.

'You should ask the adjutant if you can borrow some money, Paddy,' one of the lads kindly suggested. I was very young and naïve, and had no idea this was his idea of a joke.

'Aye, the adjutant is a gentleman,' another boy nodded in agreement. 'He won't mind at all if you ask him. Wait outside the orderly room and stop him as soon as he comes from the officers' mess.'

I did as my so-called friends suggested, and that afternoon as the adjutant marched across to the orderly room, with his sword trailing along the ground, I nipped smartly across to him, saluted, and spluttered out my well-rehearsed script.

'M…may I have your permission to speak, sir?'

Timing, it seemed, was not on my side, for just at that moment the drum major spotted me as he was coming across from his quarters. Looking as if he was about to explode, he ran full gallop to where the adjutant and I were standing. With a scarlet face, he saluted the adjutant and told me in no uncertain terms to clear off at the double.

'That's alright, drum major,' the adjutant said with a curious glance in my direction. 'Leave the boy with me.'

As the drummie saluted and marched off, he threw me a glowering look. For once I didn't care, and took the opportunity to explain to the adjutant, thread through needle, my sorry position. I prayed he'd understand.

'Alright, boy,' he said, after a moment of contemplation, 'I *will* give you a loan to buy some new clothes with. But how do you propose to pay me back?'

Being inexperienced with regard to money, I quickly suggested: 'I'll repay you at the rate of one shilling per week.'

To my surprise, the adjutant burst out laughing. 'How about we discuss the terms later?'

I thanked him and saluted before marching across the road back to my room.

What a shock the lads got when I told them about my meeting. They called me a cheeky idiot and various other names, but I pointed out that I was only following their advice.

'You nutter,' they responded. 'We were only having you on!'

The following morning a tall non-commissioned officer marched me down to Thomas White's outfitting shop in Aldershot where I was fitted out completely, from my overcoat to my suitcase. I even received a pair of gloves.

Dublin, 1927: Paddy posing for a photograph with his parents, while on leave from England.

Back at the barracks I began to pack for my trip, and didn't tell anybody about my scarlet jacket that I'd hidden in the bottom of my case. I was proud of my regiment and after much deliberation had resolved to show the Irish that the British Army wasn't scared of wearing the king's uniform. I know now this was a foolish and reckless thing to have done, as I'd been kindly provided with expensive civilian clothes so I'd neither break the Anglo-Irish Agreement nor risk my life in doing so.

Passing through the customs shed in Kingstown Port, just outside Dublin, the poor customs officer nearly fainted when he saw the contents of my case. At first he thought it was fancy dress but when I explained to him what it represented he made the sign of the cross.

'God Almighty,' he gasped. 'The British Army is back!'

I was flattered by the promotion. Up until that moment I'd felt like nothing more than a very small, insignificant soldier.

My father was waiting for me at the docks, as usual, and as I walked up to him he passed me a welcome nip of the 'Creator', as whiskey was known in Ireland. It warmed up my whole body in an instant. The British War Office had sent me home by third class and I travelled the whole way in steerage. Anyone who knows the Irish Sea will understand how soaked I got coming over. Every wave splashed against the side of the ship and I emerged on the shores of the Emerald Isle dripping wet and freezing cold.

Mother was delighted to see me, as always, and I felt sure my presence back home made her feel well again. My brothers and sisters were equally thrilled to have me home, as were all our neighbours in the village. I remember dressing up in my uniform and marching through the streets of Chapelizod, showing off to everyone who passed. They stared in amazement, and the barefoot urchins of the district gathered around and asked if I was a prince.

'He's not a prince,' one of the cheekier ones called out. 'He's just an advert for Drummer Dyes!' This was a well-known brand of fabric colouring, which had a picture of a scarlet-clad drummer on the front of the box.

I wasted no time in visiting the lovely Phoenix Park, which was just as green and beautiful as I remembered it. I went to see my old school, which was now garrisoned by the Irish Free State Army, and then on to a photography studio in Dublin where Mother, Father and I had our picture taken together. I took that snap wherever I went to remind me of home. When times got tough I'd gaze with fondness at my dear old father, standing proudly with a chest full of medals. I was standing beside him in my British Army uniform. Here was undisputable proof that I'd defied the Irish by wearing my British uniform, and lived to tell the tale.

Chapter 4

Royal Stations

In the years before the Second World War there were four royal stations for the ceremonial Guardsmen, and each year the companies would take it in turns to swap around. Two companies were stationed at Wellington Barracks in Westminster, close to Buckingham Palace; two more at Chelsea Barracks; one at the Tower of London; and a final company at Windsor Castle. In 1928 it was my company's turn to go to Windsor. Excitement was in the air as we packed and prepared to leave, and I got the distinct impression that this particular station was the most popular with the Guards. Rumour had it that the prettiest of girls, with a fair eye for a scarlet-clad Guardsman, graced the banks of the river Thames.

That morning, reveille sounded at the earlier time of 4.00 am. As we lined up for a quick breakfast of one boiled egg, a hunk of bread with a pat of margarine on top, and a drop of unsweetened tea (sugar was always absent in the army), all the non-commissioned officers were dashing around, roaring their heads off, and almost everyone lost their name that morning.

After breakfast and armed with my drum and the others with their flutes, we marched up and down the barracks playing *The Point of War* – an old custom of yesteryear, which originated when calling the troops from their village billets to parade.

With our company commanders mounted on their fine chargers, and with drums beating and bayonets fixed, we awaited the order.

'Quick, march.'

We marched through the barrack gates towards the railway station, passing a few weeping sweethearts who weren't permitted to come along with us.

Arriving at Windsor after our 20-mile journey, we found the streets were lined with musical bands and crowds of civilians who'd all gathered to watch the spectacle. The sun was gleaming on our naked bayonets as we drew near to our new home. It was nice to receive such a welcome, and I immediately saw the stories were true: the girls were very pretty.

To the usual roars of infuriated NCOs, we unpacked and settled into our new and rather pleasant accommodation at Victoria Barracks, just a stone's throw from the historic castle. No troops were allowed out on our first evening, so after our usual trip to the NAAFI for fried eggs and chips, we turned in.

Windsor Castle was a popular residence with the Royal Family, who lived there during the summer months; and the friendly townspeople were extremely fond of the Guards. Our main duty was to form the Castle Guard, which mounted on the barrack square every day. Tourists beheld the sight of Guards in scarlet and gold marching out of the barracks and up the hill towards the castle, and many a romantic date was made. One chap I knew used to write out his rank, name and number onto various slips of paper and surreptitiously scatter them around the streets like confetti as he marched. He was cured of this particular habit when he was sent to the gate one day and was set upon by about half a dozen teenage girls who'd all called for him at the same time.

There were two barracks for the Guards at Windsor. One was for the Household Cavalry at Combermere, whilst we Foot Guards inhabited Victoria Barracks. The Cavalry lads could spin the tallest of yarns, especially if pretty ladies were listening, and a special story was the one about the horse with the green tail. The chaps would delight in telling a captivated beauty that this mythical beast's tail was more precious than the Crown Jewels themselves. It was said the horse was so exceptional it was kept locked away from daylight in the depths of the castle; and God help the fair maiden who was so tempted to see this rarity that she agreed to an underground tour with her hulk of a storyteller. She always came back much the wiser. This joke went sour some few years later when a 14-year-old schoolgirl was thus attracted and trouble ensued when her irate father had to be escorted off the barracks.

Yet despite the odd hiccup, life was enjoyable here. All the Guardsmen loved this royal station and it was hard to believe this picturesque little town was only some 20 miles away from the Smoke. The train service was good and many chaps went for weekends away to see their parents and friends. I, being so far from my own home, was quite contented to stay.

The castle grounds ran down to the crystal waters of the river Thames, which was teaming with fish, and on the grassy banks there'd often be a carnival or a fair of some description. There was an abundant supply of punts, boats and canoes for hire, and it always amused me whenever I spotted a couple of straight-backed Guardsmen drifting past in full uniform, complete with scarlet tunic and forage hats on straight. It would have been an offence to sit with no headdress on, or to have one's tunic buttons unfastened.

Off duty, the officers were deluged with invitations, and Smith's Lawn in Windsor's Great Park was the scene of many lively games of horseback polo.

For us boys, various fatigues were allotted during the day, and one that was given to me and a friend of mine called George Burt was to weed the entre lawn armed with nothing but an ordinary eating fork. What a job that was! There we were, kneeling uncomfortably on the hard ground for hours on end while life passed us by. Each time the Royal Guard marched past, we jumped painfully to our feet and stood to attention, and then fell back to our knees to continue the work. We weeded and weeded, and when I finally stood up at the end of the day my legs gave way under my weight and I collapsed back to the ground. Poor George ended up with fluid on his knees. We were relieved we didn't have to use the same forks at dinner that evening, and tucked into welcome plates of shepherd's pie.

The illustrious nineteenth-century sculptor Sir Richard Westmacott was responsible for the huge Copper Horse statue that still stands within the Great Park in a direct line from the castle. It was commissioned by King George IV and depicts his father, George III, in Roman attire. This majestic sculpture was unveiled in 1831 in the presence of the Royal Family and members of the council, and a collective gasp of horror emanated from the onlookers when they first beheld the horse. According to the legend, they'd been affronted by the absence of stirrups. Whether there was truth in this or not, I cannot confirm, but it was rumoured that the designer, Vincent Gahagan, who assisted the distinguished sculptor, committed suicide not long after the unveiling by hanging himself from a tree close to the horse. It is said the copper king is pointing his outstretched finger directly towards the tree from where the unfortunate man ended his life. However, it's an undisputable fact that the Romans never used stirrups, so the designer was quite accurate in his depiction. This being the case, the true motive for the crowd's reaction remains a mystery to this day.

It's funny how these stories become distorted over time. Whilst Mr Gahagan did indeed lose his life in tragic circumstances less than a year after the unveiling of the Copper Horse, it wasn't suicide. The unfortunate man was working on his next commission, a 12-foot statue of the late British prime minister, George Canning, when part of the sculpture fell and crushed Gahagan to death.

I always admired the Copper Horse, for it reminded me a little of a much smaller bronze sculpture at Rushmoor Arena, depicting the Duke of Wellington mounted on his charger, facing Waterloo. Legend tells that the sculptor concealed a bottle of whiskey inside the horse's tail. If so, it must be very mellow by now, for the effigy was first unveiled in 1846! The bottle was apparently placed there so that when Wellington meets Napoleon in heaven, they can drink to each other's health.

During my time at Windsor I met an elderly ex-Guardsman who'd long since retired but was still living in the town. The tales he told about his time in the regiment left us all enthralled, and one day he related the curious incident of John Hatfield, the sentinel stationed at Windsor Castle during the days of King William III.

One dark and starry night, Hatfield had been pacing the terrace walls of the castle, counting down the minutes to the time when he'd be relieved from duty. The hour of midnight was fast approaching. The night was calm and clear; and far over to the west, unseen and unheard, was the City of London.

Midnight came and went but no relief appeared to release Hatfield from his lonely vigil, which officially ended at the stroke of twelve. Considering his duty was done, he sat down at the side of the rampart to wait but still nobody came. The minutes ticked by and Hatfield closed his eyes just for a second, but soon fell fast asleep. The belated relief found him snoring the castle battlements off some while later. Asleep on duty and caught in the act was a crime punishable by death, and poor Hatfield was placed under arrest.

The ensuing court martial seemed cut and dried, for the facts presented left no doubt as to his guilt. He even admitted being asleep, but John Hatfield astounded all when he stated with unyielding certainty that he'd been awake long enough to hear Great Tom, the bell in the Clock Tower at Westminster, proclaim the hour of midnight with thirteen strokes. The truth of this startling statement was met with great doubt, and the court rejected it out of hand. To hear the clock from such a distance, and that it struck thirteen … well, whoever heard such a ludicrous plea? Hatfield was duly condemned to death but he wasn't going to accept his fate so easily.

'Great Tom struck one note too many,' he insisted, 'and as God is my witness I heard it, as clear as day. That's how I knew my watch had ended.'

Had Great Tom really ushered in the hour of midnight with a baker's dozen strokes? This sensational story soon hit the newspapers, and reports began pouring in from various witnesses who'd been roaming the streets of Westminster that fateful night. They claimed to have also counted thirteen strokes as the bell chimed over the hushed city. The pile of evidence to substantiate his story became so tremendous that Hatfield received the king's pardon at the eleventh hour and was granted his freedom.

John Hatfield lived until the ripe old age of 102. He went to meet his maker on 18 June 1770, and was always thankful to Great Tom for the inexplicable mechanical error that saved his life.

The Guardsmen on duty in 1928 told us that when all was quiet and the night was serene, they too could sometimes hear Great Tom's successor, Big Ben, chime the hours, though it never struck thirteen.

One couldn't expect to visit places like Windsor Castle, steeped in centuries of fine history, and not expect to encounter some lingering ghosts from the past. Many of the sentries who were situated on the East Terrace often echoed the story of the sad and mysterious little lady in grey who could sometimes be seen on a bitterly cold night wending her spectral way along this dark and lonely part of the castle. Some of the older Guards confirmed that sightings had been reported for many a long year, and one happened during my time at the castle.

I was attending the rounds one moonlit evening, and as usual I was armed with my hurricane lamp, which more often than not went out. This normally happened as we rounded the East Terrace, and a blast of cold night air would threaten to knock us off our feet.

'Halt, who goes there?' a sentry called out, as we approached his post.

'The rounds,' I answered.

'Advance and be recognized,' the sentry replied, and after hearing the password he instructed: 'Pass, rounds. All's well.'

We proceeded to visit the various watchmen on guard that night to ensure they were alert and on top of their job.

We always took care to watch our step within this ancient stone castle after sundown. It was so dark in the wintertime that all the nooks and crannies looked grey and shadowy when the weak light from our hurricane lamps fell upon them.

As we turned the corner onto the East Terrace I flashed the lamp to give the sentry the tip that we were coming, but we received no response. I sent another signal but still we weren't challenged. The rounds were brought to a halt and a couple of us were sent to investigate. A few yards from his box lay the sentry, flat on his back and out for the count. Hastily, and not too gently, he was picked up and returned to the guardroom. He appeared to have been in a dead faint and it was several minutes before he came to. When probed for an explanation, as no doubt was asked of John Hatfield many years before, the startled sentry told us he'd witnessed something so inexplicable it surely had no mortal place in this earthly realm.

'I saw a lady in grey approaching my post,' he said, looking as ashen as the character he described. 'I challenged her but she failed to stop. I received no reply on my second and third challenges, so I lunged forward with my bayonet but no flesh did it penetrate. It simply passed through thin air. I remember no more until I came round.'

There was no court martial for this chap as he'd not been the first to tell this strange story, and likely not the last.

There was another peculiar happening at Windsor Castle that I can well recall but barely explain. One night, just the same as any other, a sentinel had been standing on guard for a long time, looking out over the gardens in the area where the Royal Family stayed during the summer. Suddenly, he saw someone – or something – moving about in the grounds.

'Halt, who goes there?' he challenged, but received no answer.

Though it was dark, he could make out the shadowy outline of several human-shaped figures advancing towards his post. He called out to them again, but without a sound the gathering slowly continued to creep towards him under the cover of foliage and moonlight. Who were these men and what were they up to? The sentinel challenged one final time, but still the strangers didn't respond. Fearing for the safety of the castle, the sentinel opened fire on the moving figures, and all fell still.

The alarm was raised but a subsequent search of the grounds found no trace of any bodies. In fact, no evidence was discovered to suggest that anybody had been there at all. The following morning, as sunlight flooded the scene of the incident, the stone statues that reposed in the gardens were found to be riddled with the sentinel's bullets. He swore that he'd seen the figures walking towards him, hence his actions. We all believed him, for we knew it would take something quite extraordinary to distract a well-trained Guardsman while on duty.

A colourful Guard Mounting ceremony took place every day at Windsor. After the Guards had formed up and been inspected on the barrack parade ground, we'd march up to the castle headed by the Corps of Drums and Colour Party. This was always a popular event with the public, who'd crowd the streets with their cameras, eager to capture memories of the pageantry, or even catch a glimpse of the Royal Family.

It was customary for the captain to take sherry with the equerry-in-waiting while the senior NCO mounted the Guard. One morning, the captain removed his sword and laid it on the hall table while he quaffed his sherry, but on returning he couldn't for the life of him find his weapon anywhere and faced the dreaded possibility of parading improperly. Just as he began to feel the sweat gathering on his brow, he heard laughter coming from outside. Upon investigation he found a young royal nobleman standing with sword in hand, which he was using to charge his trembling nanny with some offence or other. Though the officer's eyes were bulging with rage and his face as scarlet as his tunic, he politely addressed the nobleman with humility when he went to retrieve his sword.

Whenever a member of the Royal Family walked past a Guardsman, he was required to present arms in salute. The young and Right Honourable George Lascelles, grandson of King George V, found this custom particularly amusing. The mischievous 5-year-old decided to entertain himself one day by running past the sentinel on duty, who'd come to present arms, and then dash past again to another present. On and on this comical routine went until the perspiring sentinel was about to take the little lad to task himself. Fortunately, a passing nanny caught the boy and administered a hearty rebuff.

My partner in crime George Burt and I once got into a spot of bother over the Guard Mounting parade. George was the bugler for the Old Guard at the castle, and I was the bugler for the New Guard Mounting. As the New Guard arrived on the quadrangle to receive its trumpeted present arms from the Old Guard, George brought his bugle up to his lips with a flourish, and with an odd flash of forgetfulness, sounded *The Pioneers' Call* by mistake.

'Show that silly fool up with your salute,' said the voice of the NCO of the New Guard.

I shot my hand behind my back, took a firm grip on my bugle and pulled it towards my lips, but something had gone wrong. The bugle cord had got stuck. Sweat began to roll down my spine, and I was suddenly all too aware of the hundreds of pairs of eyes upon me. I pulled and tugged and at last got the bugle up towards my chin, but it wouldn't come any further and I found myself looking sadly into the wrong end. I did eventually manage to get some kind of hideous sound out of it, but the NCO was far from impressed.

I joined George in the guardroom some hours later, where we were both charged before being marched under escort to the adjutant. Our excuse was that our bugles were blocked, and the punishment was quite aptly to clean out all the bugles in the Corps of Drums the following weekend. We dutifully soaked all the instruments we could find in a bucket of hot water mixed with soda, as instructed, and then returned them all to their pegs. In our haste there was something rather essential we'd forgotten to do.

Monday morning dawned and brought with it the returning drummers who'd been away on weekend leave. A feeling of murder must have filled their hearts when they entered the barracks and found a room full of rusted bugles. It was only then we realized we'd forgotten to dry them. To make matters worse, the water had dripped all over everyone's white Blancoed equipment. George and I got the lecture of our lives and endured the wrath of the drummers for a long time afterwards.

The year was 1929 and I'd reached the age of seventeen. I'd been lucky enough to win the featherweight boxing championship of the Brigade of Guards and had also done well in the army championship, though I'd been beaten in the finals by the skin of my teeth.

I didn't have time to dwell on my defeat, for the time had come for us to leave the delightful little town of Windsor and travel to the bustling capital city. I was looking forward to my first guards at Buckingham Palace, St James' Palace and the Bank of England, for I felt nothing but veneration for these great and historic institutions. I had the naïve impression that at 'Buck House', as we termed the first, and 'Jimmy's', as we called the second, we'd be permitted to wander freely about the palace corridors on our mission to personally guard the king and queen. I also thought that while at the bank we'd watch the money being printed, and stand guard over tottering stacks of wet notes piled high on the floor. I was soon to discover that the reality was rather different, and not quite as glamorous as I'd imagined.

The crowds were cheering and the bands were playing as we marched out of the gates of Windsor Castle for the last time. Even the mayor came to see us off. Once at the railway station, we departed amidst a wave and a lover's kiss. Some of the lads even broke into an impromptu chorus:

> *Her golden hair in ringlets fair, her eyes like diamonds shining,*
> *Her slender waist with carriage chaste, may leave the swan repining.*
> *Ye gods above, O hear my prayer, to my beauteous fair to bind me,*
> *And send me safely back again, to the girl I left behind me.*

To those immortal words we steamed out of Windsor and on to smoky London. The stirring notes of the *Coldstream Regimental March* from *Milanollo* were played as we marched through the great iron gates of Wellington Barracks. We received a hearty welcome from the colonel of the regiment before being ushered away to our barrack rooms, which overlooked St James' Park. Over to the left loomed Buckingham Palace. As I gazed out of my window in wonder, it felt strange to think I was stationed here when, centuries earlier, a mighty king of England had apparently decreed that from henceforth no person bearing the name Rochford should ever be permitted to serve in a royal palace again. He was, of course, King Henry VIII, who it was said felt so betrayed by the

Rochford family – not least Jane Boleyn, the lady-in-waiting who'd arranged secret meetings between Catherine Howard and her clandestine lover – that he banished all Rochfords to the Emerald Isle with the warning that they were never to return. Jane was the wife of George Boleyn, Second Viscount Rochford, who'd been infamously convicted of incest with his own sister, the king's second wife: yet another reason for the portly monarch to strike us off his Christmas card list.

Many tides had come and gone with the passing of the years, and it seemed as though the current king didn't have any objections to my presence. Countless were the royal guards I took at the palace, and I relished every moment, from the Changing of the Guard to Trooping the Colour. We, the drummer boys, felt a little like monkeys at the zoo: we performed behind iron railings as the public peered in, though I must say, they never threw in any peanuts to us. It was a privilege to encounter so many different people, from Alfonso, the exiled king of Spain, to the little old lady who had special permission from Queen Mary to sit in the palace garden whenever she wished. Though the lady was just a commoner, she'd been presented with her own key, and was allowed to come and go as she pleased. I've sadly forgotten her name, but not the sixpence that she pushed into my hand as I bent down to pick up her umbrella for her one cloudy afternoon.

Though they called them the Roaring 20s, industrial strife was beginning to take hold all over England, dragging the country down into a state of depression. The protesting 'hunger marchers' were descending on London from every corner of the nation, and a general strike loomed large. My company was prepared to turn out at a moment's notice at the first sign of violence. Full marching kit was hanging on the pegs in anticipation and live ammunition had been issued. Eventually things quietened down, although everything was hanging on a thread at one point. We all felt the sense of misery in the air; and the countless unemployed people, without any means of a livelihood, struggled to make ends meet.

As ever, we Guardsmen were kept busy from dawn until dusk. After a thorough inspection at the barrack gate, including lifting up the soles of our shoes to see if they were in good repair, off we'd march to Hyde Park, neatly dressed in scarlet. It was always interesting to walk up and down the 'Monkey Run', the path that cut through the park to the Marble Arch; and no doubt the composer of the marching ditty *Round the Marble Arch* was a spectator who saw us.

Though we were strictly forbidden to walk out with a girlfriend it wasn't long before everybody had one. A lot of the foxier boys claimed they had a 'sister' and so evaded this rule. In most cases the girls were from private service, so the chaps were never short of a supper at the residence where they worked. One of our brighter boys selected a girlfriend in the region of 15 stone, and we rather cruelly nicknamed her *Fat Fan*. She fed her man well. He used to return to the barracks laden with parcels of food, the likes of which we'd never seen before, and we'd all hope he was in the mood for sharing. If he wasn't, we'd creep out of bed at night when he was asleep and help ourselves from out of his locker.

There was a secluded little place called 'the Dip', which was a favourite destination of lovers after the sun had gone down. No Guardsman ever dared sit on the grass in daylight while in uniform, so he'd only take his sweetheart to the Dip after dark. Before long the air would be filled with the different company bugle calls, whistled by all the courting Guardsmen to let the other lads know they weren't on their own.

One evening while out in London, I stopped to ask a civilian the time. To my pleasant surprise I found myself standing face to face with a young man whom I remembered from long ago. His name was Cyril. I'd shared the same dormitory as this fellow while we were at the Duke of York's School together, and always got on well. I was pleased to learn he'd done well for himself and was now in private service as a footman to a well-known nobleman and Tory politician, Sir Philip Cunliffe-Lister. Cyril was residing in His Lordship's family home on Ebury Street, and he invited me to call to see him on my next evening out. This I did, and had the good fortune to meet all of the household staff and enjoy their hospitality and friendship for many years to come. I'd often go to dinner at Ebury Street and share a meal with my new friends in the servants' dining room. It was delightful to be waited on by the pretty kitchen maids, who served us wholesome three- or four-course dinners, including wine. This became something of a tradition, and it was eventually suggested that I should keep a suit of civilian clothes in Cyril's room so that every so often I could change out of my scarlet uniform and go for a night at the theatre, or even to the pictures, with him and the other members of staff. Being underage I was forbidden from wearing civilian attire, but I was young and carefree, and was eager to have some fun.

One evening over the Christmas period I'd been to see a show with some chums and had arranged to meet Cyril outside the residence at 10.30 pm so I could nip inside and change back into uniform, as I had to be correctly attired and back at the barracks by midnight. I arrived at the agreed time and waited.

And I waited.

It was one of those nights when the frost nipped at your fingers and cheeks, but I kept waiting in the lamplight as the falling snow dusted me in a light sprinkling of lace. The minutes ticked silently by, and still Cyril didn't turn up. The servants' entrance was locked and it seemed as though everyone had gone out for a Christmas tipple, so there was no way of letting myself in. At 11.00 pm I became rather worried, for a couple of policemen were eyeing me suspiciously. Inevitably, after several more moments of loitering outside His Lordship's residence, they approached me.

'What are you doing here, young fellow?' one of them asked.

'I'm a drummer in the Coldstream Guards,' I began, wondering how on earth I could explain the situation to them. Mercifully, however, they believed my sorry tale, and advised I should wait a further half hour. If my pal still hadn't turned up, they suggested I should knock on the front door.

There was still no sign of Cyril by 11.30 pm, so with hesitation I approached the front door of the four-storey town house, and after a gulp or two, pressed the bell. I only had to wait a few seconds for it to open, and into view came the earl himself, dressed in a fine dinner jacket. He glared down at me with a cool stare and I lamely recounted my story. Disbelief was etched all over his well-bred face.

'You do not expect me to believe this tripe, do you?' he scoffed. 'I'm afraid you will have to go away.'

I backed away to avoid being whacked in the nose as the door slammed shut, and was just beginning to wonder how much trouble I'd get into if I was caught trying to force a window open, when Cyril appeared by my side, completely out of breath. He'd been having such a good night that he'd lost track of the time. As soon as he let me in through the servants' entrance I raced to his room, threw my uniform on and dashed away again across snowy London. I made it back just as Big Ben was chiming the introductory tune before striking midnight.

It was 1930 and the time had come for us to make our annual move. This time we'd been posted to Chelsea Barracks, and I was particularly excited because this was the year when I'd come of age. We packed up as meticulously as if we were going to an overseas station, though we were only moving a matter of a few miles. As always, we quickly settled into our new home and got into the usual swing of things.

Not many weeks after our arrival we received an order to lay our kits out for an impromptu inspection. For some reason the adjutant had a sneaking suspicion that something was amiss and he was keen to catch us unawares.

'Lay out your kits!' the drum major bellowed as he strode in through the door, while the adjutant and his Alsatian remained out of sight.

As we hurriedly turned out lockers and kit bags, whispers could be heard being passed around the room.

'Anybody got a spare bar of soap?'

'… a comb?'

'… a button stick?'

'… a tin of Blanco?'

There was always somebody who was deficient in something, and equally there was always the astute one who had two of everything, and would help out a comrade in distress. Unfortunately for a poor boy named Stan there was no spare soap, so in desperation he placed a portion of dirty-looking cheese in the spot where his soap was normally laid. Thinking he'd got away with it he breathed a heavy sigh of relief; but just as the adjutant came to check this chap's kit, the Alsatian, Sally, caught a whiff of something rather tasty indeed, and she gobbled up the chunk of cheese in one gulp.

'Where's your bar of soap?' the adjutant growled at Stan, noticing the empty space.

'Sally's just eaten it, sir,' said Stan, as a titter of laughter left the lips of his comrades.

The adjutant asked how much it had cost and without turning a hair Stan replied: 'Threepence, sir.'

At once the adjutant put his hand in his pocket and produced the required sum. Handing it over to Stan, he uttered: 'I'm very sorry.'

The Bank of England Picquet was a picturesque military operation that had the unequivocal purpose of meeting all security requirements at the bank. It was originally posted in 1780 to guard 'the Old Lady of Threadneedle Street' during the time of the Gordon Riots, when anti-Catholic protesters got carried away with themselves, and rioting and looting across the City of London was rife. Though the riots were eventually subdued the tradition of the picquet endured, and each evening at 5.45 pm one officer, one drummer and fourteen Guardsmen would march 6 miles from Chelsea Barracks to the bank. This was no fun in the summer months, when scarlet tunic and bearskin cap was the order of the day. We used to spend most of our time praying for rain, because when the weather was dreary the officer commanding the Bank Picquet would usually buy us all tickets for the Underground instead of making us march.

Come rain or shine, a small civilian lady of about forty years of age used to march alongside the picquet every evening. Sadly, I never got to know anything about her, who she was or why she marched with us. Some said her husband was killed in the Great War. If that was so, no doubt he was from a Scottish regiment, for she always dressed in traditional Highland attire. One evening she failed to turn up for the march, and after that we never saw her again.

For one young ensign, it was his first duty as Bank Picquet commander and he felt extremely proud as he swung through the streets at the head of his immaculately dressed troops. A lone piper was leading the way. Ahead, the ensign saw that the traffic lights had turn to red. He was in full swing and didn't want to be stopped, so he directed the piper to head down into the Underground. It seemed an ingenious solution to march down the steps, along the subway and up the other side. I barely recall what the ladies said as they emerged to find their privacy invaded by fourteen burly Guardsmen, one crimson-faced officer with his sword drawn, and a piper merrily screeching out his music. It quickly dawned on the young ensign he'd taken a wrong turn and had led his party straight down to the public lavatory.

It was said that the bank was impossible to break into, but we all knew that was just a myth. This illusion was shattered the day a Guardsman on patrol outside the bank witnessed, to his horror, a dishevelled head protruding from a narrow air-chute that originated somewhere within the building. Before the sentry had time to react, an arm appeared from out of the wall. The body slowly followed closely behind, and the whole figure sank to the floor in an untidy heap. The intruder was thin and emaciated, with facial hair almost down to his armpits. He looked as if he hadn't eaten or shaved for weeks. The man was arrested on sight, and under interrogation revealed that he'd spent many weeks squeezing into the bank on the instruction of a person or persons unknown. If he succeeded in his task, he'd apparently been offered a substantial sum of money, enough to go abroad with and disappear forever. The intruder didn't have anything of value on him when our men apprehended him; so the question remained: if he hadn't gone in there with the intention to steal, why had he pulled such a risky stunt? The true motives for his actions, and the mastermind behind them, have never been disclosed.

On 1 April 1930 I officially turned a man of eighteen years, and was allowed much more freedom than before. Once the duty of the day was done I was permitted to wear civilian clothes, smoke, drink and even be seen in the company of a girlfriend. Being a good Catholic boy I'd never set foot inside a public house before, so I decided I might stop off to have a celebratory drink as I made my way back from Cyril's to the barracks. I stepped smartly into what I thought was an average public house, but as soon as I entered I could tell something wasn't right. An unsettling silence descended and many an interested gaze fell on me. At first I thought I must have done something wrong. I glanced around the room and noticed that the patrons were both male and female, and nearly all of them seemed uncommonly distracted by my presence.

'What can I get you?' the barman asked.

Not really knowing what to order, I requested the first thing that came into my mind.

'Ooh,' came a seductive voice from a table to my right. 'She drinks a Brown Ale, does she?'

For a moment I thought the voice was female until I looked closer and found it belonged to a man; though only just. A chortle of laughter greeted his remark and my cheeks began to burn. Eager to leave, I downed my drink in one and went to place my empty glass back on the bar, but not being used to alcohol the beer rushed straight to my head and I missed by inches. The glass dropped straight onto the floor, scattering broken shards in all directions. With many exclamations of sympathy from the gathering, I departed in haste, too embarrassed to even offer to pay for the damage.

I was relieved to find my bus had pulled up outside, so I went to hop on board but heard the sound of footsteps hurrying along behind me. I turned and found the softly spoken man had followed me.

'What's your hurry, love?' he said, or something to that effect. I don't quite remember his exact words, for I was so perturbed by what happened next that I lost all sense of reason.

The man reached out a finger and stroked my cheek. That was enough to make my innards boil. With one hand clinging on to the rail of the bus, I whipped the man a beauty right across the chin with the other. He dropped to the pavement like a ton of bricks. At first I thought I'd killed him, but as the bus pulled away I noticed him stir. The conductor was so amused by the whole incident he didn't charge me my fare.

I later learnt that particular public house had a certain reputation around town, and made a mental note never to frequent it again.

The year 1931 saw us on the road to the grim Tower of London. It was always a cold and miserable place, and I felt sure that all the personalities who'd had the misfortune to be imprisoned there over the centuries wouldn't have been at all sorry when their hour of execution came.

Once a royal residence, the Tower had since been put to good use as a fortress, a prison, and a place to house the Royal Mint and public records. King James I, a great lover of wildlife, expanded the royal menagerie at the Tower, and traces of this were still evident by the presence of the ravens that hopped about, cawing and sometimes swooping down on tourists who looked like they might have had a packet of biscuits or a bag of chips on them. Hector, one of the cheekier ravens, was supposed to be 199 years old, and he'd a nasty habit of pecking at the legs of lady visitors. The birds used to make their nests on the walls of the Old Tower during my time there, and legend tells that the Tower will crumble and England will fall if the ravens ever depart. To ensure the safety of the country, one of our sergeants had the great responsibility of caring for the birds. Each had its own unique identification number and set of records, and food rations were put out to encourage our feathery friends to stay. The tamer ones would be fed by hand, though sometimes they'd catch the sergeant's finger in their sharp beaks and give him a nip. This hand-feeding was eventually stopped as the visitors thought the cries of pain issuing from the lips of the sergeant were put on for their entertainment, and that the ravens were trained to perform. Howls of laughter could often be heard, much to the annoyance of the sergeant. He was a great animal lover, nonetheless, and had a pet dog called Bruno who went with him everywhere. The pair could often be seen together

1931: Paddy (marked with a cross) and his comrades on manoeuvres.

in the NAAFI, and the sergeant would regularly share a beer with his faithful friend, pouring the dregs into the dog's food bowl.

A fine tradition that went on at the Tower of London at 10.00 pm each evening was the Ceremony of the Keys, during which the Tower was officially locked up by the chief yeoman warder. Ever since the Crown Jewels were stolen back in the seventeenth century, the chief constable never took any chances regarding their safety. A special security system was rigged up so an alarm would ring in Scotland Yard and Buckingham Palace if the treasures were ever tampered with. This sounded once during my time at the Tower. On hearing it we Guards turned out in number, armed to our teeth and prepared to apprehend the malignant felon, but to our hilarity he turned out to be just a little mouse having a nibble on one of the wires.

We were kept so busy at the Tower that we didn't have time to concern ourselves with the darker, more sinister matters that were looming on the horizon. Newspaper headlines were prophesising the arrival of a deadly foe, and as the months went by their warning became starker:

'CRITICAL DAYS AHEAD'.

'FASCISM SWEEPING THROUGH GERMANY'.

'HITLER'S THREAT OF "HEADS WILL ROLL"'.

And, most ominous of all: 'WORLD WAR TO END CIVILISATION'.

We all knew these sensational headlines were merely the means to sell more papers, and never gave it a second thought. After all, everybody knew the Great War had been the war to end all wars, and surely Germany wouldn't be foolish enough to come looking for another thrashing.

However, the fallout of these international political skirmishes landed firmly on our doorstep one day when we learned that Captain Norman Baillie-Stewart, a highly regarded officer of the Seaforth Highlanders, had been placed under close arrest and imprisoned in the Tower for allegedly spying for the Germans. This was a terrible shock to Great Britain who until then had placed so much faith and trust in her armed forces. By all accounts this officer had fallen in love with a beautiful German girl who, like many others working in England as officers' servants, had had the secret mobilisation plans of Britain in the event of war handed directly to her.

It was at around this time when a sort of anti-war movement began within the exclusive circles found in places such as Mayfair and Grosvenor Square. The British upper classes began to join together in what was called 'a link of happy understanding' with Germany, and the ill-famed Herr Von Ribbentrop, Hitler's ambassador in London, began seducing the rich with his lavish parties. Champagne was flowing freely on the tables in London as the oily Von Ribbentrop slipped his way into diplomatic houses, with the intention of gaining high-ranking friends across the Western world. He even had the nerve to goose-step into Buckingham Palace on one occasion, and upon leaving gave the king a Nazi salute. This caused much comment but in real English style the whole affair was overlooked as a show of bad manners from a sore loser.

Such matters were quickly forgotten, however, for my battalion had been detailed to file the Guard of Honour for Their Majesties King George V and Queen Mary. As usual, we spent many hours polishing and preparing, and consequently my second-best pair of boots were so clean that they glinted. They looked so fine, in fact, that I was tempted to wear them on this occasion even though they had a small hole in the uppers, just on the inside by the bottom of the big toe.

The great day finally dawned, and as I donned my sparkling footwear I felt a slight twang of apprehension in my stomach, but I'd made up my mind and wasn't going to change it. I half wondered if one of my superior officers would spot the hole during the initial inspection on the barrack square, but to my relief, it wasn't noticed.

To the great roars of command by Regimental Sergeant Major 'Tibby' Brittain, we duly marched into the arena at Earl's Court.

'Eeeeeyes front!' he roared, as a gathering of nearby ladies squealed in delight, and we all stood to attention to await the arrival of the Royal Family.

After presenting arms and dipping the battalion Colours to the strains of the National Anthem, played by the regimental band, the king came down the ranks. I was praying that he'd pass me by. As a single bead of sweat meandered down my brow, I watched him draw closer from the corner of my eye. Just as he reached me he stopped, like my heart nearly did. He looked down at my boots; then his eyes snapped back up to my face.

'How old are you?' he asked.

'Nineteen years, sir.'

'Your boots are very clean,' he remarked, before continuing on his way down the line.

I glanced at the drum major and saw the look of love etched on his face. I breathed a deep sigh of relief. My holey boots hadn't let me down.

In the days before indoor plumbing was common, some local authorities used to provide public bathhouses for their townsfolk. These were a little like swimming pools, and one such establishment could be found at Ealing. This particular

1930s: Paddy (left) and a friend looking smart in their uniforms.

venue was hired by the British Army, who transformed the whole building into a boxing arena. It was here where I took part in a triangular match between the Coldstream Guards, the Grenadier Guards and the Guards Training Depot. The ring had been placed over the first class bath and the changing room was in the cubicles for the second class bath. There was much excitement within the ranks, as any contest between the Coldstreamers and the Grenadier Guards was always a blood match. I couldn't wait to get in the ring and do my regiment justice. Mutt Morton and I were the first opponents and I knocked him out quite easily in the second round, with a left to the face followed by a right cross.

After the match I returned to the changing room, where I met the company sergeant major of the Irish Guards, a champion boxer himself. We had a good chat and he invited me to show him the dive that had won me the Brigade Diving Championship earlier in the year. Without thinking, I peeled off my boxing gloves, stepped onto the diving board and prepared to take my well-drilled plunge.

'I wouldn't do that if I were you, sonny,' echoed the voice of the bath attendant from somewhere below.

'Don't worry about me,' I called, eager to impress the CSM. 'I'm the champion diver for my regiment. I know exactly what I'm doing!'

'I don't doubt it, but the baths are currently being emptied for cleaning,' the attended explained, 'so I'd advise you not to go in.'

I was at that awkward age when one doesn't listen to advice. I leapt proudly into the air, did a one and a half somersault and struck what little water there was left in the bath. I hit the bottom of the pool with the bridge of my nose. The cool, blue water around me suddenly turned warm and red. I felt dazed and confused, but didn't lose consciousness. Though my face throbbed and my whole body ached I managed to drag myself out of the bath, where I sank down by the wall in a puddle of water and blood. The town mayor and my commanding officer came to see me from the makeshift arena, and after some first aid and a plaster stuck ceremoniously on my nose, I was declared fit to go back into the boxing ring to receive my cup. I just about managed this, but felt nauseous and wobbly after losing so much blood.

The following morning I was allowed an extra hour in bed, where I stayed hidden under the blankets pretending to be asleep. I was in pain for a good few weeks afterwards, but on reflection I think it was my pride that hurt the most.

With our royal duties completed, we were due to arrive at Warley Barracks in Brentwood, Essex; and it was here where I had my first romance.

1930s: preparing for a bout.

There was another boxing match coming up and though we were kept busy from dawn until dusk I was keen to get in as much training as possible. One day I went out alone for an early morning run. I was trotting along a leafy lane when ahead of me I noticed a pleasant looking country inn called The Thatcher's Arms. From one of the windows I saw two pretty young faces gazing out at me. They smiled as I drew nearer, and I decided it wouldn't hurt to step inside for a few moments to have a swift drink. It was an unseasonably chilly day and the warmth from the crackling log fire greeted me as I stepped over the threshold.

'What you running from, soldier?' giggled one of the girls, who I noticed was wearing a servant's uniform.

I puffed out my chest and tried to look impressive, though that was always difficult with my slender frame. 'I'm a boxer in the army, and I'm preparing for my next fight. It's going to be a tough one, but I'm well up for the challenge.'

The girls exchanged incredulous glances and I was mortified when they both burst out laughing.

'You're pulling our legs. You're far too little to be a boxer.'

'For your information,' I began, hoping my cheeks weren't as red as they felt, 'I happen to be the regimental champion. I have trophies to prove it, as well as a scar on my nose. See?'

'Well,' chuckled the second girl, 'if *you're* the champion, the boxing world must be very hard up.'

She lit up the whole room with her radiant smile, and I thought she was absolutely beautiful. She had long, dark locks that were bunched up on top of her head and bright rosy lips that reflected her name; and I hardly failed to notice her familiar accent that reminded me so longingly of home.

'You're Irish,' I grinned.

'Yes,' she said, looking embarrassed. 'What about it?'

'Only that I'm Irish too. I'm a Liffey-sider.'

'Go away with you,' she said, rolling her eyes. 'You're too English sounding. I know your game. You're just trying to get off with me!'

'No, of course not!' I insisted, perhaps a little too eagerly. 'Anyhow, you're the one who smiled at me as I was jogging by. So it's clearly you who's trying to get off with me.'

We all giggled, and I found I couldn't tear my eyes from the girl's lovely smile.

'What's your name?' I asked her.

'Rosie,' she said, 'and this is my friend, Ruth.'

We stood chatting for a good half an hour, during which time I learned that these two girls were employed by Ruth's father to work at the inn. As I was leaving they invited me to call round on my next evening out, which I did with pleasure, and over time we three became good friends. I even used to help out by serving in the bar every now and again when I was off military duties.

That Christmas I called at The Thatcher's Arms to say so long before I went to Ireland on leave, but was so moonstruck by the lovely Rosie that I stayed with her at the inn for two whole weeks. I had my own room, of course, and sent my poor old mother a telegram saying: 'Further delayed; will arrive tomorrow.' I never did, but I had one of the nicest Christmases I'd ever experienced.

After a period of shy courting I made a cardinal mistake. I introduced my sweetheart to one of my sergeants, and not just any sergeant. This one was a tall, handsome, muscular man with a tongue like velvet and a right hook that would fell an ox. Though it's sad to relate, it's perhaps hardly surprising that that was the last I ever saw of my first love.

Chapter 5

Beside the Tideless Sea

The year 1936 was a fateful one. Our beloved King George V had been ill for some time but news of his death came as a grave shock. Britain and the Commonwealth were plunged into mourning. Our monarch had led us to victory in the Great War, commanding respect from all four corners of the earth.

In the months leading up to his death, as his health declined, speculation in England was rife. Would the Prince of Wales accede to the throne? This question was on the nation's lips. Our wilful prince remained unmarried and his name had been associated with that of the divorced American, Mrs Simpson, who at one time was married to a Coldstream Guards officer, Captain Simpson. This was indeed a rather scandalous affair, but the gossipmongers were silenced once and for all when the cries rang out: 'The king is dead. Long live the king!'

King Edward VIII was proclaimed.

George V was laid to rest at Windsor Castle and we had the honour of an inspection in full Guard Order. We stood to attention on the parade ground, and as the new king passed by looking at our scarlet tunics, which of course were our best, I couldn't help noticing the look of displeasure on his face. He sighed and turned to address the commanding officer.

'Often when I have looked out of the castle window, I have noticed that the drummers' tunics look very clean when mounting, and very shabby on dismounting,' he remarked, with a disapproving shake of his head.

'Sir, the air is sometimes very dusty on the parade ground,' Lieutenant Colonel Whittaker replied, clearly doing his best to remain polite, 'and that's why the tunics may sometimes look a little off-colour. There's not much we can do about this, I'm afraid.'

Despite the commanding officer's reasonable explanation, new tunics were purchased at the extortionate cost of £9 19s 6d each, which the regiment could barely afford. We were warned that if we soiled them, stoppages would be made to our pay at the sum of two shillings per week. Needless to say we were less than impressed, and felt our new king had got off to a shaky start.

However, we all agreed there was still plenty of time for him to grow into his father's shoes.

Meanwhile, far across the North Sea, the political struggles in Germany were deepening. During the 1930s the country had been in fear of Communism and in desperation had looked anywhere among her own people for a leader, someone strong who could see them safely through the dark times. Ex-Corporal Adolf Hitler had pushed his luck by making impassioned soapbox speeches in the troubled streets, pledging to create a greater nation for all the German people. He gained more and more power, and his Nazi Party began to make headway in the political arena. Joseph Goebbels belched forth his propaganda to all and sundry, whilst Hermann Göring, desperate to get young Germans into the air, had urged these young, impressionable men to take up glider sports as a hobby. Göring, of course, was a fighter pilot in the First World War with a great many kills to his name.

The *Horst-Wessel* song, or *Horse-Weasel*, as it later became known, rang out through the streets of Deutschland as the general populous surrendered to Hitler's deceits.

> *Clear the streets for the Brownshirts,*
> *Clear the streets for the Stormtroopers!*
> *Already millions, upon seeing the swastika, are filled with hope,*
> *The day of freedom and bread is dawning!*
>
> *The storm warning has sounded for the last time,*
> *We all stand ready for the fight!*
> *Soon Hitler's flags will fly over all the streets,*
> *And our bondage will only last a short time more!*

The fate of Germany now lay in the hands of one man: the aged president, Paul von Hindenburg. He could have stopped Hitler from ever coming to power, but the president's sanity was in question. He was eventually talked into handing the reigns over to the self-proclaimed Führer, and Germany's delight was fanatical. Delirious people packed the streets as the man who would surely lead them to greener pastures took control of the country. They dared to dream his rise to power would bring an end to mass unemployment, street riots, and baton charges that had plagued their everyday lives. In triumphal celebration the brass bands played, banners were waved, and the so-called Stormtroopers appeared in the towns and cities, gathered as one in military formation. Deutschland was once again on the march and it seemed as though nobody, save for two valiant men, had the guts to stop her.

From Westminster the eagle eyes of Winston Churchill and Anthony Eden were watching. Both of these politicians had persistently campaigned for Britain's rearmament in the event of war, but their fellow ministers treated these men as though they were reptiles. Heads turned away, eyes looked to the ground and ignorance reigned. It wasn't that they didn't care; it was just that nobody wanted to believe that another war could be on the way.

While the world turned a blind eye, the Nazis began strutting about like masters of the universe. The Jews were to be the brunt of their attack. These poor men, women and children were seized in the streets and even in their own homes. Women's heads were sheared; aged men were made to scrub the pavements; Semitic shops were looted; and books were burnt. The German Jews who'd fled their homes to seek solace in the Holy Land fared little better, for the native Arabs objected to the sheer volume of immigrants, and land ownership became a volatile issue.

In England, the War Office began trying out experimental manoeuvres, testing new equipment and calculating just how long we could march on as little food as possible. We soldiers were training and marching, day and night.

1930s: with army comrades enjoying a break.

Rumour had it that we'd soon be sent abroad, but nothing was ever confirmed to the 'rank and file' until the last moment, so we learned the news from idle gossip. Some called it the grapevine, although in the Guards the world over it was always in the WC where one heard what was really going on. That was the only place where one could talk freely without being overheard.

One WC rumour spoke of a new type of super weapon that was in development. It was called the 'Bren Light Machine Gun', a name only spoken in whispers. We still had the old Lewis automatic gun – and by then I'd mastered the fifty-seven known blockages – but it was said that one only needed to press the trigger of the Bren and all hell would be let loose. This was one rumour we all hoped would come true.

Many changes were being made in the army, and not only where our armament was concerned. For one thing I was now a lance corporal, and my company had been moved to Stansted on manoeuvres. One day I was passing a group of officers when one of them called me over.

'Tell the sergeant major to come and see me at once,' he instructed.

I knew from the urgency in his voice that something was going on, and soon we all knew what it was. Our battalion was being sent on active service to Palestine, where trouble was reaching breaking point. Not only were the indigenous Arabs incensed by the mass immigration of European Jews, but there was also open rebellion against British rule, and it was apparently down to us to keep the peace.

Our men were trimmed to fighting fit. Though discipline was down to the last blink of an eyelash, we were only human, and still young and naïve. Our inexperience meant that most of us lacked the understanding of the sort of dangers that lay waiting for soldiers in an active war zone, and most of us were looking forward to the adventure. I for one had always wanted to visit the Holy Land and was filled with a feverish excitement, never once fearing that any kind of harm might befall me.

As it happened, our first tour of Palestine did indeed turn out to be more of a holiday than a military operation. It was almost as if Mr Thomas Cook was there in person to guide us around, as we seemed to do more sightseeing than fighting; shooting more films than bullets. Rumour had it that when the rebels heard the British Guards were on their way, they decided to ask for a truce, so all was calm and peaceful when we arrived in October 1936.

We started our journey as we meant to go on, setting sail on board the luxurious liner, SS *Laurentic*, which had been chartered especially for us on its return from a Mediterranean cruise. As we steamed out from Southampton

Docks, the regimental band, which never failed us, was there in all its glory, playing martial airs. The last notes I heard were the immortal strains of *Auld Lang Syne* before the shores of England vanished into the blue.

We were six to a cabin, and to us, used to being cooped up in the hold with a filthy old hammock alongside a couple of dozen sweaty bodies, this felt like a luxury. Our days at sea were filled with concerts, swimming in the ship's pool, setting obstacle courses for each other along the decks, and firing live ammunition at balloons. Early one morning I was taking a stroll along the decks, playing my mouth organ to while the time away, when I happened to pass the ship's padre on his way to the little chapel. He was carrying what looked like a stack of hand-drawn posters.

'You play very well,' he noted. 'I'm going to be putting on a talent show tonight for all the troops to enter, and there'll be a prize for the best turn. Pass the word around the ship and make sure your name is down. The details are on these notices, which I'll be pinning up around the ship for everyone to see.'

I was rather flattered by this. I'd been playing the mouth organ since my young days at Mount Sackville, purely for my own amusement, but until that moment it never occurred to me that anyone else would possibly be interested in listening to me. I thanked the padre and went around telling all the lads about the concert, and was surprised by the number of men who also owned harmonicas. A few of us decided that, with some practice, we might play well together, so we began to prepare a routine we could perform.

We were third on the bill that evening and though the competition was tough – with some of the lads having formed a rather decent barber shop quartet, others reciting poetry and some even dancing a ballet – our performance received a standing ovation, and to our astonishment we won first prize: about a ton of cigarettes. The commanding officer, who'd applauded and cheered with the rest of the audience, took me to one side after the concert and told me to carry on with the group, as it would be a booster to morale during the bleak days that lay ahead.

Our liner docked at the city of Haifa on 1 October 1936. We crammed the rails to get a good look at this new land and were greeted by the sight of an enormous crowd of barefoot natives who'd gathered in their hundreds looking for money. They were all in rags, and looked extremely thin.

It was winter back in England, but here the sun was a glowing red ball, searing down upon us. The surrounding hills were earthy and bare, but on top of Mount Hebron there was a white covering of snow. It reminded me of Mother's Sunday tea table, adorned with its spotless tablecloth.

1930s: Paddy and his boxing trophies.

The whole battalion paraded off the ship and formed up in line by the side of the docks. As an added bit of swank we'd been ordered to wear puttees around our lower legs and to tuck our khaki-drill slack into them like the Foreign Legion. Headed by the Corps of Drums, and the commanding officer mounted on horseback, we followed the battalion Colours, company by company. As we marched through the city and up towards the hills, we passed many British Army camps, and some of the remarks from the troops were ripe.

'Go home, Guards – the war is over.'

'Look out that you don't get your uniforms dirty.'

'You've lost your way – this isn't Blighty!'

At the time I couldn't find the right word to explain their hostile behaviour, but now I can understand. They were slaphappy. They'd no doubt experienced terrible times, having been sniped at every day by the rebels, had their trucks blown up by landmines, and had experienced all the other terrible things that come with unrest in a land torn apart by strife.

We carried on undaunted, and after some miles we finally reached our dusty encampment where we were to spend the night. It wasn't grand. There were a few tents for the officers' mess (an absolute must) and a few tents for our provisions. There was nothing else for miles; nothing except trees, rocks and undergrowth. Those of us not fortunate enough to have a commission laid out our groundsheets between two poles and hoped for the best.

We settled down that night amongst the hills, hoping for a restful sleep, but it wasn't to be. Some chaps awoke in the darkness, bathed in sweat, having been disturbed by the calls of the pyeards. These unworldly creatures reminded me of angry banshees, wailing inharmoniously in the night. The Palestinian wilderness abounded with these wild canines, which only came out after sundown.

One or two of the men were bitten by scorpions during the night, and it was no wonder. Our juicy white flesh was new, fresh and apparently tasty. Thankfully, the medical officer had a cure, and this was to create an incision with a knife or razor blade crossways over the wound, which was then soaked with iodine. It was painful but essential, for if left unattended, a wound like that could prove fatal.

I gazed up at the stars as I lay beneath them. My makeshift tent had collapsed, though I wasn't too concerned as the temperature hadn't dropped. It was surprising how close the stars seemed when one was under the Eastern sky.

Reveille sounded on the bugle the next morning as if declaring to the whole country: 'It is a beautiful morning but watch your step: the Guards are here!'

Palestine, 1938: an alleged photograph of Fawzi Bey, commander of the Arab rebels.

Before we knew it, we were up, washed, fed and ready. We were marched several more miles to a local railway station where we were rammed into the oldest looking train carriages I'd ever seen. They had the letters PSR painted on the side, which stood for 'Palestine State Railways'. We wondered how our superior officers would enjoy travelling third class, but as professional as ever, their faces betrayed no hint of displeasure at any point during the journey.

As the rickety old carriages bumped and swayed through the foothills of the mountains, my Wolseley helmet, complete with red plume and large, shining badge of my regiment, fell through the open window. It rocketed down among the sandblasted boulders and out of sight. I knew I'd be in so much trouble, and my imagination began conjuring terrible visions of a sharp–eyed Arabian rebel fingering it with delight.

'See, I have beheaded an accursed Englishman!' he declared in my mind, presenting it to his smirking leader, Fawzi Bey, who in turn would send it to the British Governor of Palestine with his compliments.

Would I lose my stripes for this? I fretted for the rest of the journey, but nothing serious happened, except a brief reprimand from the sergeant major.

'It's a pity you didn't fall out with it,' he said in his usual brusque manner. 'A right sight you'll look, marching past the general officer commanding without headdress.'

Thankfully I was issued a replacement. We Guardsmen had strict orders to wear headdress from sunup until sundown. Why this was, I'll never know, but in about 1940 this order was revoked, and the army Wolseley helmet went out of fashion.

Under the Balfour Declaration of 1917, Jewish people from every nation were given a right to establish a home in Palestine, the land of their forefathers, if they so desired. In the years preceding the Second World War, thousands of them suddenly began taking advantage of this liberty all at the same time, and were buying up as much land in this part of the world as they could.

'The Jew is pushing us out of our rightful land!' was the cry that was taken up all over the Middle East by the Arabs, their brothers, cousins and all their brethren.

The British soldier, as usual, was the man in between, and a decidedly unpleasant task it was. The intensity of hatred felt by the Arab for the Jew shocked me to my core; but whatever the natives thought about their new neighbours, the latter brought a prosperity to the land that had never before been realized by the former. Through new ideas, hard work and a fanatical love for the Holy Land, the country began to thrive. The plots the Jews had purchased suddenly began springing up with all kinds of vegetation that the Arabs had never dreamed possible, and this caused even more resentment. It all boiled down to the fact that both races of men felt that they, and they alone, were entitled to inhabit the nation, and neither could live in harmony with the other.

On a personal level I found the Arabs to be a friendly lot, and rather innocent at heart. Their carefree manner meant that they tended to avoid doing more work than was absolutely necessary. There was an old Arabic saying that went: '*Yimkin bukra fil mishmish*', which, when translated into English, meant: 'Maybe tomorrow, when the apricots grow.' In other words, never! This proverb had been handed down through the generations, and though its origins had been lost in the midst of time, many believed that it referred to a foolish Englishman who once tried to grow apricots without success.

The Jewish immigrants, on the other hand, were a hardworking sect whose resilience was admirable. They didn't fraternize much with us Tommies, and we got the distinct impression that they resented our presence in the land. With this in mind, we tried our best to remain as low key as possible for the duration of our tour.

The Mount of Olives, 1936: the ruined Augusta Victoria Hospital, where the 3rd Battalion of the Coldstream Guards were to be stationed.

The Mount of Olives, 1936: fancying himself as 'Paddy of Arabia'.

My battalion was stationed atop the celebrated Mount of Olives in a large, ruined building known as the Augusta Victoria Hospital. It had once housed German pilgrims before being transformed into a military infirmary during the First World War, but this onetime hospice was damaged, almost beyond repair, by an earthquake that struck the region in the late 1920s. Surrounded by pine and palm trees, which gave off a lovely fresh smell that whetted the palate, this decaying stone palace was our home for the next few months.

Armed with buckets, brooms and scrubbing brushes, we cleaned the place from top to bottom. Though the weather was warm the floors were marble and the rooms were incredibly large with no means of warming them up, except for the army stoves, which, when not choking one to death with the paraffin fumes, more often than not had wick trouble, and there was always a shortage of new wick.

Despite these little issues, my time on the Mount of Olives, overlooking the city of Jerusalem, was a momentous experience. Life was calm and serene, and we had little work to do. From the windows of our sanctuary one would never have guessed that turmoil was plaguing the scarred yet beautiful land below.

From the rear of the hospice we could look down into the wilderness where Satan had tried to tempt Christ. It was easy to picture the stories from the Bible with clarity as I gazed for miles across this netherworld, where no one but the desert dogs found sanctuary. Sound carried for miles out here, and in the dead

The Mount of Olives, 1936: the view over the wilderness.

Jerusalem, 1936: a view of the Holy City.

of night the distant pyeards would let out their bloodcurdling howls. It was quite some time before we learnt to sleep undisturbed, and one or two fellows would often wake from their slumber in terror, believing that the night prowlers were right beside them. Our beds were not at all comfortable, which didn't make sleep any easier. Each man was issued with three bed boards and a single blanket to sleep on, and the 'pillow' was one's kit bag; but like everything else in the army, you got used to it and soldiered on.

After a few days, which were filled with lectures on what was expected of us, we were allowed out in pairs. There was much to be seen and various tours were arranged to cover all the places of interest. Every day was a holiday, and when we weren't on patrol we went exploring.

There was the Old City and the New City of Jerusalem. I always imagined the Old City, surrounded by its thick, stone walls, had changed little since the days when those feet of ancient time had walked upon its uneven streets. The colourful shops, houses and marketplaces had been built almost on top of each other, and the narrow alleyways twisted and turned in all directions. Black hosts of flies swarmed everywhere, but through the filth and the dirt was an ever-present aroma of fresh food and incense, which helped to mask all the other smells.

Life proceeded in this land in much the same way as it had for millennia. The biblical stories that dear old Mother Patrick had told us were unfolding before

Palestine, 1936: Paddy (second from right) and friends taking a dip in the Dead Sea.

Jerusalem, 1936: Palestinian police on patrol by the Wailing Wall.

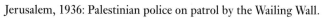

Bethlehem, 1936: a typical market day street scene.

my eyes. The prophets; the moneylenders; the beggars in rags; the afflicted; and the asses and donkeys all roamed around the streets together as one. The only difference now was that it was British soldiers, instead of Roman, who were to be seen patrolling the city.

One day we marched from the Mount of Olives to the Mosque of Omar, one of the most sacred places in the Muslim world. This was just one of the many fantastic visits that we were lucky enough to make. We'd been told to wear clean socks, as nobody was allowed inside in his footwear.

On arrival, a wily Arab at the steps to the building offered each of us the hire of a pair of sandals. We duly placed our shining army boots in neat rows outside the entrance and dropped a few piastres into his hands, trusting he'd keep them safe until we came out. Low and behold, on our return we found that two pairs of boots were missing, and the wily one was gone. He never returned, and neither did the boots. Two crestfallen Guardsmen were left on the steps of the Mosque in their stockinged feet, as neither of them had hired sandals, and remained there in humble meditation for several hours until a red-faced comrade had the chance to race back from the Mount of Olives with their second-best footwear.

Jerusalem, 1936: an Arab rioters' conference. Paddy and his men later arrested everyone in attendance.

Jerusalem, 1936: Paddy (far right) visiting the Mosque of Omar.

After exploring Jerusalem, we made our way to see the Church of the Holy Sepulchre, the place of Christ's crucifixion. After an hour or two I left full of wonder, with an affirmed belief in my Christian faith. Like many others I'd come away with a pocket full of rosary beads and some holy medals as souvenirs of our visit; but imagine my surprise when my sightseeing buddy handed me an old key.

'You're Irish, Paddy,' he whispered, thrusting the rusty old thing into my hand. 'Add this to your collection; it's the key to the tomb of the Lord!'

I blinked in surprise and asked him what on earth he was talking about.

'It, um, fell onto the floor as we were going inside,' he explained, 'so I picked it up and thought you might like to keep it, seeing as you're Catholic.'

I didn't feel too comfortable about this and felt the item should have been restored to its rightful place. I returned to the church to hand it in, but the priest simply smiled and told me to keep it as they had a spare.

The next time I travelled home to Ireland I presented the key to my mother as a surprise gift. At first she was horrified, but after I explained the story to her, she had the key plated and inscribed; and from that day forward it was most reverently handled by my family. Many years later Mother told me that every night during the Second World War she'd held the key to her heart and prayed for my safe return.

It was Christmas in the Holy City. The weather was getting cold and our time in this beautiful land had come to an end. We trooped up the gangplank of SS *Laurentic*, looking forward to returning to England, but somehow or another feeling a little sorry to be leaving. The past couple of months had been an experience that we were lucky to have had, and would certainly never forget.

Before we arrived back in England the news reached us that King Edward VIII had abdicated in favour of his brother, Prince Albert, Duke of York. This emphatic proclamation meant that our king had been Britain's shortest reigning monarch since the days of Lady Jane Grey. I recalled to mind the day of the funeral of George V, when my battalion had stood to attention as we lined the route on the Mall. I remembered the sombre expressions upon the faces of his four sons as they passed by. How could the shy and retiring Duke of York possibly have foreseen that the weighty crown was destined to rest upon his head? A great burden had fallen on unprepared shoulders; but as history recalls, he carried this burden with humility.

My final year of service in England was spent training in preparation for our attendance at the coronation of His Majesty King George VI. When the great

Chapelizod, 1936: a portrait of Joseph and Annie Rochford.

Jerusalem, 1936: the Coldstream Guards marching to church from the Mount of Olives.

day dawned on 12 May 1937, the capital city looked her best. A festive spirit filled the air; visitors, photographers and news reporters from across the world had flocked in their thousands to witness the spectacle. Even the heavy rumblings in Hitler's Germany couldn't stifle the excitement. Bunting, streamers and flags of every nation were proudly on display, and street parties were held all over the country by revellers in outfits of red, white and blue.

We were roused at 4.30 am that morning. After breakfast we took up our positions outside Buckingham Palace at the Queen Victoria Memorial. Even at such an early hour the streets were crammed with people. The rain held off until later in the day, at which point it began to pour, but this did little to dampen the enthusiasm of the joyous crowds. Thousands of scarlet-clad Guardsmen lined the roads, their bearskins groomed, and the horses of the Household Cavalry sporting glistening coats.

The procession commenced at 8.40 am, when the magnificent royal carriage drove into view. I saw His Majesty King George sitting calmly inside. He looked thoughtful and passive under his cap of submission, though it was hardly surprising. Sitting gracefully beside him was his beloved wife, Her Majesty Queen Elizabeth, and joining the royal couple were the two lovely little princesses, Elizabeth and Margaret, whose carefree smiles beamed out of the windows.

As the golden carriage passed by it was difficult to hear the word of command, 'Royal salute, present arms', because the cheers from the crowd were so tremendous. Even the corporation dustman with his horse and cart received a special cheer as he passed by.

The ceremony itself took place inside Westminster Abbey, and once our king and queen had been crowned we were marched back to barracks. On the way through the assembled throng people kept offering us drinks, which all except for one Guardsman declined. (He was punished later.) We were allowed to have the rest of the evening off, so most of us went back into London to join in the festivities. The street outside the palace was swarming with people, and many times our new king and queen, along with other members of the Royal Family, came out onto the balcony to greet their subjects and watch the firework display, which lasted long into the early hours.

It was a frosty November dawn when we received orders to relieve the 2nd Battalion of the Grenadier Guards, who were serving in Alexandria, Egypt. We were told it was to be a normal peacetime tour lasting eighteen months, and were given embarkation leave prior to our departure. I travelled home to Chapelizod for a few snatched moments with my loved ones. At the end of my brief visit my brothers and sisters came to see me off, and that was the first time

Somewhere in Hertfordshire, 1937: Paddy and the troops on manoeuvres, shortly before leaving for Egypt.

1937: HMT *Dunera*, the ship that took the 3rd Battalion of the Coldstream Guards to Egypt.

Father hadn't taken me to the docks himself to bid me a final farewell. I did wonder why that was, but when I arrived back at barracks there was too much going on for me to dwell on it any longer.

It was bitterly cold when we embarked. As always, the faithful regimental band played for us as we waved at the well-wishers who'd gathered to bid us bon voyage. Mothers, wives, sisters and girlfriends all blew teary kisses towards their men.

The air became milder as we sailed further from home, and I knew we couldn't be far from our destination. It was during the early hours one morning when I was roused by a pal and told we were finally approaching Alexandria. I went onto the deck of HMT *Dunera* and breathed in the warm, sea air. I could see bright city lights ahead, twinkling like fireflies in the distance. The Rue Corniche was a main road through Alexandria that swung down from Abū Qīr, a village in Egypt that was made famous by the sea battle in 1798 when Lord Nelson defeated the French fleet, resulting in the British landings in Egypt. The lights had the appearance of a diamond necklace draped across the skyline, which earned the road the colloquial nickname 'Queen Nazli's Necklace'. She was the beautiful and much younger wife of the late King Fuad, and the mother of the present ruler, King Farouk I, the gluttonous monarch considered by many to be one of the most crackpot leaders of all time.

Any apprehension I felt about this voyage was taken by the breeze, and as I stood in the night air, I felt a shiver of excitement. I wondered what adventures awaited me in this historic land of pharaohs and kings, where we were due to arrive at dawn.

Chapter 6

The Land of Pharaohs and Kings

British troops landed on Egyptian soil following the defeat of the French fleet at Abū Qīr Bay in 1798. At first their arrival was more or less accepted by the Egyptians until a nationalist officer named Colonel Arabi Pasha rose up and tried to force the British out. This courageous leader inspired the native masses, and in 1882 he roused the rebels into declaring war on the invaders. The British Cavalry galloped across the grey sands to meet the advancing rebels, whose artillery vomited angry jets of flames through the battle clouds. Shells screamed across the sky and tore open the ground around them. The British were falling from their saddles when the command came.

'Charge those guns!'

The stirring Moonlight Charge that followed was commemorated in both paintings and verse. A trooper of the Second Life Guards told how the British Cavalry, eager to avenge their ill-fated comrades, stared death straight in the eye and cut their way through the screaming Egyptian hordes. Gravely wounded after his horse had bolted, Trooper Bennett staggered valiantly through the enemy lines, but the Bedouins lassoed him before he could return to his unit. With a rope around his neck, he was taken before Arabi Pasha himself, who looked down at the soldier with disdain.

'The English are fools,' he mocked. 'I have 40,000 men at my command. Your feeble army will never return home; you will all be completely annihilated!'

Arabi Pasha (the Arabic word for 'Lord') had spoken too soon. The Egyptians lost hundreds of men that night and Britain was ultimately victorious. The rebels were routed in a dawn raid at Tel el-Kebir and the British entered Cairo the following month. Arabi Pasha was exiled from the land and the British ruled Egypt from then on as a protectorate.

By 1918 the Great War had come to an end, but instead of peace, unrest descended once again like one of the ten plagues of Egypt. An underground movement against the British began to stir. Scuffles broke out in Cairo and Alexandria, and a couple of prominent Egyptian radicals began to flex their muscles. Their names were Mustafa el-Nahas Pasha and Mahmoud Fahmi an-

Nukrashi Pasha. Both of these university graduates began inciting the nation's student population to go out into the streets and spill as much blood as they could. Under much pressure, the British decided to end the dominion, and in 1922 Egypt was granted its independence. An Anglo-Egyptian agreement was signed at St James's Palace, and certain terms were reached, which could be briefly summarized as follows:

1. Egypt would be a completely independent country and was to retain its sovereignty. King Fuad was then on the throne, and his son, Prince Farouk, was his heir.
2. The defence of Egypt was to remain in the hands of Britain until the Egyptian Army had been trained to take over. A British Military Mission, commanded by a major general, would oversee the training of the Egyptian Armed Forces.
3. Once this was done, the British were to move out of Cairo and the Nile Delta to the barracks at Fâyid, close to the Bitter Lake of the Suez Canal, where they were to protect the Canal Zone.
4. The police, who were mostly Europeans and British, were also to be gradually withdrawn and replaced by Egyptians.

If Britain hoped that the signing of the treaty would placate the rebels then they were to be sorely disappointed. Though Egypt was outwardly gratified, behind the smiles was discontentment. There were still many citizens who craved the complete removal of the British Army from their land, and secret factions began plotting and scheming to rid Egypt of all British influence once and for all.

Mustafa el-Nahas Pasha was a conspicuous member of the political Wafd Party, a nationalist party whose name meant 'for the people'. His liberalist views afforded him great standing among the poorer classes – of which there were many – during the 1930s. The starving masses idolized him, and in consequence he wielded great power over the land of Egypt. He did more than anybody to help improve the lives of the poor *fellaheen* (peasant labourers), and I witnessed much of his good work for myself.

Because of this man's unprecedented popularity, King Fuad and Prince Farouk greatly distrusted Nahas Pasha. When the king died in 1936, and his teenage son ascended the throne, a great rivalry between Nahas Pasha, of humble descent, and the blue-blooded Farouk was born. If Nahas could have had his way, Egypt's sovereignty would have died with the late king. How he longed to remove the prosperous young ruler from the throne and divide his riches among the people. He would have done so in a heartbeat, given half the chance, but in those days the king was backed by the powerful British, and was effectively untouchable.

Major General Aziz el-Masri Pasha was an impeccable and ambitious officer of the Egyptian Army who, like Nahas Pasha, despised British supremacy with a passion. During the First World War he'd made no secret of the fact that he was staunchly pro-German, and had been actively engaged in street riots and political revolts. For this reason tensions between him and the authorities were high.

Their mutual determination to oust Britain from Egypt united Masri and Nahas Pashas, and together they recruited a band of likeminded militant renegades. Hassan al-Banna was the fanatical head of the recently formed Muslim Brotherhood; and the debonair Lieutenant Colonel Gamal Abdel Nasser, a popular man with almost everybody he came into contact with, had begun concocting radical plans of his own. Outwardly he was shy and retiring, but behind his deep brown eyes was an ambitious and determined soul.

By the time we arrived in Egypt in 1937, the revolutionary mobs were growing restless and street riots across the major cities were becoming frequent. Political activists were once again whispering into the ears of impressionable students, filling their minds with all sorts of anti-authoritarian notions. It wasn't difficult to brainwash some of these young people, who found street skirmishes more interesting than their studies. We all knew Nahas Pasha was responsible for winding up this army of toy soldiers and letting them go, but proving it, and thereby getting to the root of the problem, was another matter entirely.

I had a cousin back in Dublin who worked as a theatrical agent at the Gaiety Theatre, and he often travelled the world in search of new stage talent. He'd once described the docks at Alexandria as the 'backside of the world'. I never understood what he meant until HMT *Dunera* docked, and I realized just how right he was. Everything was untidy and haphazard. On one side of the docks, dozens of barefoot labourers in filthy rags unloaded bale upon bale of merchandise. A wily master who had the run of the docks hired out these gangs and made a fortune from their toils, whilst the workers themselves received a pittance. They were made to run here, there and everywhere under the supervision of a man armed with a rhino whip, which he used unsparingly.

Yet despite the abject poverty that afflicted this land, the average man on the street acknowledged we Britons as friends. As we made our way along the docks, we were patted on our backs and greeted with warm words of welcome.

'Hello, Johnny!' they'd cheer, flashing us glimpses of decaying teeth. This was usually followed by the word '*Buckshees*', which meant 'tip me', as they held out their open palms with expectant expressions.

Swarms of barefoot urchins were running around beside us, dodging in and out of our legs. Their faces were dirty and they had the strangest of remarks on their lips.

'I come from Mobarak, where Husani lives.'

'Do you know Fatimah from Manchester?'

We were surprised at their knowledge of English and of England, forgetting that for nearly six decades troops had been doing just as we were, coming into Egypt from Great Britain.

As we drew up in a straight line beside the tram stop, we saw the most peculiar-looking electric tram pulling in. It was small and made entirely of wood, and reminded me of the old Dublin steam trams from long ago. The conductors and drivers were dressed in ill-fitting suits of khaki and each wore a red fez on their heads. All aboard, and with a sharp toot on the funny hooters, off we set in these swaying, wooden vehicles. Pungent smells drifted in through the open windows, and we gazed outside as the derelict scenery passed us by. Through the flies and the dust we could see that the dock neighbourhood wasn't at all pleasant. This was a place where you could have your throat cut for a farthing and your body whisked away for a halfpenny, never to be seen again. This was the place where holy men rubbed shoulders with murderers, smugglers, robbers and dope fiends, and where the prostitutes plied their trade from behind bars like caged animals.

Leaving this bleak part of the world behind us, we entered Alexandria's European quarter. In stark contrast, this district was filled with cinemas, sports grounds and well-kept properties on delightful avenues banked with flowers and palm trees.

After some 4 or 5 miles the tram stopped at a place called Sidi Gaber. Spread out on the other side of the road stood Mustapha Barracks, the great military fortress that was to be our home for the foreseeable future. We marched through the gate behind the Corps of Drums and it soon became apparent what a sprawling place Mustapha was; yet despite its enormity this was not the only army base in the city. The Royal Egyptian Navy was also stationed here, and theirs was one of the biggest bases in the Middle East. Unfortunately for them, the navy was the butt of many Egyptian jokes, as their annual naval manoeuvres consisted of moving from one part of the harbour to the other. On one occasion, one of their destroyers was sent out to sea with the purpose of finding Malta. Some few days later it returned, much sooner than expected.

'Malta *mafeesh*,' the admiral reported, which meant: 'there's no such place as Malta: I couldn't find it.'

Mustapha Barracks was just a short walk from the beautiful blue waters of the Mediterranean, and we were all rather disappointed to learn we were to be confined to barracks for the first two days of our stay. However, this proved to be a wise move, as our commanding officer, Lieutenant Colonel J.A.C. Whittaker, had decided to bring in a man with local knowledge to put us in the picture about life in Alexandria before allowing us to wander about in this strange land unprepared. Egypt was very different from Palestine, and was becoming more dangerous by the day. Riots and violence were a part of daily life, and Alexandria was infiltrated with spies. We were told they could be anyone. They could be blonde or they could be brunette, and we had to learn quickly to trust no one.

Lectures over, and with a disharmony of guidelines ringing in our ears, we were allowed to explore Alexandria in our free time. I soon began to discover the customs, places, and the dos and don'ts of Egypt for myself. Despite all the warnings, I was pleasantly surprised by the ease with which one could make friends with the average man on the street. The local shopkeepers were particularly amiable, and I once asked one of them what the strange, exotic smell of the East was.

'Have you ever seen a public urinal in Egypt?' he asked me.

'Erm, no,' I replied. 'I don't believe I have.'

'Well, there you have it, boy,' he said. 'They have to do it in the streets here, and the smell remains forever.'

The lack of good sanitation wasn't the only regressive thing about this country. For many decades the brave women of the suffrage movement had been fighting for equality in the West, and in recent years had made considerable progress in battering down the boundary between the sexes. In the East, however, women were still the inferior gender, and it wasn't wise for a local girl to be seen in the company of a man who wasn't her father, husband or brother. Matters were made significantly worse if the suitor in question happened to be a British soldier.

One day I met a lovely young lady and rather foolishly asked her out for a date.

'That would be nice,' she replied cautiously, 'but you must wear civilian clothes. And, of course, my mother, my four sisters and two of my cousins will be coming along as chaperones.'

This appeared to me to be some sort of racket to get the whole family a free treat, and I was having none of it, so I remained dateless.

Though I'd learned that the women of Egypt were strictly off limits, the menfolk were an approachable bunch who were possessed of many pipe dreams that never seemed to become reality. After lunch they used to lie in the sun until teatime and dream of the three things they yearned for the most: a gun, a horse and a wife, usually in that order. Their fourth wish was a regular supply of *hashish*. This was an illegal drug that everybody seemed to crave. It wasn't unlike cow manure in appearance, and was always carried in the top left-hand pocket of one's *jelabiya* – the white garment that the men wore, which looked a little like a nightshirt. There were only two classes of Egyptians in those days: the very rich and the very poor, and the very poor relied on the sale of this drug to earn an extra penny.

The British Army in Egypt was one of the country's major employers of working-class Egyptian men. At the barracks each company had a man known as a *dhobi*, who was responsible for washing the laundry and other such activities. These employees had begun work as children, alongside their fathers, and after the fathers had died, the sons had taken over. *Dhobies* were always spotlessly clean and could be seen dashing around the barracks in the whitest starched clothes with a bright red fez stuck jauntily on their heads. Our *dhobi* was known as Ali Cream, and he was a sharp character indeed. For five piastres (about one shilling), he'd take away a kit bag full of washing in the morning before we got up, and it'd be back before sunset, clean, starched and ironed.

No parade took place after 10.00 am in the morning, and when we weren't on patrol duties we were free to do as we pleased for the rest of the day. A taxi ride from the barracks to the centre of town cost less than a shilling; a large glass of Stella beer with plates of food to go with it cost no more than a shilling, and a good seat in the cinema cost pennies. What more could a chap ask for?

Along the coastline one could find lovely beaches with gaily painted sunshades, bathing cabins and sun-bronzed bathers, but it was the crowded streets of Alexandria that interested me the most. Here one could see every class and race of person going about their business in one united community. It was said that there were more than 20,000 Italians here; and with the Greeks, Syrians, Armenians, French, British and others, one could really appreciate that Alexandria was a truly cosmopolitan city.

On an evening the city was ablaze with lights, and the crowds were buzzing. There were plenty of places that offered entertainment, though some venues were strictly out of bounds to the common soldier, or, as the French called us, 'the other ranks'. This seemed unfair, but I later discovered one or two fairly decent establishments that were open, and I was more than contented with my lot in life.

Having settled into a new regime in this foreign land, I received an unexpected telephone call from a Mr Jack Davy who worked in Alexandria for Barclay's Bank. He was a civilian who'd given up much of his free time to look after the interests of a harmonica band formed by the 2nd Battalion of the Grenadier Guards, who'd been stationed in Alexandria up until our arrival. Jack had arranged concerts for them in venues across the city, and word had reached him about my band. Keen to continue his role as booking agent, he invited me to call to see him at his house in the hope of reaching a similar arrangement. This was the first time an English resident had asked me to visit his home, and I was made most welcome by this kind gentleman. His wife served us tea and cake on the veranda, and I felt like an honoured guest when she brought out their best china cups and saucers.

'I've heard great things about your harmonica band, corporal,' Jack said with a smile. 'As I understand it, you've been performing for the troops and you've gone down very well indeed.'

'Well, we've certainly been performing our hearts out,' I replied, suspecting that whoever Jack had been speaking to must have exaggerated our success. 'But we've been doing it out of enjoyment more than anything else. None of us are professional musicians. We just want to go out there and have a good time, and hopefully entertain our chums in the process.'

Jack placed his cup on the coffee table and sat forward in his chair. 'How would you feel about performing to a wider audience?' he asked.

A wider audience? I liked the sound of that, but surely nobody outside our circle of friends and comrades would be interested in hearing us play.

'My senior executives at the bank have asked me to find an act to perform at our staff Christmas Eve ball,' he explained, 'which is to take place at Nouza Casino. I rather hope that you and your band will be interested in this opportunity.'

I could hardly believe what I was hearing. Our first proper engagement!

'Yes, indeed, we'd be honoured,' I said, grinning like a Cheshire cat. 'If you really think we're what you're looking for.'

Jack assured me we'd fit the bill perfectly, and I left his house feeling awash with excitement. An official commitment for my little band, and for the bigwigs of Barclay's Bank, no less! The Nouza Casino was one of the most prestigious places in town, and my band mates were staggered when I told them the news.

Dressed in our white silk shirts and matching cricket trousers with red cummerbunds around our waists, we duly arrived at the agreed time on Christmas Eve. The casino was decked with all the usual festive trimmings, and we were so taken aback by the elegance of this palatial venue that we tiptoed inside, feeling completely out of place. We took drinks at the bar and fretted about the standard of competition we'd have from the resident band that was to play alongside us. We didn't have long to worry, for beautiful music, performed with utter balance and perfection, soon began drifting through the room. To our dismay the members of this band were exceptionally talented, and we knew even in our wildest dreams we couldn't compete to that standard.

With knees a-trembling we left a long line of empty glasses on the bar and prepared to take centre stage. It was only then we discovered, to our relief, that we'd spent the past few minutes fretting over a recording of a world famous band that was being broadcast over the wireless. The real resident band, it transpired, was pretty mediocre. Things went better than expected, and at about 11.00 pm the guests sent the resident band packing and we held the floor until early in the morning.

After Christmas we became inundated with engagement requests, and the Merrymakers' Harmonica Band became quite famous locally. One day our guitarist, Jimmy Norton, and I were invited to the Summer Palace for a chat and drinks with the proprietor, who wanted to hire us. This was a popular – not

Alexandria, Egypt, 1937: the Merrymakers' Harmonica Band on stage, with Paddy (centre) on the drums.

to mention expensive – hotel and resort within an exclusive residential area of Alexandria called Zizinia. I only had twenty piastres (about four shillings) to my name and Jimmy was completely broke, so we tried our best to get out of the invitation, but to no avail.

'Hold on to your hat,' I whispered to Jim as we stepped inside. 'It'll cost you an arm and a leg to get it back!'

Unfortunately, however, the well-rehearsed concierge was too quick for us and Jim's hat was whisked from his grasp before we'd even crossed the threshold. Like a man possessed I dashed after it and managed to return it safely to its owner without paying a penny.

As Jimmy and I approached the bar, I prayed the owner drank beer so at least we'd be safe for one round. Albert Metzar, who was reputed to be a millionaire, was already waiting for us. My heart sank as soon as I laid eyes on him. This chap looked so refined I thought a double whiskey would be the least he'd want. Thankfully for us, he bought the first round, and Jim and I were careful to take a long time to sip our Stella.

Mr Metzar was a charming man, and he offered my band a top engagement to play at his hotel as part of a lavish show that was being planned to mark Bastille Day.

'His Majesty King Farouk will be in attendance,' Mr Metzar enthused. 'I'll even present you to him during the evening.'

Naturally, we were thrilled, and I hit on the idea of getting the band to play the first eight bars of the Egyptian National Anthem as the young monarch arrived. This we did, and during a break in the proceedings the king actually came over and chatted to us. He was a rather plump fellow with a perfectly coiffed moustache, and though he'd crossed the threshold into adulthood he still retained all his boyish charms. I was instantly drawn to his attire, which was so immaculate that even our sergeant major wouldn't have found fault. His Majesty even appeared to have at least three or four pocket watch chains protruding from his waistcoat, though what he needed so many for, we didn't enquire. It was well known that Farouk was no fan of the British, but he was pleasant in his conversation and seemed to enjoy our show.

One of the main attractions at the festival was an exceptionally beautiful Egyptian belly dancer, and what a showstopper she was. Following her act was a slightly less alluring Australian chap called Sweeney, who, dressed as an Egyptian lovely, wiggled and danced to the delight of everyone, including the king.

Alexandria, circa 1940: a portrait of Paddy with his good friends, Yvonne and Layla Shakour.

During the evening I met a charming family who lived nearby. The two sisters were Yvonne and Layla Shakour, and their older brother was Joseph, who I learned was a friend of the proprietor. They showed great interest in our performance and invited me to join them for drinks and a bite to eat at their table. The four of us spent a most enjoyable evening together, sharing small talk and witty anecdotes, and I found my new companions a pleasant bunch indeed. At the end of the night they suggested I should take tea with their family one day. I agreed with pleasure, and the following weekend arrived at their exclusive address in Zizinia.

Their Swiss-type chalet was tucked away behind a thicket of palm trees, and from the veranda you could look down onto the golden stretch of sand beside the sea. It was a beautiful neighbourhood, and my three friends introduced me to their aunt, Vanda, and their uncle, Charles Shakour Pasha. He was an Egyptian-born Syrian gentleman who, having been educated at a public school in England, had a deep respect for Britain and our Western culture. I was entertained most kindly that afternoon, and soon became a regular visitor. Over time the Shakours welcomed me into the bosom of their family, and the six of us remained lifelong friends.

It was 1938 and the unwelcome news reached us that further troubles were brewing in Palestine. This didn't concern us, though, for we were on our way to a training exercise at Fâyid, a desolate place in the Egyptian desert beside the Great Bitter Lake. We boarded the primitive cattle trucks that graced the railways in those days and departed Alexandria, passing through Tel el-Kebir, where the British had first defeated the rebels. After a bone-shaking journey we stopped in the middle of the desert at Fâyid Station and marched the remaining few miles to our tent camp at the foot of Little Flea and Big Flea. These were two huge mountains of sand, where we were to call home. Just a few miles away lay the grey-coloured waters where trade ships from every nation waited to pass through the Suez Canal.

We spent about three weeks at this godforsaken spot, marching by day and firing our weapons by night, all the time enduring incessant sand storms, until the warning came to stand by for orders to proceed to the Holy Land on active service. This came as no surprise. It seemed as if the world was going to pieces again. In 1935 the Italian prime minister, Benito Mussolini, had declared war on Abyssinia, and less than a year later Hitler had violated the Treaty of Versailles by ordering his troops into the Rhineland. The German Führer was putting into action his plan to annex Austria, and all in all things were looking pretty bleak, to put it mildly.

Egypt, circa 1938: Paddy in the desert.

Alexandria, 1938: the 3rd Battalion of the Coldstream Guards arriving at the docks, about to set sail for Palestine.

On 14 October 1938 we sailed away from Egypt in the direction of Haifa, and could hear the crackling of gunfire and thumps of exploding landmines before we'd even entered the docks. It appeared that the Arabs had become quite the experts with these weapons since our last visit, though that was hardly unexpected, as they'd had plenty of practice.

Alexandria Docks, 1938: the 3rd Battalion of the Coldstream Guards embarking the ship for Palestine.

Alexandria Docks, 1938: Paddy (marked) and his comrades setting sail for Palestine.

Jerusalem, 1938: two rebels preparing for trouble.

We moved to Jerusalem by night and were told we were to enter the Old City at dawn. Enemy moles were all around us: they were employed in the canteens, the local tailors' shops and even as *dhobies*, so we troopers were never given the full picture of what lay ahead. We were simply informed that an armed band of rebels had captured the walled city, killing and plundering as they did so. They numbered approximately 500, and our duty was to get them out, either alive as our prisoners, or dead.

In those soundless moments before the sun had risen we slipped through the deserted streets of Jerusalem wearing canvas shoes instead of nailed boots to remain unheard. The early morning mist was tainted with the scent of gunpowder from yesterday's battle, yet the air was still. Not a single noise could be perceived save for an occasional cock crow. I felt jittery as I climbed over the gate and took up my position with the others on a high wall directly overlooking the Mosque of Omar, but we'd been warned that only in extreme circumstances were we to open fire on that holy area.

As the grey streaks of dawn appeared, the low rumble of our approaching aircraft stirred the concealed rebels into action, and all hell broke loose. Rifle and Bren fire thundered all around us, along with the thumps of grenades and the rebels' homemade bombs. I had a clear view from where I was positioned, and could see dozens of figures in black running for cover. Coming up from

Jerusalem, 1938: the Guards mining a rebel stronghold.

the narrow streets below were two Guardsmen carrying one of our comrades between them. Bright red blood was streaming from his otherwise ashen face. A grenade had been lobbed at him from the window of a nearby house.

I received orders to move my section up to the Damascus Gate. In single file, and with rifles at the ready, we made our way swiftly along the cobblestones. Several dead bodies littered the streets and terrified civilian faces peered furtively from behind their windows. As soon as we arrived at the gate I was ordered to sight my Bren gun across to the Old City from a high wall; my riflemen were to be deployed in and around the gate area. I was told I was to control all movement in and out of the city, and wire cages were erected in order to detain our Arab prisoners.

I stood on guard at my post and watched with bated breath. Every few minutes flares and explosions would illuminate the dawning skies and bullets flew across the horizon like shooting stars. When the gunfire ceased, a deathly silence fell over the city; then everything started all over again.

A band of the most fearsome rebel snipers soon began to make things heated for us. From a minaret approximately 350 yards from my post, a sniper was having a lot of fun shooting across the way whenever a target presented itself. We had orders to leave him alone for a while as this was a holy spot, but his

Palestine, 1938: Fawzi Bey with his rebel troops.

audacity made our blood boil. He'd come into view for a second to take a well-aimed shot before darting back into his hiding place like the slithering coward he was, before repeating the process. Patience has its limits, and a sudden burst from Guardsman Patfield's Bren shook the dust from the minaret. The sniper was unharmed, and he fired back with a renewed fury. That was when Patfield's gun fell silent. He slumped forward, a bullet having passed right through his neck. As he dropped dead on the windowsill where he'd been positioned, every weapon in the city opened fire.

The scene of desolation all around me was a far cry from the picture of peace I'd had in my mind whenever imagining the Holy City. There was nothing but death and hatred in this place; and as twilight fell I stood back while the blood-soaked corpses of rebels and Guardsmen were stretchered away out of the Damascus Gate.

The guns had fallen silent by now and my chaps were naturally subdued, so to cheer them up I sent Guardsman Jock Hamilton to a furniture store that had been broken into during the riots, and asked him to retrieve some mattresses and blankets for the men. It was cold where we were, but with the extra bedding we were able to settle down for the night in relative comfort.

An explosion in Palestine, 1938.

The Royal Air Force flew over Jerusalem before first light, dropping leaflets that warned people to stay in their homes while we conducted our searches for arms and rebels. If anybody was caught venturing outside, they'd be shot at.

At daybreak the Palestine Police Force began to march out their prisoners in chains, and a scurvy looking crew they were, dressed in oddments of rags, and many in bare feet.

'Don't feel sorry for them,' one of the police inspectors said to me. 'They'd slit your throat, given the chance.'

I was detailed to take a message to a party of sappers who were positioned near the Wailing Wall. I took two of my men along with me, and as we raced along the streets, we came upon a party of curfew breakers. Most of them were children who refused to budge to let us through, and were defying us to shoot them. I didn't have time for this, so I grabbed one of the youngsters by the scruff of his neck, threw him over my knee and administered a few hearty smacks. In a thrice the streets were cleared.

We delivered the message; and on our way back, as we passed by the area known as 'the Way of the Cross', a local lady beckoned me to her door.

'May I be allowed permission to take my ox to water?' she enquired.

'I'm sorry but there's a curfew on,' I explained. 'Orders are nobody's permitted to leave their homes until we've conducted a thorough search of the city. Where exactly is your ox?'

'Right here,' she replied, as if the answer was obvious.

I peered round her door and was shocked to see the family's ox faithfully observing the curfew in the living room. I also noticed there were three grown men in residence, hiding behind the petticoats and leaving the woman to do the asking. I passed on her request to the police inspector and I'm glad to say permission was granted.

Information was received on our third day of our being in Jerusalem that people were to be allowed to come out of their homes from 10.00 am until 5.00 pm, and I was given orders to search every single person who passed through the Damascus Gate. There must have been thousands of people living in the city, and I felt myself beginning to perspire just thinking about it. Nevertheless, orders were orders, and I duly waited in my position for the curfew gun to fire.

BANG!

And then they came. On foot, on donkey, on camel, in pushcarts and the devil knows what else. Holy men, beggars, the blind, rich merchants, women and children alike all surged towards me as one. The exodus lasted hours, and except for the odd wicked-looking knife, a supply of *hashish* or one or two packets of

Jerusalem, 1938: a snap of the Old City taken by Paddy while he was Guard Commander of the Damascus Gate.

cocaine that I handed over to the police, nothing of importance was discovered. Thankfully, after a week or so of this rigmarole, order was restored and the police resumed their normal duties.

Some 2,000 miles across the sea, Germany was growing stronger by the day. The Nazis were secretly developing their formidable Luftwaffe, and though the world knew exactly what Hitler was up to, nobody was brave enough to stop him. Unchallenged, his army invaded Czechoslovakia, and Poland was next. The mighty Adolf Hitler was standing four-square in Germany, with profitable and industrial lands in his pocket, ogling at the rest of Europe with greedy eyes. He thought the world was his for the taking.

So, here we were in 1938, on the brink of another world war. In two short decades our enemy had returned to the arena fighting fit. Germany was ready to go again. The question was: were we?

Chapter 7

White Sand and Red Blood

Every town and village in Palestine had to be searched for weapons and rebels, and this was no easy task. One day we received orders to move to Jaffa, the place where the juiciest of oranges were grown. Though it sounded like a charming place, the houses in this poverty-stricken town were ramshackle and many were without roofs. Sanitary arrangements were nil and the residents lived in the shadow of a terrible disease called trachoma, which causes blindness.

We surrounded the town before first light and moved in at dawn. An odd assortment of weapons was found and lots of suspects were caged off in the market area, and a scruffy bunch of vagrants they were, too. We sat them all down in

Jaffa, 1938: clearing up after the mobs.

rows, and each in turn was escorted to a spot some few yards from an army truck concealed behind a large canvas screen. Inside the truck was an Arab informer, who was peering out through a narrow slit in the canvas. When the prisoner under questioning was a well-known bad boy, the chap behind the screen would tap the driver of the truck on the shoulder, and off to the 'dangerous group' the suspect would go, with much weeping and wailing. This went on for hours, and my job was to keep the prisoners on the move to and from the truck.

Day after day our searches continued, well into the winter of 1938. We travelled from one crumbling town to the next, and spent Christmas in Jerusalem. Being a Catholic, I received special permission to attend a candle-lit carol service in the holy city of Bethlehem along with a handful of other chaps. It was a cold drive but well worth it, and I'm sure even non-believers would feel a presence in Bethlehem at Christmastime. Though the peace was there, the goodwill to all men was sadly lacking, and orders were that we had to carry our loaded guns into the Church of the Holy Nativity. It was sad to look around this holy place and see so many weapons of war, but I knew it was for our own protection.

The New Year heralded the departure of our commanding officer, Major General J.A.C. Whittaker, who'd been summoned back to the United Kingdom

Nablus, 1938: trouble in Palestine.

Palestine, 1938: the Guards in charge of 'Pam-Pam' guns.

to take up another post. We were sad to see him go, for he'd been with us for a long time and was like a father figure. On his last day we paraded and cheered him on his way, and later stood to attention to await the arrival of the new commanding officer. My Bren was mounted on a tripod nearby, but unfortunately as Lieutenant Colonel John Moubray arrived, one of the chaps slipped off the wall he was standing on, grabbed my Bren on his way down and accidentally pulled the trigger. A burst of noise rang out as bullets and tracer flew into the air, lighting the sky like a firework display. Nobody was hurt but we were all left red-faced. The new commanding officer took it in good humour, and dryly remarked that he'd never before received such a welcome.

One afternoon a party of men were sent out on a recce up in the rugged Hebron Hills, some 20 or 30 miles south of Jerusalem. All was going to plan until one of the party's trucks broke down. The unseen Arab rebels who'd been lurking in the hills saw this as their chance, and sniper fire rained down all around the stranded soldiers. Our quick-thinking troops managed to get their truck going again and made their escape unharmed; but as they rounded a bend in the narrow track, they were met by a line of boulders that the rebels had heaped across the road. Passage was impossible. The lads jumped off the trucks to attempt to push the boulders aside, but as soon as they stepped foot onto the gritty road, another volley of shots smacked into them from the hills, and poor

Palestine, 1938: Paddy firing his gun.

Ramleh Military Cemetery, Palestine, 1939: the funeral of Sergeant Jack Langdon.

unfortunate Sergeant Jack Langdon, a good pal of mine, was shot dead by a bullet to the back of the head.

The sun had gone down by now and the desert was getting cold. In the East there was no twilight; it just got dark. Ammunition was low and with only one flask of water per man and no blankets, things looked grim. The lads huddled together beside their vehicles, facing every direction from where a possible attack might come.

Menacing jeers from the concealed Arabs echoed all around the darkened skyline.

'Come on, Johnny!'

'What are you waiting for?'

'I think they're afraid!'

Receiving no answering fire, the rebels presumed that the British were all dead, but they were badly mistaken. Our boys were simply waiting, dry-lipped, for the right moment in which to avenge their fallen comrade. With every crunch of sand beneath the rebels' feet, the troops knew they were becoming surrounded, so they stayed as still and as silent as they could. As soon as the Arabs were close enough, the soldiers pounced. Within minutes it was all over; the rebels were killed to the last man.

Jerusalem in the snow, 1939.

The year 1939 had brought with it a blanket of snow that settled high on the hills, turning Jerusalem into a scene from a Christmas card. There were only a few weeks left for us in this trouble-torn country, and these were spent patrolling and searching every nook and cranny of the settlements. Though most people co-operated, there were still some who wished us harm, so we were supplied with special armour-plated trucks with sandbags packed on each side in the event of the vehicles running over landmines. Our driver, Guardsman Walton, christened our truck *Helene* after his wife, and we were sent all over the place in her.

One day we rounded up all the males in the village of Bethany to conduct our security searches, when all of a sudden crowds of weeping, wailing women surrounded us, demanding that their husbands were to be returned immediately. One of our chaps, Guardsman Stan Lee, was a bit of a comedian and he began attempting to entertain the ladies while we got on with our jobs in peace. He offered them rocks to sit on while he danced, told jokes and even serenaded a passing donkey. The women, it seemed, were less impressed than the braying jenny, and after a while stones began to fly at us. One well-aimed shot hit the regimental sergeant major on his tin hat, which sent him spinning.

'Fix your bayonets and charge them!' he cried in anger.

Some of the men began to obey, but one of our stalwarts, Sergeant Chick Bryant, refused.

Palestine, 1939: Paddy (crossed) and his men on patrol in their truck, *Helene*.

'Not on your nelly, sir,' he shouted, gesturing for the men to stand down. 'These are innocent women.'

The crowd continued pelting us with stones and we stuck this out as long as we could before some of us snapped and lost patience. We took the women over our knees and spanked them like they were naughty children, which had the desired effect. The crowd suddenly backed away, allowing us to complete the task in hand. When we'd finished we handed the men back, and everyone went home happy.

There was no doubt that during demonstrations tempers were frayed and the hot young soldier, at the end of his tether, administered the occasional kick in the pants to the hostile Arab rebel. As unacceptable as this was, it was better than putting a bayonet through him or blowing his head off. I never witnessed a single act of cruelty by the disciplined and well-trained British soldiers, but I can relate some of the terrible things the Arabs did to the British. Two privates of the Black Watch Regiment were stabbed in the back one Sunday afternoon in Jerusalem. Then there was a British soldier who walked into a village by himself and was found the next morning on the roadside with his throat cut and a long line of ants eating his carcass. Another chap went to the outside lavatory in the dark and a rebel threw a grenade into the privy. Two young men from the Special Investigation Branch, not more than twenty years of age, were strangled in the Holy City. A man was shot while lying wounded in hospital, and one chap had a grenade slipped into his haversack and was blown to pieces. Things became so bad that we received new orders: shoot to kill; but I for one found this a difficult order to obey. One day in Jerusalem I gave a rebel the hardest smack in the mouth he was ever likely to receive, and let him go free. I was in hot water from my adjutant for a long time afterwards, but I was in the Holy City and could hear the church bells ringing. I simply couldn't bring myself to kill him.

We received intelligence that a rebels' hideout was concealed somewhere by the shores of the Dead Sea, so we moved down into the Jericho region, where we were ordered to search the entire area. The territory was vast and possessed an eerie calm that unsettled me. There were rocky peaks and hillside caverns all around us that led to who knew where. Not knowing where to start, or even what we were looking for, we spread out in smaller groups. My party entered a deep catacomb near an ancient settlement known as Qumran, and after a while I heard one of the lads calling out.

'What's this in here? Hello! I think I've found something!'

My men and I filed across to the spot where Guardsman George Nightingale was gesturing. He'd found a collection of stone vessels that were sealed at the top, resembling confectionary jars. There were about thirty in total, all caked in dirt, and it was clear by their condition that they'd been in this cave a very long time. As we began to inspect them we found they were stuffed with what felt like seeds. In the middle of each was concealed a kind of yellowing parchment, some of which was rather badly damaged.

'This looks like wog writing,' one of our brighter lads articulated, handing me one of the ancient manuscripts.

None of us could read the words and we hadn't a clue what to do with them so we called for the company commander to come and examine them for himself.

'Well, perhaps they were put here by the Palestine Survey Department,' Major Pereira suggested, after careful consideration. 'Leave them as they are, as they're no doubt of some special significance.'

So, these precious relics of the past were left undisturbed for another three decades until the Dead Sea Scrolls, as they became known, were 'discovered' by a Bedouin boy, out searching for his stray goats. I cannot convey how many times over the years those immortal words 'if only …' have run through my mind.

April arrived, and after six busy and gruelling months in Palestine, we returned to resume our duties in Alexandria. Jack Davy had been busy while I'd been away and had managed to get us a thirty-minute slot on the Egyptian State Broadcasting System, the local radio station. My band mates and I were naturally over the moon by this, and when the exciting day arrived we all piled into the studio. With our eyes fixed on the red light that was to signal we were live on air, we began playing our signature tune, *She'll be Coming Round the Mountain When She Comes*, followed by a host of other much-loved melodies. Unfortunately, our enthusiasm ran away with us, and we raced through our programme with minutes to spare. To relieve the desperate DJ, who was frantically gesturing and mouthing 'Carry on!' we played chorus after chorus of our opening song.

Our little hiccup appeared to go unnoticed, and afterwards everyone said we'd put on a brilliant show. We even got headline recognition in the local papers. Wally Metcalfe, Jock Hamilton and Jimmy Norton were all mentioned by name, receiving special praise for their solo items. The best part was that the Merrymakers had given the 3rd Battalion good press in Egypt, and that meant the world to us.

It's often surprising what a difference a couple of months can make. By July the papers were filled with news of a different kind. I was sitting in a tram on my way back to Mustapha Barracks after visiting my friends in Zizinia when the Egyptian conductor came over and pointed out an article in the local *Egyptian Gazette*. It stated that the Germans were preparing to invade Poland.

'Well? What are you British going to do about this?' he demanded.

I was unable to offer any kind of answer. The thoughts of a war were far from our minds. Had not Hitler, Mussolini and Neville Chamberlain all agreed there'd be no war? I'll never forget the night when that wonderful news came

Alexandria, 1939: the Merrymakers' Harmonica Band, during one of their final performances. Paddy can be seen to the rear, on the drums.

through. We'd been invited to play for the British Royal Navy on board a ship in Alexandria Harbour. The deck had been rigged into a stage by the sailors, though all around one could see that preparations were in progress for a quick move in the event of war. The navy, at least, was ready.

At around 11.00 pm the captain came on stage and announced that an agreement had been reached between Hitler and Chamberlain.

'I have returned from Germany with peace for our time,' the prime minister had told the nation, clutching a folded piece of paper upon which was written the Anglo–German Declaration.

Great cheers rolled across the harbour as the captain relayed these words, and a feeling of relief washed over us all. My band and I were even invited to the wardroom for a celebratory drink, which we enjoyed to the full.

It was Sunday, 3 September 1939. I was off duty and lazing in a deckchair on the beach with a friend of mine from the Regular Army Reserve of Officers. The sea was calm and blue, and the sun was shining down on us. It was still summer here. My friend's lovely wife, a German lady, had gone up to the promenade to buy ice creams for us all. The water looked tranquil and inviting, so I was about to suggest going for a quick dip when I suddenly heard something that made my stomach lurch.

'Britain's declared war on Germany.'

What did she just say? It couldn't be true.

The words of my friend's wife had sent my head into a tailspin. A chill spread throughout my body as though an unseasonably cold wind had whipped around us, causing the little hairs on the back of my neck to stand to attention. All along the beach people were looking alarmed and some were dashing back home.

'So, what does a good soldier do now, Paddy?' I heard my friend ask.

I didn't know. We both rose to our feet.

'Reports back to barracks, I suppose,' I replied, though my voice didn't quite sound like my own.

My friends returned to their home on the seafront and I made my way back to barracks. The guard commander quietly told me not to panic and advised me to go back to where I'd come from, as Egypt was a neutral country so the war didn't affect us.

In Britain, however, things were changing at an alarming speed as her citizens prepared for the worst. Blackout regulations came into being. Air raid shelters were dug; children were evacuated from the big cities, and British troops were sent to France.

We in Alexandria waited with a prayer. The bitter truth was Britain wasn't in a good position. We fell far behind Germany in terms of weapon production, and needed two things: time and allies. News was coming in that many countries in the Empire were lining up with us and I wondered if the Americans would hang fast, as they had done in the First World War. The Chamberlain government quickly gave way to one composed of all three political parties, and was called a 'national coalition'. Mr Winston Churchill headed the government, and thanks to his motivational speeches on the radio, the British held firm. His vigour and determination was just the tonic that was needed at this desperate hour.

At Mustapha Barracks we were digging shelters and wondering how long we'd stay in Alexandria. We were just a few weeks short of completing our eighteen-month tour abroad and returning to Blighty. The war had changed all of that now.

On 11 June 1940 the Merrymakers' Harmonica Band had been booked to make a final appearance. Standing in the wings at the Fleet Club, waiting to go on, the master of ceremonies announced to a crowded house that Italy had declared war against Britain and France, and their fighter planes were heading our way. He called last orders and bid the best of good fortune to us all.

The wives and families of our comrades were packed off to South Africa for their own safety. They tearfully left us at Sidi Gaber Railway Station, no doubt fearing that would be the last time they'd get to kiss their husbands farewell.

Just as expected, the Italians came over in droves that Saturday night and dropped plenty of bombs. Most of them fell over Sallum, a coastal village on the Libyan border, but a landmine exploded in a populated district and killed several people, mostly Italian civilians.

Taking our place in a larger unit comprising several other regiments, mainly anti-aircraft batteries, we slipped out of Alexandria in full battle order before first light. By now I was a full sergeant, and though that was a proud achievement, I was charged with the huge responsibility of safeguarding the lives of others. The thought of letting any of them down filled me with dread, but, as ever, I intended giving my best.

It's strange what goes on inside a soldier's head when he suddenly realizes that war, the thing he's spent his entire life training for, is now at hand. Troops fight their best when defending their homeland, yet here I was, thousands of miles away from my own home, preparing to defend somebody else's country. Even though Egypt was still neutral, the Egyptians were sitting on the frontiers with Italy, just waiting to be invaded.

Ali Maher Pasha, the Egyptian prime minister, was openly pro-German and I'm afraid to say that during the first few months of the war, Egypt assisted Germany in many ways. I even heard that King Farouk sent a personal telegram to Hitler, thanking him for preparing to invade his country. Whether there was truth in that, I cannot say, but the way I saw it, the Egyptians didn't want or even appreciate our help, so why were we bothering to defend their country, risking our lives, when they were aiding our enemy?

We were told there were a thousand or so Allied troops dug in at Mersa Matruh, the great resort for the rich on the shores of the Mediterranean Sea. We were to join them to help to defend the frontiers of Egypt against the advancing Italian Army, which by that time had a strong foothold in Libya. It was reassuring to know we wouldn't be facing the enemy alone, and this was the motivation we needed to keep us going as we rolled on and on across the Egyptian wasteland.

At first glance the Western Desert looked deceptively peaceful, but the blazing sun burned down relentlessly upon us until the backs of our necks ached. After several hours the dust made our throats dry and water was scarce. The only provision we had in abundance was cigarettes, and I smoked and smoked until my tongue felt like fur.

The further we travelled the more amazed we became, as there wasn't a single trench or a scrap of barbed wire in sight. In fact, there were no defensive preparations whatsoever; just sand and more sand, and the odd native riding on his donkey. To where he was going, goodness only knew.

We paused every so often and were told to prepare our own trenches, which had to be dug at every halt. I despaired at this job, for it felt as though we were digging our own graves. Out came our sand mats and shovels, and with sweat rolling down our bodies we heaved, shovelled and toiled beside the winding desert road, cursing throughout, as was a soldier's prerogative. None of us could understand why this work hadn't been carried out already, or why there was no evidence that thousands of Allied troops had already passed by. Surely, though, this was all part of the grand plan, and the real barricades were just over the horizon.

The truth was there were no defences, for there were no allies waiting for us. We were all alone; a very small force indeed, standing solo against some half a million singing foes, armed with all the modern tested weapons of warfare.

We entered Mersa Matruh late in the evening on 24 July 1940, and were surprised to find it was nothing more than a ghost town. Not a single soul was to be seen. This once thriving seaport had been reduced to a deserted settlement of roofless houses. The population had clearly evacuated before the bombs had begun to fall.

We brushed away our tracks to prevent the enemy planes from spotting us, and made our encampment for the night. The sun went down like a flaming red ball of fire, and that was when the sand fleas came out to play. We howled like wild desert dogs that night, but once I'd settled down in my 'grave', with my groundsheet at the bottom to keep out the damp, the itching didn't bother me so much. With an army blanket as my pillow and my great overcoat covering me, I fell asleep, though I was awoken several times as the enemy droned overhead. I hummed a tune to keep my mind distracted as the occasional shell whistled across the sky and then thundered to the ground nearby. This explosion was the only 'comforting' aspect of shellfire: it was only after you heard it you knew you were still alive.

At dawn we found ourselves on the move again, this time to take up positions along the rocky escarpment that divided Egypt from Libya. Our mission was to hold fast for days, weeks, if not months, and keep the Italians at bay long enough for Britain and the Allies to spin a web in which to catch them on the Egyptian flats.

The Italians had barricaded themselves within a place called Fort Capuzzo, not far from the Egyptian frontier. This was our enemy's strongest base in Libya, and thus one of our main targets. Having successfully managed to cut the water pipeline that fed into the fort, a secret ambush was planned, and our fighting patrol was sent in to attack. Without a sound they made their way forward towards the great stony fortress, and within seconds of reaching it our men began flushing the enemy out. The bombs from our aircraft rained down around the stronghold, and everything was covered in sand and debris. Thick columns of smoke billowed from the ruins, and we were elated by this early victory. Many of the Italian dead were left to rot, and with the heat and abundance of flies, getting too close to Fort Capuzzo wasn't pleasant for a long time after the battle.

Summer was an ordeal in the desert. The sun beat down without pity and everything was red hot to the touch. 'Shade' was a forgotten word. Some of our chaps were struck down by sun blindness; and with the rays of the sun dancing across the sand, one's mind conjured visions of refreshing silver lakes. I'd only ever read about the phenomenon of mirages before, along with the stories of circling vultures that followed the weary traveller. All of a sudden these things were no longer just myths printed on the pages of books; they were tangible hardships, ones that were now part of my everyday life.

Daily bathes in the sea helped to save our sanity but the salt aggravated our sunburn. I once saw a chap from our unit climb out of the water and peel an entire length of skin from his shoulder right down to his elbow.

Our water ration was one single bottle per day, and this was for all purposes. A morning shave was a painful art and a rub down with a damp towel served as a wash. The smallest cut left unattended could easily turn septic, though it was difficult to keep clean. Once our daily ablutions were over there was often very little left to drink, and what there was, was always red hot. Ice-cold beer was a distant memory, though various types of cigarettes were out on issue. We weren't allowed to smoke after nightfall as a match could be seen up to 2 miles away, so we made up for a lack of nightly cigarettes during the daylight.

Daily fare consisted of breakfast, lunch and a main meal after sundown. Breakfast was half a mess tin of tea; one small portion of bacon; half a packet of army biscuits; and a slab of tinned margarine. Lunch comprised half a packet of biscuits; half a tin of bully beef; and a few sips of water. Our main meal was much the same as the one at midday, except the bully was boiled or shaped into something like an Irish stew.

Letters from home were few and far between, and letters out were always censored. Before we came out here I'd met a pretty French girl, Frannie, at one of our concerts in Alexandria. We'd only seen each other a couple of times, but one day, feeling lost and lonely stuck out in the middle of the wilderness, I wrote a love letter to her. I poured my heart and soul into every syllable of that composition. It took me hours, and a great many pages besides. When I'd finished the only officer available to censor it was a fat ex-ranker who wasn't at all pleasant. With a grunt he took hold of my letter, settled himself down on a couple of petrol tins and read every word with seemingly utter mirth. As I stood to attention in front of him, watching the smug look spread across his face as he pored over my private words, I seethed with embarrassment. How I wished I had a match to send him soaring to kingdom come.

After what felt like hours, the officer finished reading and gave me a hard stare, before signing the pages with his pencil.

'Shakespeare himself couldn't have put it better,' he remarked, dryly.

That did it. As he handed me back the letter I grabbed it from him, tore it into a thousand pieces of confetti, and marched off in a huff. I never heard from Frannie again.

August 1940 found the Battle of Britain in full swing. Though correspondence was slowly trickling in from parents and friends back home, we had no idea just how serious things really were. We were only just getting over the shock of hearing about our withdrawal from Dunkirk and it was something like a miracle to us to learn that some 200,000 British soldiers had been evacuated.

We were positioned in a cove on the edge of the Mediterranean Sea near a British stronghold called Sidi Barrani, east of the Libyan border. At about midday on Friday, 13 September I took a party of men over to the sea for our daily dip, leaving my Bren gunner on duty. As we were whiling the time away, digging crabs out of the sand with a stick, an Italian shell rocketed close overhead. When it landed, the whole earth began to quake. Unable to keep our footing, we fell to the ground and grasped hold of the sand in desperation as more explosions erupted all around us, some missing us by yards. The blasts were so forceful they lifted my entire body off the ground. We were under attack!

After a few moments we began to raise our heads. Puffs of smoke were issuing from the Italian escarpment, and we knew we had to make it back to the cove to re-join our company. We must have looked ridiculous as we scrambled to our feet, completely naked, and dashed across to our position, clinging on to our boots and uniforms for dear life. I remember thinking how awful it would have been to be captured like this, but we were spared that day, and made it back unscathed, save for a terrible ringing in our ears.

The whole of our forward troops were on the move back towards Mersa Matruh and there was no doubt in my mind that this was it: at last, the fly was being drawn towards the web, and he was buzzing over at an alarming speed.

The night was drawing in as we reached the perimeter of the deserted seaport. Having made it through the gates, we were met by a British major who told us to take up positions on each side of the road, as the town was set for a pasting that night and there was to be no movement.

The moon shone brightly after darkness had fallen. It was a clear night, perfect for bombing, and it wasn't long before the drone of Italian aircraft could be heard. Dozens of them came over, and we were pelted left, right and centre. Fortunately no one was hurt where we were, but the brave Egyptian station master at the Mersa Matruh railway station lost both his legs. He'd refused to quit his job at the start of the war, and was later honoured with the MBE by the ambassador in Cairo.

At daybreak we were informed that the Italians had captured Sidi Barrani. This meant we were to remain in this devastated ghost town for the foreseeable future, and were to make all the necessary arrangements for a lengthy stay. My lads and I dug a big hole in the sand for us to reside in, and named it the Ship's Hold. We divided our living space into two rooms, and sizeable ones at that.

There were six of us in total and each had his own homemade wooden bed, three on each side. The other space we turned into a sitting room, complete with a wooden table and box chairs. Hanging on the walls were hurricane lamps; and we also dug a large WC at the far end of the dugout. We were relatively comfortable here, and one day I received a parcel full of books from my three good friends in Zizinia, so we started a lending library. Outside our back door we constructed a round gun pit with sandbags for walls. We cut a sloping ramp, like a tunnel, running up to the top with just enough room for two men to move up to the position where we could use our Bren to good effect.

My main job, while stationed at Mersa, was to man sentries throughout the day and night. The sentry on duty had a whistle on which he sounded short blasts in the event of aircraft approaching. However, we soon learned that the desert dogs were experts on aircraft warnings and would begin howling long before we heard the planes. One or two of the posts actually adopted a dog because they came in so handy at night when the visiting officer came round to inspect the men. The dog would start to howl, giving the chaps just enough time to hide the cards and money, as gambling was strictly forbidden.

After several long, tedious months our job began to get us down. Our numbers were slowly diminishing through sickness and injury, so I was loaned a Guardsman from general headquarters to help us out. His name was Frankie Ashton, and he lived with my men and me in the Ship's Hold. One night Frankie's turn came round for sentry duty so I gave him a gentle prod on the shoulder to rouse him.

'Wake up, Frankie,' I yawned, entering the Hold after several aching hours cooped up in the gun pit.

The Guardsman opened his eyes but made no other attempt to move at all. His face was blank and his gaze distant. I nudged and addressed him again but still he remained motionless. I suspected then something was wrong, for he was normally quick to his duties.

'Come on, you lazy blighter, up to it,' I said, a little firmer this time.

After a moment or two Frankie staggered to his feet, and without a word of acknowledgement disappeared towards the gun pit. Thinking nothing more of it, I returned to my bed. My mind soon began to drift and I must have dozed off. How long I was asleep, I cannot be sure, but what seemed like seconds later, Jock Hamilton came bursting in.

'Sergeant!' he cried.

'What's wrong?' I croaked.

'Frankie's acting oddly. He's … well, I think you should come take a look at him. I'm not sure what to do.'

As I followed Jock into the night air, I discerned the most beautiful singing I'd ever heard in my life. It was a man's voice, but I couldn't work out where it was coming from. It was as if the desert itself was singing, every note drifting around me in the gentle breeze. I couldn't understand the words, for they weren't English. Even the dogs were silent as they listened, entranced by this haunting lullaby. Jock led me into the gun pit, and there was Frankie in a theatrical pose belting out a ballad from an Italian opera.

'That will do, Guardsman Ashton,' I said. 'Do you want to give away our position?'

'It's no use, sarge,' Jock said. 'He won't respond. I've already tried.'

I had no idea what had come over my Guardsman but I knew I had to shut him up somehow. It wouldn't have been surprising if the Italians had heard him all the way over at Sidi Barrani.

'What *is* he doing?'

'I've no idea,' Jock said, looking pale. 'But the queerest thing is, sarge, Frankie can't sing. Believe me, I've heard him try. And he's never been to Italy, and as far as I know, he certainly can't speak the lingo.'

This made no sense to me, for here he was, plain as day, serenading the life out of the Bren gun in fluent Italian. I walked over to face my unlikely Beniamino Gigli.

'Alright, what's all this about, Frankie?' I demanded, but he did nothing to acknowledge he'd even heard me. I raised my voice. 'Guardsman Ashton, you are on sentry duty. I order you to desist this nonsense at once and return to your post.'

All of a sudden Frankie wrapped his bear-like arms around my waist, picked me up as effortlessly as if I were a rag doll, and began swaying to the lyrics. I felt the hairs on the back of my neck stand up. What was going on? Normally Frankie was a shy, placid type of man. It was just as if he'd been possessed. With Jock's assistance I was able to release myself from his grip, and we managed to steer Frankie back to his bed, where he rolled over and fell straight to sleep.

The next morning he rose for his breakfast looking as fresh as a daisy. He seemed to be acting himself but just to be sure I escorted him to the sick post. To my surprise, he returned moments later with a note saying he'd been diagnosed with stress and was to be excused duty for the rest of the day. I found this rather perplexing and went to have a word with the medical officer.

'Lots of funny things happen in the strains of war,' the medical officer asserted, after I'd questioned him. 'This case isn't unusual.'

Jock and I spoke to Frankie later on but he refused to believe a word we told him about the incident. In fact, he couldn't remember anything at all about the night in question. He did, however, make a full recovery; so full, in fact, that his newfound gift disappeared back to wherever it had come from, and I'm sorry to say I never heard his beautiful singing voice again.

Since our withdrawal, Sidi Barrani had become one of Italy's most fortified advanced posts. The entire area was defended by an assortment of anti-tank obstacles and anti-aircraft guns, the best technology had to offer; and our mission was somehow to recapture the town.

We weren't too aware of the months of the year or the days of the week any more, but we could feel the weather was getting colder and suspected winter must be setting in. All that was certain was that we were preparing to slip out of Mersa Matruh under the cover of darkness and give those Italians the spanking they were asking for. My lads and I were attached to a forward company and knew it was going to be a case of 'do or die'. Lieutenant Colonel Tom Bevan was commanding my force and if ever a man could move, it was he. Our company travelled west for what seemed like hours and eventually we went over the escarpment at a place called Sofafi.

'Follow me and keep close,' the major ordered; so away we went, further and further into the darkness, heading towards our fate.

We spotted derelict and dummy vehicles, placed at intervals here and there by our men so the Italians would think we were a stronger force than we really were. Drawing closer to our destination, we were instructed to move forward to a position and dig in some distance from the Italian strongpoints. With everyone in situation and our air force ready to fly in for the attack, everything seemed perfectly tied up, save for one burning question: would we live to see the dawn? All I could do was hope and pray.

At zero hour we moved forward on foot, but very little happened. We met no resistance, and it appeared as if the Italians had all cleared off already, which was worrying. Was it a trick? Sergeant John Toole from the Carrier Platoon volunteered to go forward with a vehicle to find out what was happening. He bravely entered one of the Italian forts only to find the place utterly deserted, or so it appeared. On his return journey the fort suddenly sprang to life with hundreds of fire-breathing Italians. Within seconds we were advancing, and boy, did we move. We ran into heavy bombardment from the enemy but my men and I managed to take cover behind a dip in the sandy hills. Wondering what to do, for there was no use just staying there, I called back asking if anybody had seen

Lieutenant Colonel Bevan. A signal truck behind flashed a message in reply, and in so doing it gave away our position.

'Take cover!' I yelled.

We were belted with mortar fire. Ammunition whizzed over our heads, bursting at the top of the slope.

After what seemed like an age, the shelling and mortaring died down and my men were finally able to press forward. To our great relief, as we marched through the dusty air, we saw our forward gunners with their 25-pounder field guns belting away at the fleeing Italian Army. It was a sight for sore eyes.

The battle continued all day and well into the evening. By nightfall my little band of men were ordered to rest, though the thumping of shells, the thudding of bombs and the rattling of small arms could be heard all around.

Early next morning, after not much sleep, the jubilant-looking regimental sergeant major approached me.

'It's all over,' he said with a smile and a mop of his brow.

This was welcome news.

'What happened?' I asked.

I could almost feel the anxiety seeping out of every pore in my body. Despite the odds, I'd survived, along with many of my friends and comrades.

'The Wops have packed up, and we've taken about 6,500 of them prisoner. There they are, coming in now.'

Away on the road was column after column of prisoners being marched out of the bombarded town of Sidi Barrani. I couldn't help but notice that almost all of them were carrying suitcases, as if they'd already packed in advance. We later learned that they were so sure of capturing Alexandria that they'd brought suitcases full of civilian clothes to wear when off duty.

The fleeing Italians left a great many things behind; and along with the prisoners, we'd also captured weapons, materials and other supplies. Of particular note was a huge collection of band instruments. It seemed we'd denied the Alexandrians a lavish victory parade by their Italian conquerors. I could have just imagined them strutting down Rue Corniche behind their massed bands, and it was satisfying to know that we, a small and ill-equipped force, had been their stumbling block. The whole of Sidi Barrani was littered with guns, lorries and tanks, and it took some time to get things under control. One or two of our lads found some peaked caps and matching coats, and astride Italian motor cycles they had the time of their lives, speeding up and down the town, giving the Italian salute to all and sundry.

The commander of the Italian forces was now in our custody. We nicknamed him General Electric Whiskers due to his large moustache. We were told our part in the war was drawing to a close, and the sooner we got the prisoners under control, the sooner we might move. I was detailed to escort a column of captives from Barrani to Mersa Matruh, where barbed wire compounds had been set up to detain them until they could be transported to the various prisoner of war camps that had been set up. This was no easy task, for there were thousands of prisoners and thousands more on their way. I began to wonder how on earth I'd achieve this hefty task.

At the main road leading towards Sidi Barrani, I spotted what looked like a broken-down Italian lorry, ideal for carrying troops in. The back was open and I could see the inside was stacked full of letters and parcels. I went around to the driver's side to see if I could get it to start, and was surprised to find a tiny Italian soldier sitting there with a look of contentment spread across his face. I gestured for him to jump down from his seat, and he obliged. He was the shortest man I'd ever seen; he couldn't have been any taller than my old mother.

'*Bonjourno*,' I bid him.

'*Come sta?*' he asked.

'*Molto bene, grazie*,' I replied. My Italian wasn't fluent but I knew that meant 'I'm very well, thank you.'

It turned out this chap could speak fewer English words than I could Italian ones, but through gestures and basic words I learned his name was Tony. He'd been employed to deliver mail to the Italians, and when the battle had started, he'd shut off the engine and stayed put. He wasn't going to participate in the fighting, and had remained in that spot ever since.

He tried to explain his feelings with regards to Hitler, Mussolini and Winston Churchill by placing three matchsticks in the sand, one to represent each leader. He pointed to 'Churchill' and said: '*Buono*', which meant 'good' in Italian.

His allegiance thus assured, we gave Tony the task of helping us load the truck with prisoners. Once it was full we all headed off for Mersa Matruh. The journey was long and tiring, and it took several trips over a couple of weeks before all the prisoners had been transported. Once the gruelling task was over, we thanked Tony for his assistance and allowed him to go on his way. He'd been a great help to us, and at the gates of the prison camp we waved as Tony marched off into the distance with his suitcase under his arm.

That night, the Italians dropped bomb after bomb on our camp, and we had to pack up and leave at top speed. How they knew our location was a real mystery; it was just as if they'd received a tip-off.

Chapter 8

Into the Blue

After months in the wilderness our job in the desert was done, and the powers that be decided to send us to Cairo, where we were to be stationed at the British military barracks on base duties. A period of leave was granted before we departed, and setting off back towards Alexandria was my happiest moment in a long, long time. With my pay packet tucked neatly into a large wallet and my kit shining bright, I made my way towards the railway station.

The old desert train puffed and groaned its way across the dusty landscape, and when I arrived at Sidi Gaber Station I found that my friends at Zizinia had sent a car to collect me. I was driven to their home, where I'd been invited to stay for the next few days, and the very sight of it was like a mirage, rising up before me. I received a warm welcome from the Shakour family, who were all delighted to see me alive and well. I was able to put their minds at rest about the war, though heaven help me: the number of white lies I had to tell!

I had my first hot bath in months, and seeing my reflection again in the mirror was a most peculiar sensation. My whiskery face looked much thinner than I remembered, and extremely tanned. After changing into a loose summer suit and joining my hosts on the veranda, I savoured a delicious glass of iced Stella beer. It tasted like nectar. My bedroom smelt like fresh linen, and when I retired for the night it was a pleasure to climb into a soft bed and lay my head on a feather pillow.

The following day I telephoned one of my favourite dining places, which always offered a good cabaret show, to reserve a table for the six of us. I was astounded when my request was refused because the club was now out of bounds to 'other ranks'. I soon learned a great deal had changed since I'd left Alexandria. Before 1939, officers and other ranks had never mixed in the same social circles, but the Second World War had altered a lot of things. The proliferation of all ranks in the city while on leave was generating friction at the local entertainment venues that were still open to everyone. This resulted in the authorities instructing the proprietors to admit officers and civilians only, excluding lower ranks of the army altogether. After everything we common soldiers had gone through in recent times, we now found ourselves being shunned so dismissively. One city centre bar even erected a sign declaring: 'Out of bounds to dogs and other ranks'. The only places left open to the returning heroes looking to forget their troubles were the brothels and backstreet bars.

The one way of getting around this dreadful rule was to disobey orders by wearing civilian clothes. Joseph Shakour let me borrow one of his suits, and we boldly went ahead and booked a table at our restaurant. Though it was satisfying to openly defy the authorities, I kept looking around me throughout the evening, praying I wouldn't bump into any officers who might recognize me.

Much was happening back home in England. The Battle of Britain was over. Our brave fighter pilots returned home victorious, full of spirit, determination and song.

> *We're gonna hang out the washing on the Siegfried Line,*
> *Have you any dirty washing, mother dear?*
> *We're gonna hang out the washing on the Siegfried Line,*
> *'Cause the washing day is here.*

Though we'd won the battle we were far from winning the war; and with the threat of a German invasion looming over every household in the land, the British public began arming themselves with anything they could lay their hands on. All eyes were cast in the direction of Hitler's invasion barges that were supposedly moored up all along the North Sea coast, waiting to transport some half a million or so goose-stepping Huns to our shores; but the people were ready.

'We shall fight on the beaches, in the fields, in the streets and in the hills. We shall never surrender.' Winston Churchill's pledge was on the lips of every man, woman and youth.

Yet Hitler stayed his hand. Germany's failed attempt to destroy our RAF had, for the time being, at least, laid to rest any grand desire the Führer had of invading our Sceptred Isle. The fear that Churchill would fulfil his promise of setting fire to the English Channel if Gerry so much as put a single oar into the water was undoubtedly keeping the Nazis awake at night, but nobody seemed to know for sure if or when Hitler's dreaded 'Operation Sea Lion' was due to commence.

It was the cusp of 1941, and we in the 3rd Battalion found ourselves stationed at Qasr el-Nil Barracks in Cairo, wearing out the barrack square with our hobnailed boots. The British Army hadn't occupied these premises for forty years, and the generations of bugs that had settled there since the turn of the century didn't take too kindly to our presence. Once a week we'd whip out our blowtorches and burn the blighters to a crisp, then scrub the floors from top to bottom so no marks would be left.

Thanks to the war, a great deal of money had begun pouring into the capital city. The ancient streets were thick with Allied troops on leave, and they all had one thing on their minds: spending their troubles away. As Cairo's nightlife began hotting up, the locals started to become rich overnight. Honky-tonk bars opened up all across the city, and women down on their luck took to the streets, looking for battle-worn Tommies to kiss better. With so many thousands of troops on leave, the pimps and prostitutes began a roaring trade. The city found itself in a crazy state of slap-happiness, and things became so bad that at the height of the troubles a brothel was opened in more or less every other house on the main street through Cairo.

Egypt was the land of the quick-fingered, and pickpocketing was operated on a scale that could barely be imagined. Like in so many parts of the Middle East in those days, there was a growing resentment against occupation, and the best part of the Egyptian police force was focusing its resources on the universities, where hot-headed students were in a constant state of rebellion. The influence these boys had over the hungry masses meant that they were more or less running the affairs of the country, and this presented a grave threat to public security. Groups of well-dressed Egyptian students were regularly espied sitting outside coffee houses, sipping their drinks and talking in whispers as they observed the people passing by; and I often wondered if they ever attended to their studies.

With the police preoccupied, lawless thousands were running around the city unchecked, so my battalion was detailed to assist the military police on street patrols. Two sergeants would go out with one military police NCO; and as well as apprehending the local vagabonds, our duties included monitoring the conduct of the troops on leave. I lost count of how often I had to stop Tommy and tell him to do up his collar, or to swing his arms up.

Overall, I found Cairo to be a most unpleasant place indeed. The enchanting stories of pharaohs, pyramids and prehistoric treasures soon became obscured by clouds of flies, dirt and the ill intentions of so many of its citizens. I was marching back to barracks one day after attending a meeting at the local Royal Antediluvian Order of Buffaloes lodge when a scruffy young bootblack approached me.

'Shoeshine, Johnny?' he called out.

This didn't please me in the slightest, as we in the brigade prided ourselves on cleaning our own.

'*Imshee, wallad*,' I replied, which meant: 'go away, boy'.

To my disgust, the *wallad* spat all over my feet before vanishing into the crowd with a mischievous laugh. With mucus dripping over my toes, I had no option now but to get my shoes cleaned, so two young rogues began to polish them for me. Standing on top of two rickety footstools, and feeling rather silly, I waited as they rolled the bottoms of my trousers up and applied a liberal amount of sheen to my boots. Before they had chance to finish, the lads suddenly caught sight of an approaching policeman and away they fled at top speed, leaving me balancing in my bare shins several inches higher than the rest of the population. I was astonished when the passing constable finished off my shoes for me, and then held out his hand for payment when he'd done.

Further along the street I bumped into a rather suspicious-looking chap who flashed me a sinister grin.

'Good for the stomach, Johnny,' he said, offering me a smoke of the infamous hookah water pipe, which was no doubt filled with more than just tobacco. 'Make you strong to fight the Germans!'

Needless to say I ignored him and carried on my way.

There was one particularly filthy area of the city that was home to the spies, spivs, thieves and murderers, all living in close proximity to one another. It reeked of sickness and decay; and it was here where a comrade and I were sent on patrol one evening. We couldn't have taken more than a few steps along the road when an irate Greek came rushing up to complain that some Australian troops were wrecking his joint. We followed him along the grimy backstreet and up a flight of wooden stairs that led into a brothel. The long, dark corridor was lined with closed doors, and I shuddered to think what was going on behind them. As we passed, one of the doors creaked open and a pretty, painted face peered round at us. The girl's golden hair was bunched up in ringlets on the top of her feathered head, and the scent of perfume was intoxicating.

'Hello, shortie,' she taunted, fluttering her long eyelashes at me. 'How did *you* get into the Guards?'

I tried to ignore her giggles as we made our way towards the dimly lit bar at the back of the building, where we found a gathering of Aussie soldiers, somewhat the worse for drink. From the look of things they'd smashed a door in, and one of the patrons had a large purple lump billowing from his forehead. After a firm reprimand and a threat to report them to their commanding officer if they didn't pay for the damage, the bother was settled; but just as we were about to leave I noticed the tallest Australian had his jacket undone.

'Button up your jacket, soldier!' I instructed. 'You look a disgrace!'

The soldier, it seemed, didn't take too kindly to a little British Guardsman issuing him orders. This gorilla of a man suddenly reared over me, revealing his enormous stature, and his icy stare morphed into a smirk.

'Are you speaking to me, runt?' he growled, to a ripple of laughter from the other Australians.

I couldn't believe what I'd just heard. In all my long career I'd never before been addressed with such disrespect.

'May I remind you, private, you are …'

Before I could finish, the giant grabbed hold of my collar and lifted me into the air, almost raising me above his head. I thought he was going to throw me out of the window, but my screams of protest alerted him to the fact he'd succeeded in putting the wind up me. Without another word he set me back down, did up his jacket and strolled away down the corridor with his pals, all laughing their heads off.

I glanced sheepishly at my fellow sergeant.

'In future,' he said, 'I'll do the talking. No one will ever take any notice of you.'

Across the sea in Italy, Mussolini was still reeling from the crushing defeat of his army at Sidi Barrani. In need of a new legion of warriors to reinforce his dwindling numbers, the Italian prime minister looked to Germany for assistance. Upon Hitler's personal command, a new expeditionary unit was formed. The Afrika Korps was an elite fighting force under the leadership of the decorated Field Marshal Erwin Rommel. His distinguished capabilities earned him the nickname 'The Desert Fox', for he was cunning, stealthy and certainly not a foe to tangle with.

It was springtime 1941. I'd just stepped outside the Al' Americano after a few drinks with some pals, when we were stopped by a military police patrol.

'Report to your unit forthwith,' we were told.

This sounded serious, and soon everything became clear. Arriving back, we were informed that we were to return to the Western Desert post-haste. There was no time to lose, for the Afrika Korps were sweeping across the same region where we'd belted the Italians. Rommel had struck south of the Libyan city of Benghazi, pushing our forces back to the Egyptian border. We still held the Libyan port of Tobruk, though the fate of the soldiers defending the town hung by a thread. Several legions had tried to relieve the troops, but all attempts had failed, and Jerry had captured the Egyptian barracks at the top of Halfaya Pass, or 'Hellfire Pass', as we'd renamed it, making passage impossible. It was my unit's mission to clear the way.

After a bone-shaking journey, we arrived at a place called Marble Arch in the midst of the Western Desert. We were all fighting fit, but still hadn't learned to conquer the desert's *khamsins*: scorching, unbearable winds that blew through the sands. The Arabs reckoned the devil himself was present during such sandstorms, and this I could well believe. We fell foul of these hellish weather conditions many times as the wind blew towards us at ferocious speeds. Many of the chaps were sick; nostrils, mouths and ears were filled with sand, and even our weapons became clogged with this wretched stuff. Movement was impossible and we were pinned down at Marble Arch for forty-eight hours while we waited for the storm to ebb away.

I'd managed to hang on to two bottles of Stella beer that I'd smuggled along with me. I buried them in the sand, hoping they'd cool, but each time I touched them the glass burnt my fingers. It was agonising to feel so desperately thirsty yet not be able to drink. I slumped to the floor in despair, feeling wretched, even wondering if life was worth living. I lay there for goodness knows how long, hating the bloody war and everything about it. Groans of misery were audible around me, but I hadn't the will to care. The only consolation, if you could call it that, was that the enemy must have been suffering the same as we were.

On the third day the wind dropped and peace descended. With the sun shining down from the clear blue skies, it was difficult to believe we'd experienced such an unworldly storm. It was as if we'd awoken from the dead.

Jerry had firmly 'dug in' around the Sallum Barracks on the Egyptian frontier. As night fell, we slipped up the desert slopes to join the forward companies in a surprise attack. Our drivers were Indian, and unfortunately a mix-up in communication meant the timing of the attack didn't go as expected, so our plan failed. Our own artillery ended up shelling our forward company, with several casualties. The whole operation was a complete disaster, and to top it all, the Jerries must have known we were coming, for their guns were fixed; they'd been waiting for us. Our lads were cut down as they charged into battle. We lost some fine men that night.

Morning dawned over the escarpment and few of our chaps had returned. One poor soldier was left gravely wounded between two sand dunes. There he lay in the searing heat, bleeding to death, until he was discovered some hours later, barely alive. The Jerry machine-gunners held fire while a brave

Guardsman went out and brought him back. There was no Victoria Cross for him or the dying soldier.

I was ordered to move across to the extreme left-hand corner of the escarpment, where my men and I were to watch for any movement from Jerry. It was a pleasant morning as we drove across to set up our positions; one would have hardly believed we were in the middle of a war. Across the way, the exotic long-beaked birds were going about their business, warbling and probing into the sand in search of a tasty morsel or two as we began mounting our weapons.

Then, without warning, eight fearsome black shapes rolled up to the edge of the escarpment and belched fire towards our positions below. They were Jerry tanks. Within seconds we were surrounded by an inferno. Guns were knocked out; overhead shells burst into a thousand splinters that rained down around us, and our brave, dying gunners continued shooting as they went down. One of our weapons opened up and with its first two rounds it knocked out two of their tanks. These powerful war machines just rolled over the top of the escarpment as if they were toys.

I turned my truck around and raced as fast as I could across the salt flats to the commanding officer's truck. I found him standing there, staring straight ahead.

I saluted. 'Enemy tanks on the left, sir.'

'Yes, I heard them,' he said in a dismissive tone that clearly indicated that was the end of the conversation.

So, that was it. There were to be no reinforcements; my men and I were to face the enemy alone.

I dived back into my truck and took up a position covering the road leading to the escarpment, and there I waited, gun at the ready. I didn't have to wait for long, but it wasn't Jerry who came towards me. Our own trucks began rolling down from over the top, one after the other, all of them devoid of troops, save for the drivers. I stopped one and found a friend of mine from the Cairo days; we'd both attended the same Buffaloes lodge. He was covered in blood and was badly wounded, his arm hanging to his body by a string of flesh.

'Jerry's coming,' he managed to utter in that, his dying breath.

It's funny what the hands start to do before the mind begins to function. Before I knew what I was doing, I found myself tearing up the letters I had in my haversack. Some were from Rosie Malone, the girl I'd known in England, who'd sent me a few words since her beau had moved on; but most were from my mother. The same thought kept spinning in my head, over and over again:

'At least if I'm to be taken prisoner, Jerry won't be able to track down my loved ones.'

After what seemed like an age, the commanding officer gave the order for us to withdraw. For some reason or other, as we started to pack up and flee, most of the lads began laughing like drains. What there was to laugh about, I didn't know, but before long we were all joining in. I think we just laughed for laughing's sake; otherwise we'd have drowned in our own tears.

The year 1941 was drawing to a close and we were on the move again, though where to was anybody's guess. Since the day we joined, we Guardsmen never asked questions; we simply did what we were told, knowing that one way or another everything had to end, either on a battlefield in the prime of our lives or as old men in our beds, having shared the stories of our great adventures with our grandchildren.

The grapevine had it that somewhere out west a secret allied army was forming under the command of a legendary figure named Vladimir Peniakoff who'd once worked in Cairo as an engineer for a sugar manufacturer. In his spare time he'd made a remarkably detailed study of the Western Desert. Popski, as he was dubbed, began instructing his own band of men on how to blow dumps, cut off the enemy's supplies and pass valuable information back to the Allies. This legion went under the name 'Popski's Private Army', and did much to help the war effort. Their first mission was to sabotage the Fox's supply of fuel and other rations; and the knowledge that they were out there somewhere, hounding the Jerry wherever they could find him, lifted our spirits more than I can say.

Popski's men were based at a place known as the Siwa Oasis, which sounded much more inviting than where we were headed. We were making our way towards Sofafi, a place that didn't even deserve a name. It was bare, rocky and unremarkable, and where even the regimental sergeant major commented that if he'd known there were such places in the world, he'd never have enlisted.

In true Guards' style we shook off any personal feelings and tried to make the best of this bleak situation. After an evening supper of the usual warmed bully and tin of tea, we sat around our 'Fitted for Wireless' truck and listened, entranced, to the heart-warming notes of our heroine, Vera Lynn. Next came the stirring words of Winston Churchill, urging us to tighten our belts by one more hole and carry on with as much grit and determination as we could muster. He was followed by the voice of Alvar Lidell, telling us the latest news from London, to which we listened intently before rolling ourselves up in a single blanket to keep each other warm and attempted to sleep.

Except for a few aircraft attacks, there was little excitement at Sofafi, and I was glad when we finally left. We moved further and further into the west, onwards to nowhere. We saw nobody as we negotiated miles and miles of nothing. Strange thoughts pass through the minds of men, especially during the stresses of combat; and as we travelled through the abyss I remember thinking this was the perfect place to build cities to house all the homeless people in the world. I left my thoughts in the desert wasteland, and we hurried on through the great swirls of dust that shot up around us. I swore that if I ever got through this war, I'd never again go to places where sand could be found.

We stopped and made camp as night fell, and, as ever, the stars hung like diamonds from a midnight curtain. They seemed so close it felt as if we could reach up and touch them. With a full and troubled mind, it was tricky to sleep. Remembering about a half-smoked cigarette somewhere in one of my pockets, I started to grope around. It was then I felt something slide past my hand with an ominous hiss. Striking a match, I saw I had two asps for bedfellows in my little hole in the sand. Needless to say, I quickly dug another hole.

The next morning reports reached us that there were four Jerry tanks patrolling the area, and we were ordered to keep a watchful eye open. Unluckily for us, the Jerries spotted us first, and as soon as we were in range they opened fire. Machine-gun ammunition exploded all around, and four of our gunners were hit. Gunner Sheldon, of the Royal Artillery, was seriously hurt. The bullets from the tank had ripped the flesh from his face, and he died in my arms.

I emptied his pockets into a large handkerchief and removed his two identity discs from around his neck. The brown disc was tied to the small bundle of belongings, and the other – the green one – I tied to his left wrist, as we'd been instructed to do in such situations. As I wrapped the dead gunner in a blanket, one of the other lads began to dig a grave. Together we committed his body to the earth and covered the remains. In my mind I was taken back to a time when my family and I were on holiday by the beach, and we used to bury each other in the sand for laughs.

When we'd done, I noticed an old photograph on the ground. I picked it up and was greeted by the sight of this poor young man smiling up at me. I knew at once it must have slipped out of his pocket. The cheery likeness had evidently been captured a few years before the war. He was posing hand in hand with his wife and two young children, a boy and a girl, strolling along a seaside promenade. I've never forgotten the image of their happy faces, nor the inscription on the photograph: 'With all our love, darling. Pray God you will be safe and home soon.'

In that moment, if I could have got my hands around the throats of Hitler and Mussolini, they would have died much sooner than they were destined to.

'Come on, Paddy,' I heard someone shouting.

'Get moving, sergeant,' another voice commanded. 'You're holding up the convoy.'

The wind was howling and sand was biting into our cheeks, getting up our nostrils and in our mouths, but I was determined that my fallen comrade was going to have a headstone. So, together with the lad who helped me dig the grave, we constructed one out of an empty petrol barrel and painted his name, rank and number on it. We placed a couple of large rocks on top to protect the grave in the hope of keeping the jackals off. I recorded its coordinates on a map for sending to the Imperial War Graves Commission, so they could find him after the war and re-bury him properly, side by side with all his fallen brothers.

I didn't sleep a wink that night. I just lay there, suddenly realising it was Christmas Eve and wondering if the man's wife and children were decorating their tree in faraway England, thinking about Daddy and wondering what he'd be doing on Christmas Day.

I was standing by my truck, waiting to know what our next move was to be, when I was sent for by Lieutenant Colonel John Moubray.

'Have you any idea what's happened to my WC stand, Sergeant Rochford?' he asked.

I blinked in surprise. The commanding officer always carried this wooden stand around with him wherever we went, for his own personal use.

'No, I'm afraid I haven't, sir.'

'Then I'd like you to go and find out,' he said, waving his hand in dismissal.

Perplexed, and having no idea where to even begin, I went to ask our medical officer, John Eyre, for advice, but he, too, was just as stumped as I was.

'The last time I saw the wretched thing was yesterday, at our last position,' he informed me, scratching his head.

Being a key witness, I took John to report back to the commanding officer, and he told him exactly what he'd just told me.

'Well then, please take your truck and locate it for me,' Lieutenant Colonel Moubray said, as if we should have thought of this earlier.

Ammunition was still falling and most of it was landing in the area where we last remembered witnessing the squatting-down of the commanding officer; but orders were orders, however dangerous or ludicrous they seemed. Dodging shot and shell, we combed the desert and duly found the lost WC, recovering it without injury. We expected at least a hint of praise when we returned in triumph, but even that, it transpired, was too much to hope for.

'Make sure it's not lost again,' the commanding officer simply directed before dismissing us both.

Of all our wartime duties, guarding the commanding officer's privy had to be the most ridiculous one of all.

It seemed, however, we had it easy. Back in Britain, the government was at the end of its tether with the Egyptian authorities, who were doing little to help us win the war. The British Ambassador to Egypt, Sir Miles Lampson, was ordered to give a final ultimatum to King Farouk. In short, he was to dismiss his pro-German prime minister, Hussein Sirri Pasha, and replace the entire government with a new regime. If Farouk failed to comply, he was to lose the throne. Naturally, the brazen young king was enraged, but Abdin Palace had been surrounded by a wall of British Army tanks and armoured cars with weapons that had the power to blow the palace to kingdom come, taking the Royal Family with it. Farouk had no choice but to agree. The wily Mustafa el-Nahas Pasha, leader of the Wafd Party, was duly appointed prime minister, for Britain was confident she could twist this chap's arm if need be. Nahas had, after all, been one of the political leaders who'd signed the Anglo–Egyptian Treaty, thereby earning a degree of trust with the British.

By giving in so willingly to these demands, Farouk had hammered the first nail into his own coffin. The once popular young monarch was now being openly derided by his subjects for showing such weakness, and the ultimatum had served to breed even more hatred towards Britain. The young and impressionable Egyptian officers who were coming into the army were riled and angry. Gamal Abdel Nasser was among them, and he wasn't one to take things lying down.

Chapter 9

My Broken Body

Shells and mortar bombs were getting ever closer as we fled across the desert. Looking over my shoulder, I saw what I thought was a formation of British trucks on our tail. I waved and gave the reversed V-sign, a habit amongst troops to show friendliness, but to my horror, instead of returning the compliment, a crowd of Jerries began pouring out and started mounting their weapons. There wasn't a moment to lose. I raced forward with my section, taking cover behind a mound of earth where we readied our Bren. The sand swirled in a blinding cloud as I gave orders to Drummer Charlie Baker to send word to the rest of our company.

'Okay, sarge,' he called, leaping back into his truck.

It was then I felt as if the weight of the whole world had fallen on top of me. I was trapped face down in the sand and couldn't move. I heard my bones crack as my body was crushed; it was if I'd been clamped in a giant vice.

'Mother of God!' I think I screamed, though perhaps I just thought the words, for there was no air left in my lungs to emit any sound.

It was only after the colossal pressure seemed to lessen when the realization of what just happened began trickling into my mind. As Charlie's truck had pulled away, it caught my jacket and dragged me straight under its wheels. I'd borne the entire weight of the vehicle as it travelled over my left shoulder and up towards the back of my head, missing my skull by a fraction of an inch. How I escaped I'll never know, but by some miracle of God I did. I couldn't see, and every breath was agony. Then I felt someone next to me, dragging me through the sand and rolling me onto my back.

'Jesus Christ, Paddy,' I heard someone say in a Scotch accent. It was my pal, Sergeant Douglas Watson, to whom I owe my life.

'Dougie, am I blind?' I beseeched, reaching out and grasping his arm. 'Are my eyes alright?'

'Take it easy, Pad,' he soothed. I felt a handkerchief wiping something wet from my face. 'Your eyes have been filled with sand, that's all. You're going to be fine.'

With the help of Dougie and another pal, Jack Noble, I was taken to a military ambulance and handed over to the care of the medical officer. After a quick examination of my injuries and a few bandages applied here and there, he declared: 'There's very little I can do for you, Sergeant Rochford. Just lie still a while.'

John Eyre had been having a busy time of things lately, so I couldn't blame him for not having much time for me. There were countless numbers of casualties and the man lying beside me in the ambulance was nearing his end. He'd received the full blast of an enemy shell, which had cut right across his stomach.

Outside I could hear explosions all around us but I cared little. I laid there in a daze, slipping in and out of consciousness, while my fellow patients proceeded to die. As the more seriously injured men passed away, things became quieter for the medical officer. It was only then he found time to look me over, and pronounced temporary blindness caused by shock, a broken shoulder, several shattered ribs and torn ligaments in the knee.

The battle outside began hotting up and it sounded as though the ambulance and its occupants came close on several occasions to being blown sky high. In the end it was Mother Earth and not Jerry who helped to break the springs in my bunk, for we were tossed about so much as we raced across the bumpy terrain of the desert.

I fretted about the lads in my truck. Had they got away okay? Did they get hold of any more petrol? We'd been down to our last drop and I shuddered at the thought of them lying stranded in the middle of the wilderness. I wondered where I was being taken. Was I, like the other wounded troops, headed for a makeshift desert hospital somewhere in the middle of nowhere, where I might as well be dead? Or would I be lucky enough to make it back to Cairo, or even Alexandria? These and many other questions were racing through my throbbing head, making it hurt even more.

By nightfall there was only one other wounded man left in the ambulance, and he was in a bad way. He'd been hit by a bullet in the lung and wasn't expected to last much longer. He'd lain motionless throughout the journey until the early hours of the morning, when he'd become agitated and began to murmur.

'Mother,' I heard him call several times, and I think he said 'Lillian,' but I couldn't be certain.

I managed to move my good arm onto his pillow. I wasn't quite sure why I did this, but looking back, I suppose it was to let him know he wasn't on his own. He shifted his head so his cheek was touching my fingers, and with a final rattle from deep in his lungs, he slipped away to meet his maker. He'd fought the good fight, as thousands of men were doing all over the world, and as thousands more were destined to do before Hitler's bloody war ended. I wish now that I'd learned the poor chap's name so at least I could have got word to his parents and sweetheart, just to let them know they'd been in his thoughts at the end.

The few men that were left of the battalion were committed to battle again. I was a dead loss to them and they couldn't have carted me around in my present state, so I was handed over to the 12th Light Field Ambulance, which set off through a blinding sandstorm.

The old spark stayed alight, though I was in tremendous pain. The two orderlies sat in the back with me helped to make light of the bumps and jolts. I was suffering from spasms of crushing agony in my chest, but when the pain ebbed we were able to chat, which proved a welcome distraction.

At some point in the journey the driver lost contact with our convoy and we became well and truly lost. Someone was watching over us that day, for we eventually ran into a convoy of Polish troops who were making their way to Tobruk, where we were heading, so we were able to follow them. I was amazed by the array of fresh bread and wine the Poles had to offer, and by the time we arrived in Tobruk my head was light from all the alcohol I'd consumed.

Those who once passed through Tobruk Hospital would no doubt remember the feeling of terror that stalked the wards night after night as the spineless Italian fighter pilots rained down their bombs upon the wounded men. I felt defenceless in my hospital bed, unable to walk, as bomb after bomb showered down around us. Between the explosions came the cries of the wounded, etching those frightful nights in my memory for the rest of my days. One of my injured comrades and fellow Merrymaker, Guardsman Tom Elliott, was with me in hospital, having lost a leg in battle. During an air raid he'd become startled and had fallen from the operating table, breaking his nose as he landed on the floor. I wondered if the Italian bomber would have been proud of his actions, had he seen the result of his handiwork.

When it became too dangerous for us to be there, we were divided into groups and informed we were to be transported to Egyptian hospitals by sea. They laid us out on stretchers along the dockside, where gentle hands began lifting us onto the ship's deck. It was then I knew I must have died and gone to heaven, for I saw something so beautiful it must have been an angel: a female face. It was a sight I hadn't seen for a long time, for all the attendants at Tobruk had been burly medical officers. Had I finally succumbed to my injuries? No, I told myself, for I was still in too much pain. If my body had been working properly,

I would have reached out and touched the lovely face that was peering down at me with smiling eyes.

'Is it true you're a sergeant in the Guards?' the nurse asked, extinguishing her own heavenly halo with that single sentence.

'Yes,' I sighed, waiting for the inevitable comment.

'But you're so small,' she chucked. 'Did you slip in through the back door?'

'I've been marking time for twenty-two years,' I said. 'Perhaps my legs have worn down.'

That afternoon aboard the ship, two charming nurses helped to bathe me. They removed the huge pad of cotton wool that had been secured over my facial cuts. I was handed a mirror, and whilst my head looked like a swollen punch bag, I was told there wouldn't be any permanent scarring, and was thankful for that, at least. The nurses examined my bruised cheeks and told me how far a blush reached. I'd never really wondered about that before, although I'm certain mine must have extended down to my ankles. Even to a disciplined Guardsman with years of battle practice, being bathed like a newborn babe by two pretty young ladies was one of the most daunting experiences of my life.

Feeling a little more comfortable for the first time since my accident, I settled myself down for the night. Before I drifted off to sleep, the ship's medical officer began doing his rounds. He told me the first port of call would be Alexandria, where I was to alight and transfer to a hospital in the city. I couldn't believe my luck. I was returning to my home away from home, close to my good friends, Jack Davy and the Shakours.

As soon as we docked, I was on my way to the 64th General Hospital. I settled in well, and it was beneficial to experience some restful nights, free of Italian air raids. Though the skies were deceptively silent, I knew the war must have reached a desperate stage, because one morning a tall, military moustachioed major from our battalion came to visit. His greeting was shamefully brief.

'I'm sorry you chaps are missing all the fun,' he said, the sound of his large boots echoing through the ward, 'so do try very hard to get well, and don't stay here a single day longer than is necessary. Hospital is no place for a Guardsman. You're all much needed on the front line.'

Tom Elliott, who'd transferred with me, was unable to move an inch. He was in tremendous pain, and was at that time waiting to have his remaining leg amputated. I'm sure the major meant well and didn't mean to be unkind, but I sometimes wondered if he even popped his head round the hospital mortuaries on the off-chance there might have been some Guardsmen who were still breathing!

The weeks passed quickly and in what seemed like no time at all I was allowed out on day leave to visit my pals, who only lived a few tram stops from the hospital. My civilian clothes were waiting for me at Zizinia, fresh and aired, and though I spent just a few hours in them, I shall always remember strolling along the sea front in good company, feeling at peace with the world. A few days later my old friend Jack invited me to attend the Barclay's Bank tennis championships. I even had the honour of presenting the silver cup to the winner with my one hand, as the other was still strapped up. Seeing the inquisitive looks on people's faces, Jack took much delight in telling everyone I'd been run over by a tank.

'No!' they exclaimed in horror. 'How on earth did you survive?'

Everyone I met was keen to hear my story, and I'd never felt so popular in all my days.

Returning to hospital at the end of the tournament was a precarious undertaking. It was rush hour in the city and I was cattle-prodded into a rickety old tram, where I found myself squished between a crowd of civilian Arabs and Egyptian soldiers. The journey did nothing for my aching bones. There were always far too many passengers aboard than those old trams could hold, and that was just on the inside. To avoid paying the fare, a great deal more of them could usually be seen clinging to the exterior like spider monkeys. Frequent were the reports of people who'd slipped and landed on the tracks, sometimes losing a

Alexandria, 1942: all smiles before tea. Paddy with his British and Egyptian friends, while wounded on leave.

limb, or worse, their lives. The authorities were getting tired of this, so they sent Egyptian policemen, armed with rhino whips, to wait at various tram stops, ready to lash the trespassers off the sides.

Many sympathetic eyes were upon me as I stood in the carriage, covered in bandages and sporting an empty jacket sleeve. Not wanting people to get the wrong impression, I slipped my bad arm up through my collar and took my cigarette out of my mouth. The expressions of pity turned to shock, and then to grins.

'I'm delighted to see you still have your arm,' one lady passenger said to me. 'I thought you'd lost it.'

'I've been run over by a tank,' I told her with a wry smile.

If ever a Guardsman was detached from his unit, he was expected to return as soon as possible. This had been drummed into our heads from a young age, so it came as a bitter blow when I was examined by the medical board and regraded from A1 to B2. These were medical categories, and whilst the former signified that a soldier was in tip-top condition, the latter meant he was deemed unfit to fight on the front line and was restricted to base duties only. The feeling that I'd let my battalion down was difficult to bear. I didn't share this news with anyone, for I had no intention of being given base duties when so many of our men were out on the battlefield, risking their lives in the firing line, in need of all the relief they could get. There were no two ways about it: I had to return to my line as soon as I was able.

The following day a driver arrived at the hospital to collect some of the A grade Guardsmen who were being discharged and sent back to duty. My ward was all hustle and bustle that morning as a bomb had been let off outside by a gang of renegades, so in all the commotion it was fairly easy for me to sneak away unnoticed and join the other Guardsmen in the back of the truck. I made some excuse about being late for roll call, and one of my pals helped me into the vehicle just as it was pulling off.

The summer solstice of 1942 was approaching, and our diminishing band of men was based at a military camp in a desert village called El Daba, some 100 miles west of Alexandria, on the shores of the Mediterranean Sea. There were only a small number of troops here when I arrived, for the rest of my battalion had found themselves caught up in a hostile campaign in the middle of the Libyan Desert, having come face to face with the Desert Fox himself. News of their progress came trickling in over the coming days, and by the sound of things our lads were in desperate straits. The grapevine had it that some of our bravest and most respected officers had either been taken prisoner or killed, including our own Lieutenant Colonel Tom Bevan. He'd died from the wounds he'd sustained during a courageous struggle.

It wasn't long before news reached us that Tobruk, our remaining stronghold in Libya, had fallen to the enemy. It was said that 25,000 of our men had been taken prisoner, with thousands more killed, wounded and missing in action, including hundreds of Coldstreamers.

I struggled to process the information. Hundreds of my pals were lost; and if I'd not made such a foolish mistake in the desert a few months back, I'd have more than likely been among them.

Second by second the hours ticked by until some heartening news reached us. Our valiant Major Tim Sainthill had refused to surrender, and about 180 of his Guardsmen had fought their way out through the bombs and the minefields. As they made their way back across the desert they'd rallied other surviving troops from the South African regiments. All told, this band of survivors had swelled to over 300 men. By some miracle they made it safely through the clouds of war and on to the home straight, only to run into a column of German soldiers. Yet their luck hadn't quite run out. With quick thinking, they removed their headdress and waved to the unsuspecting enemy who, thinking they were their own chaps, waved back and let them go.

It was a jubilant evening when these happy stragglers began to arrive at our base. I even saw two men kiss one another as they embraced. Normally that sort of conduct was unheard of in the Guards, but nobody minded that night.

Tales of our harrowing defeat came in thick and fast. Several drummers from my platoon, including the great comic, Stan Lee, had escaped from Tobruk and had made their way to Mersa Matruh, never knowing that Jerry had got there first; and into the bag they went. I hoped to goodness he'd destroyed the photographs of the *Comic Stormtroopers* comedy show we'd put on before the war. Stan had taken the part of Hitler, and he'd looked uncannily convincing.

We slept soundly that night but in the early hours of the morning we received a shelling, which told us the Germans were hot on our tail. We pulled camp, tents and all, and when the place was completely bare we moved off leaving nothing for Jerry to claim. We even filled in the WC so he'd have to dig all over again if he wanted to use our base as a camp.

We journeyed throughout the remainder of the night and reached our new position before dawn had broken. This place was called El Alamein: just another name for nowhere. Nevertheless, it was a British-controlled nowhere, at least for the time being, and it was our job to see it stayed that way. We were told

Mustapha Barracks, Alexandria, 1939: the Coldstream Guards in fancy dress. It was all fun and games, just before the war.

a special message for our unit had been received from Winston Churchill himself, who'd issued us with the select task of holding this line at all costs until reinforcements arrived. In short, we were asked to 'do or die' for forty-eight hours more. Would we be strong enough to hold on until then? We'd heard the cavalry would be bringing a fresh supply of weapons and armour; welcome news indeed. Throughout the course of the war we'd been so ill equipped we may as well have been fighting with nothing but a stick, and now even that was blunt. I knew if ever there was a time to call upon the store of extra energy that was supposed to rest behind our elbow, this was it.

It was some hours after sunrise when things began kicking off. One of our petrol lorries was dive-bombed by a German aircraft and both the driver and passenger were burnt to death in their seats. Their smouldered remains were visible in the cab, and RSM Len Rowlands asked for volunteers to get them out. I volunteered along with a Guardsman from Headquarter Company, and together we sweated in the hot sun, struggling to remove the bodies. It was an almost impossible task, for the heat from the explosion had caused the cab of the lorry to twist into a mangled wreck. The effort made my shoulders and ribs ache, but I fought to hide my pain. More volunteers came forward, and between us we managed to disassemble a sufficient amount of the exterior to allow us to slip inside. As we pulled the charred corpses out, parts of them fell off. Their feet had become wedged underneath the pedals and I had to retrieve them. The smell made my stomach heave.

After committing the bodies to the ground, I was sent for by the commanding officer, and the stony look on his face told me that whatever was coming next wasn't going to be anything good. Without a word he presented me with a medical record that had arrived fresh from Alexandria. My heart sank when I saw 'B2' stamped across the page. I knew I'd be found out eventually; I'd just hoped for a chance to do my bit in battle before then.

'I admire your loyalty, Sergeant Rochford,' he said, 'but as I'm sure you'll understand, I'm duty bound to ensure that every single man I send into battle has the highest possible chance of returning to me safely. That includes my wayward sergeants who seem to think that military regulations don't apply to them. I'm sorry, old chap, but I'm afraid there's no way I can permit you to stay with us.'

I knew then, as I stood before him with throbbing ribs and an aching arm, that it would have been pointless trying to convince him I was fit and healthy enough to stand side by side with my comrades. I was of no more use to my battalion, and that was a bitter pill to swallow. I already felt like a yellow belly and this made everything seem so much worse, but everybody wished me well when I left. I was grateful for their support.

The left-out-of-battle detachment, where I was transferred, had formed up at a place on the edge of the desert called Mena, on the outskirts of the capital. The poor chaps who'd been left out of the 'fun', as the officers termed it, were having a hell of a life here. One of the sergeant majors at the base seemed to really enjoy making life dammed uncomfortable for the unfortunate soldiers, many of whom still hadn't recovered from their traumas. They were booked left, right and centre, and for absolutely nothing at all, whilst each morning the officers would swan in at whatever time suited them from where they'd been roughing it at the nearby Mena House Hotel, having spent the night in a soft bed, with a private bathroom and a push-bell to summon their attendants. It was all so unjust but I tried not to let it bother me. I kept my head down and got on with life as best I could, hoping that one day my lot would improve.

Rumour had it that the British authorities had placed King Farouk under house arrest within his palace at Abdin in Cairo. It seemed Britain was taking no chances with this crafty monarch. They'd even moved his yacht, and that of Prince Mohammed Ali Tewfik, the heir presumptive, from Ras el-Tin Harbour in Alexandria to Lake Timsah at the town of Ismailia, part of the Canal Zone. The reason for all this was that Farouk was partial to the Italians and his palaces were infested with them: they'd filled every role within his household staff, enjoying the king's protection throughout the war.

Our detachment was bursting with speculation, and it was funny how the rumours were spread. We'd no proper toilets at Mena, and had to make do with going behind a small mound in the desert in the shadow of the pyramids. This was the perfect opportunity to spin a yarn or two before heading back to our duties. One rather appropriate story I heard while squatting was the tale of an unfortunate patrol of Guardsmen who'd been sent out to spy on the Afrika Korps. With only the light from the desert moon to see by, the patrol, flat on their tummies in the undergrowth, had seen the Jerries relieving a couple of Italian sentries. Bursting to go, the Wops nipped over in the direction of our watchers and commenced to urinate into the underbrush, soaking the hidden Guards. They'd been ordered not to move from their position at any cost, so our poor lads just had to lie there and bear it.

'Hey, Paddy,' one of the young lads called out one day as I was squatting behind my little mound, 'I heard a smashing rumour today, and this one came directly from the officers' mess. Mick Laycock said he'd overheard the company commander telling one of the senior officers that they're sending us to a place called "The Land of Milk and Honey". They say it's a place that has an abundance of everything, including fresh spring waters and brothels galore!'

We were leaving. This was the best news I'd heard in a long time. I was sick and tired of life in Cairo, and this new place, the Land of Milk and Honey, sounded far more appealing. The lads and I never guessed it would be Syria.

Chapter 10

The Egyptian Army

In the autumn of 1942 the Allied forces, fortified by weapons and manpower, dealt a terrific blow to the enemy at El Alamein. It was one of the greatest artillery barrages ever devised, and within twelve days the Hun was rolled back and out of the Western Desert. In the evening moonlight and shadows, the roar of the guns from El Alamein could be heard over in Alexandria, some 70 miles away. Under the leadership of the brave General Montgomery, our sappers went forward, marking the minefields with white tape. The infantry, with their shiny new bayonets and tremendous guts, followed closely behind. Their victory heralded the turning of the tide; the Desert Fox's days in Egypt were numbered.

I, too, was leaving the sands of Egypt for the first time in years, though I was headed for a training camp at Syria, along with the others from our detachment. Up until 1941 the country had been under the governance of the Vichy French, but, fearful that Hitler would attempt to use this territory as a launch pad for his assault on Egypt, the Allies had liberated the land from Nazi domination.

It was a long and tiring trek from Cairo to Syria, but when we finally arrived my first impression was of how clean everything seemed. The cleanliness of the locals, in comparison with the Egyptians, was striking. We were greeted with smiles and waves, and began to look forward to a comfortable stay.

We settled down some 30 miles west of the city of Damascus, under the shadow of Mount Hermon, the summit of which was covered with a perpetual blanket of snow. It would have made a picturesque view from our billets, but unfortunately we were provided with windowless cattle huts in which to sleep. There were no electric lights or running water, or anything even vaguely resembling a commodity. So much for the 'abundance of everything' we were promised; but despite this, life presented few real problems. The only shooting we had to contend with was out on the ranges where we went to practise our firing, trying out the brand new weapons that were on issue.

Our days comprised training exercises, patrols and little else. The weeks dragged by, and in 1943, with their mission in the desert complete, the 3rd Battalion of the Coldstream Guards came to join us. A harsh winter had fallen, and thick snow had settled all around. My feet were frozen and there was nothing I could do to put the warmth back into them. I had it easy, though, for the fighting troops were sent away into the icy hills on a week-long training exercise. I, of course, was left behind, along with three of my pals from the desert days. We decided this would be the perfect opportunity for a lads' night out: a luxury we'd promised ourselves many moons back, as we lay hungry and thirsty in our scorpion-infested holes in the ground. We booked a table at The Grand Trianon in Damascus, which was an 'officers only' venue, but we didn't worry about that for I'd become friends with the manager.

Money was no object that night, as we'd been putting by for this evening for a long, long time. We ordered a bottle of Scotch each before being ushered to our table by the white-gloved maître d'. The food was delicious; we ordered five courses, and after a moreish dessert of crème brûlée we settled down with our cigars to watch the after-dinner cabaret, when the drinks began to flow like water. With a cocktail of whiskey, vodka and exhilaration pumping through our veins, we lost track of time and inevitably missed the leave truck that was waiting to pick us up in the market square.

I awoke the next morning in my bunk with a thumping head, and was informed by the mess waiter that I was under open arrest, and likewise my pals. Try as I might, I just couldn't remember anything from the moment I stood on the table and proposed the health of the Free French. How we got back to camp I'll never know, but the three of us were duly charged with missing the leave truck – a fair charge – and we accepted our reprimands with good faith.

February came and time was called on our stay in the Land of Milk and Honey. The cunning Rommel was on the offensive once more, so our troops were called back to action. Having already suffered significant losses, our battalion was merged with other diminished forces, including the 6th Grenadiers and 2nd Scots Guards; and this new band of heroes was officially named the 201st Guards Brigade, affectionately termed Two-O-One. Together they raced some 1,500 miles into the desert to hunt down the Fox and slaughter his sly old pack once and for all.

Unable to tag along, I was sent to the Infantry Training Depot on Egypt's Canal Zone. The sergeant major, Baggy McKinley, was from the Scots Guards, and a fine man he was. Along with a service comrade, Platoon Sergeant Major Sam Cowley, the three of us became firm friends. We got through dozens of pints during our evenings in the mess, so we'd eat orange peel the following morning to mask the smell of alcohol prior to the company commander's inspection.

I'd been promoted to company sergeant major, and though I didn't get the pay of the rank, I received an extra four shillings per day. There was little out here to spend it on anyway, and apart from drinking there wasn't much for us to do. The Canal Zone was a bleak part of the world, and I sometimes wondered why we were even bothering to defend it. After a few months I began to feel restless, wishing there was something more useful for me to occupy my time with. Utterly fed up, I got in touch with a friend, Charlie Youner, whom I'd met through the Buffaloes before the war. He was the chief engineer of Prince Mohammed Ali's private yacht, and as the craft wasn't currently in operation, he said I could go down to Lake Timsah and make use of it any time I liked. Not wanting to pass up this chance, I invited my two sergeant major friends to lunch on board, and they were greatly impressed when we arrived. They teased me something rotten, claiming I'd made it all up about being friends with the engineer and was nothing more than a stowaway, but we had a grand time that day and many other days that followed. I made full use of the yacht before I left the Infantry Training Depot.

I soon learned that rumours circulated at the depot just as quickly as they did in other divisions in the army, and one morning, having heard I was feeling blue, the company commander sent for me.

'I understand you're up for a new challenge, CSM Rochford,' he said. I braced myself for a lecture, thinking he was about to accuse me of being ungrateful of my current situation, or of failing to pull my weight, but then I noticed a smile in the corner of his lips. 'How do you feel about taking a commission with the British Military Mission?'

I looked at him in surprise. 'Sir?'

'The Egyptian Army requires a military adviser at the Small Arms Training School at a place called Almaza just outside Cairo, and I've recommended you for the job.'

I was staggered. I hadn't seen that coming. The position sounded appealing and I accepted the offer without hesitation, but it was with some sadness that I left. I wondered if I'd miss the Guards' way of life; the only one I'd ever known. Would I fit in with this new unit? I knew there was no point dwelling on this now, for I'd cast my die, and it was time to begin a new life with the Egyptian Army.

I reported to the British Military Mission Headquarters, which was situated between Heliopolis – the great 'City of the Sun' – and the garrison town of Abbassia. I was greeted by a man called Captain Franklin, who welcomed me to the Mission and gave me an address in Heliopolis where I was to live. My flat was pleasant and came with all the home comforts one could wish for. I shared the building with a handful of other soldiers who also worked as military advisers, and I settled in quickly to life on a bustling street.

Major General Aziz el-Masri Pasha was once the chief of staff of the Egyptian Army, but he'd been dismissed at the request of the British Ambassador, Sir Miles Lampson, owing to his anti-British tendencies. One of his worst offences was passing our plans on to the enemy, yet for whatever reason, General Masri wasn't placed under arrest. I for one was amazed that somebody like that was allowed to remain at large. As was to be expected, the deceptive general took full advantage of his freedom by trying to cause as much trouble for Britain as possible, and he wasn't alone.

Over in Iraq, an Arab nationalist officer named Rashid Ali al-Gailani formed an alliance with the Nazis and began a bloody revolution to attempt to overthrow the pro-British government. General Masri, upon learning of the coup d'état, tried to flee Egypt and join forces with Gailani. With the help of two Egyptian wing commanders, Hassan Zulfiqar Sabri and his brother, Ali Sabri, Masri attempted to fly to Iraq in a stolen Egyptian Air Force aeroplane, but the British got word of this conspiracy and the plane was forced down over Heliopolis Airport, where the trio were arrested. The two air force officers faced a court martial. One was transferred to the regular army as a captain with loss of promotion for five years, whilst the younger brother was allowed to remain in the air force, but also faced a five-year loss of promotion.

General Masri, who'd once again wormed his way out of jail, began mixing with the junior officers in the army. There was a social venue known as the Egyptian Officers' Club in Zamalek, an affluent suburb in the west end of Cairo, where he'd spend many an evening boasting that one way or another he'd oust Britain from Egypt once and for all, and then boot the king out after them.

An alliance was formed that became known as the Free Officers' Movement. These defiant young officers, with plenty of spare time on their hands, used to gather together and dream of an independent country led by a strong army. Much older men than they held all the senior ranks and there was no retiring age. It was the same old story: it wasn't so much what you knew but who you knew, and many of the junior officers felt they were being overlooked. Disillusioned, and sick and tired of all the 'bull shine' parades, these chaps were eager to seek out the company of the sympathetic ex-chief of staff.

Colonel Gamal Abdel Nasser was a prominent player in this underground movement. Unlike many other Egyptians, Nasser was one of the few men who actually began to put his ideas and daydreams in motion. It was because of his influence that the movement grew from strength to strength.

I first heard of the Free Officers in 1943 when I was posted to the Egyptian Army and began mixing with its officers; but who was I to voice my concern about them, and who would choose to listen if I did?

I arrived at the entrance to the Small Arms Training School on my first day, full of apprehension. Unfortunately, no transport had been arranged for me so I had to make my own way on foot. I'd seen the school from a long way away, resting on top of the high ground. From the road it had seemed like a short distance to walk. How deceptive that turned out to be. It was a long, hard slog over the sand, with the Eastern sun blazing down upon me; and when I finally reached the gate I must have looked like a dishevelled wreck.

I always took my first impression of a unit by the sentry at the gate. In this case, he was the shortest and scruffiest soldier I'd ever seen in all my life. He looked like a pile of rubbish that had been dumped in a heap, ready for the corporation dustman to sweep away. His rifle was casually propped up by the side of a sentry box that hadn't seen a paintbrush in many a year. He was dressed in a threadbare uniform that fitted where it touched, and his boots were down at heel. The only thing neat and shiny about him was the dazzling smile he flashed me.

'*Marhaba*, Johnny,' he said, which meant, 'Welcome, English soldier.'

I passed through the gate and ahead of me I saw a long line of what appeared to be offices; opposite these were rows of wooden huts. Further to the rear were miles and miles of sandy wasteland, a perfect place for weapon training. In search of the commander, I made my way towards the central office. I received a few curious stares from passing soldiers, sporting their fez headdresses. A handful saluted, if you could call it that, and I wasn't at all impressed by their slipshod approach to discipline.

On a board outside one of the offices was written something in Arabic. Though I had a fair knowledge of the language, like many Europeans I couldn't understand the written word. Assuming I was in the correct place, I knocked on the door and was invited to enter.

Sitting at a table in the centre of the room was an Egyptian red-tabbed lieutenant colonel. He stood up when he saw me, shook me warmly by the hand and offered me a seat. I couldn't help notice the man was strikingly handsome. He had dark and chiselled features, and, unlike a lot of senior officers I'd known, his smile extended to his eyes. He introduced himself as Seif el-Yasin Khalifa, and expressed his surprise when I told him I was his new infantry adviser. He told me their previous adviser had also been an Englishman, who'd apparently caused a fair bit of trouble for the school, resulting in a court martial. Thereafter the Egyptians requested for the Military Mission not to appoint another English adviser under any circumstance. I didn't want to be fired before I'd even started, so I decided to put things straight.

'Actually, I'm Irish,' I said, and the colonel's face lit up.

'Well, this is very different,' he said, leaping to his feet and shaking me by the hand for a second time. 'We love the Irish people, for you, like us, are still fighting for your ideals.'

I smiled back, but couldn't help commenting: 'You don't like the English much, do you?'

The colonel returned to his seat and lit a couple of cigars.

'In a way, no,' he replied, and I could tell he was choosing his words carefully. 'They have been in my country for a long time and yet they have never learnt to understand us, or even try to help us. Not really; not where it matters.'

The more we chatted the more I got to like my new colonel. He was young and enthusiastic; and after a few cigars and several cups of strong black coffee, he offered to show me round. I saw things that day that may well have made others laugh, but I was more inclined to cry. I couldn't believe what a ramshackle state this place was in and was disappointed to find I was going to have to start my work from scratch.

The Egyptians' method of training was years out of date and the instructors couldn't even read. I passed a squad of men who were practising firing their weapons from the ground. One chap actually had a handkerchief tied around his left eye, and on closer examination, I found that not one man could ever hope to hit a target, as none of their guns were properly sighted. There were no weapon pits, battle courses, or, for that matter, anything suitable at all.

Colonel Khalifa explained to me that the trainee soldiers were currently preparing for an annual appraisal, during which their skills would be assessed. This sounded worrying.

'Do all the trainees fire weapons as part of this test?' I asked.

'Oh, no,' he replied, waving a dismissive hand. 'We have a shortage of live ammunition, so only one selected man actually fires, and if he passes, then all of the squad passes too.'

I couldn't quite believe what I was hearing, and my shock must have shown on my face.

'The government gives the army 250,000 Egyptian pounds per year,' he explained. 'This does not go very far.'

After the tour, the colonel showed me to the office where I'd be working. I'd never had my own office before and was excited by the prospect. Inside I found several other Egyptian officers who, on introduction, stood up and shook hands with me.

'*Ahlan wa sahlan*,' they bade me, which meant: 'You are welcome with us.'

One of the officers clapped his hands twice and into the office, at the double, came an Egyptian soldier, grinning from ear to ear. After a few quick words in Arabic, which I didn't understand, the soldier took up a crouching position at my feet. Feeling slightly uneasy, I asked the officer what this was all about.

'This soldier is your servant,' he told me. 'Should you want anything – a coffee, your shoes cleaned – this man is at your disposal.'

It took me a while to get used to having this man around, following me about like a playful puppy, but we got on well and I found him to be an enthusiastic worker.

I learned a lot about the Egyptian Army over the coming weeks. Conscription was compulsory for all the fit and healthy Egyptian men. After their eighteenth birthday they were compelled to serve in the army for anything up to three years, unless they could find the sum of E£25. If so, they could pay their way out of military service. If not, they were apprehended and taken from their village under police escort to the nearest town, where they were handed over to the military. The fittest and tallest men were earmarked for the Royal Bodyguard, and the remainder, however small and feeble, were drafted to the infantry.

The Royal Bodyguard was the king's private army. This elite force of men was equipped with all the modern weapons of warfare, while the regular Egyptian Army was still training with obsolete weapons. Farouk remained deaf to the pleas of his officers. As long as his Bodyguards were suitably equipped, what did it matter about the rest of the army?

One day I spotted a crowd of new recruits in rags and tatters, their hands tied together with string, being escorted along the Abbassia Road. They were surrounded by Egyptian soldiers who were armed with rifles to keep the unfortunates in line. I wished there was something I could do to help, and decided the only chance I had of making any difference at all would be to enrol on the next military training course that was held each year in Palestine. I went to the British Military Mission headquarters to speak to Captain Franklin. He listened intently to what I had to say, and at the end of my pitch he told me he wouldn't stand in my way.

'But remember,' he said, 'if I agree to pay for you go to Palestine, I expect to see dividends on your return.'

With a shining bright kit that would have been a credit to my former regiment, I departed from Cairo Station in full marching order and soon found myself back in the biblical land of Palestine. I arrived at the training camp shortly after dawn and was directed to the dining hut, if you could even call it that, where I was served a small portion of cold breakfast.

'Well, well, if it isn't Paddy Rochford,' said a voice behind me.

I turned around and found myself face to face with one of our ex-sergeants, Chick Bryant, with whom I'd served in Palestine before the war. He joined me at my table and we had a good old chinwag. He too was working with the Arab forces, and neither of us could believe what a state the country's army was in. We made a pact there and then to put up with all the little discomforts during the course, knuckle down and learn all we could. We worked seven days a week, from early morning until late at night, then after a couple of drinks we'd retire to our tent and spend the remaining hours swotting. We'd get a few hours' shut-eye before rising the following morning to do it all over again.

One morning some of our comrades awoke to find their tent had been stolen during the night. The only clues left were the tracks of camels' feet, galloping away into the distance. The Arabs truly were grand masters in the art of stealing.

At the end of the course we'd all become experts in the use of modern weapons. We took our exams and waited outside the commanding officer's office to be told the results. Chick and I were sent in together, and were thrilled to be informed we'd both passed with the highest marks. Our hard work had paid off!

I arrived back in Heliopolis first thing the following Sunday. After a clean-up, I reported to Mission HQ and handed my results on a slip of paper to the general service officer. I was duly promoted to paid warrant officer class II and it wasn't long before I'd completely reorganized the syllabus at the Small Arms Training School.

We divided the school into three wings. Two wings were commanded by Major Ismail Mohammed and Major Ali Amer whilst the third went to Captain Hassan Zulfiqar Sabri, the brother of Wing Commander Ali Sabri, who'd been caught up in the Iraqi scandal a couple of years earlier. I supervised the digging of training pits, built a battle course and arranged with Egypt's Ministry of Defence to procure some modern weapons. Patience wasn't one of Colonel Khalifa's virtues, and he was eager for the new weapons to arrive. To speed things up, I telephoned my good friend from the New Zealand forces, Captain Keith Collins, and asked to borrow some of theirs until ours were delivered. He agreed, so I went over to collect them.

Among the Kiwi weapons was a Sten Mark V with a bayonet attached. Being a brand new issue, it caused quite a stir in the Egyptian Army, and it vanished from sight shortly after it arrived. When I asked Colonel Khalifa if I could have it back, he turned a deep shade of crimson.

'This I cannot do,' he remarked, and that was the end of the matter.

I went to ask Mission HQ for their help, and after a lengthy telephone call to the Ministry of Defence, I received the same response.

'You'll not see it again,' Captain Franklin began, replacing the handset, 'because it's with the Egyptian Army chief of staff. It seems there's nothing much you or I can do about it.'

'Why, what's happened?' I demanded. 'The weapon isn't mine, and I'm honour-bound to return it to its rightful owners.'

'Let's just say King Farouk is rather partial to anything new,' Captain Franklin said. 'Reading between the lines, it sounds as though he spotted the Sten and insisted he should have it. His chief of staff, not wanting to incur the king's anger, duly obliged.'

In the end, the New Zealanders kindly agreed to make a formal presentation of the weapon to the king, although it was all done rather reluctantly.

It wasn't long before our own weapons began arriving and I demonstrated the 2-inch mortar to the troops. The school had previously used the French 60-millimetre, until a terrible accident occurred. A bomb was dropped into the base of the barrel and struck the firing pin. The course officer forgot to remove his hand from over the end of barrel, and he lost it when the bomb came hurtling out. I also demonstrated the new projector infantry anti-tank, known as the PIAT; the 4.2-inch mortar and the Thompson machine carbine.

With the help of Colonel Khalifa, I talked the school commander, Brigadier Suleiman Bey, into joining us in a demonstration assault course run. He agreed, but unfortunately lost his hat and got stuck in a hole. This didn't seem to dampen his enthusiasm, and he even suggested putting on a demonstration for the king's chief of staff. I wasn't happy about this, as the man was still in my bad books, but I didn't want to let the commander down so I set about organizing a show.

There was quite an audience when the big day arrived. I stood at the front of the display ground, and after a brief opening talk, picked up the first weapon and took aim. I pulled the trigger and the spring went forward with a rattle. The missile went hurtling forwards and exploded in the dead centre of the target. Delighted shouts rang out from the bank of spectators.

'*Mabrouk!*'

'*Bravo aleik!*'

Brimming with confidence, I turned to my audience and said: 'If some of you would like to follow me, I'll show you how to blow something up.'

My colleagues and I ushered the dubious crowd to a reasonable distance. One of the advisers, a chap called Dick Dodds, insisted we used about 2 yards of fuse for the demonstration. I disagreed with him, thinking it should be shorter, but Dick was as stubborn as a mule and wasn't going to change his mind, so we compromised, but still it was far too long. We lit the fuse and retreated behind a small rise in the ground.

Nothing happened.

We waited and waited but still there was no explosion.

'I suppose we'd better take a look to see if the fuse has gone out,' I suggested.

Just as Dick and I rose from behind the bank there was an almighty thump that rattled the hills, and we fell to the ground, covering our heads with our arms. When the smoke cleared, I looked up and was amused to see the chief of staff galloping away at top speed, hotly pursued by the other spectators. I can't say I was sorry.

'Serves him right,' I thought.

A few days later I was called into the commander's office and was introduced to the brigadier in command of Egypt's Infantry Division. He'd heard about my demonstrations at the school and asked if I'd take my 'wondrous weapons' and do the same for the 1st Infantry Brigade.

'I promise nobody will run away this time,' he said, with a twinkle in his eyes.

I was honoured by the invitation, and the following week Dick and I went over to the Infantry Division to put on our show. To our amazement, we found that the brigadier had turned it into a red carpet event and had invited a host of dignitaries. The chief of the British Military Mission was there, as was the major general and hundreds of senior officers from both the Mission and the Egyptian Army. They'd even brought in a military band from the Royal Bodyguard, and a fine set of musicians they were, too.

'All of this for our measly little weapon demonstration!' Dick muttered.

We both agreed, on second thoughts, that this should be an all-Egyptian show, and tried to disappear into the massed array of VIPs. After all, we reasoned, our appointments were to act as advisers only, and felt our Egyptian colleagues were more than capable of demonstrating the weapons themselves. Our plans were soon altered when the brigadier's voice from a loud speaker came echoing across the arena.

'Where is my friend, Mr Paddy Pasha? Please ask him to come to me to begin the demonstration.'

With a red face I made my way over to his side. I explained we thought it'd be best if we took a back seat, having already briefed a couple of the brigadier's own soldiers on how to conduct the presentation. The brigadier looked at me as if I'd insulted his wife.

'But you don't expect those two donkeys to demonstrate a thing like this, do you? Please show us yourselves.'

All eyes fell upon Dick and me, and nervously we began the demonstrations. The booms and blasts from our weapons were followed by 'ooohs' and 'aaahs' from the assembly, and when we'd finished, we heard clapping and appreciative cheers from the crowd.

'*Jayyid jiddan*!'

'*Mabrouk*!' they were shouting.

After the show, the brigadier took Dick and me by the arm and led us into an enormous marquee. The interior was decorated with multi-coloured bunting and the tables were laid for a banquet, with white-jacketed and red-fezzed waiters weaving smartly between them. We were given the seats of honour; and a spectacular feast, as only the Egyptians could offer, was served.

Several months passed at the school and our first course had come and gone. To my delight, the troops told us they'd enjoyed every minute of it. I'd scrapped the useless entrance examination, which had changed little since the Boer War days, and replaced it with a more informative opening lecture. It was drastic but fruitful, as it woke the chaps up and made them understand that even though the Second World War was not really theirs, they were still a part of it. Smoke bombs were set off around the students, and with the help of a few thunder flashes and phosphorous grenades, we achieved the desired effect. We proceeded to talk about the various weapons; and to round everything off, a few colleagues would make a surprise attack with bayonets, drawing very close to the now interested students. The course proved to be popular, and news about us travelled throughout the Egyptian Army. Even the king took a keen interest in following our progress.

When I first arrived at the school, food rations were meagre, but now we'd organized a dining room with tables and trestles, and nobody had to sit crossed-legged on the floor anymore. Food was gradually becoming more plentiful, although meat was a rarity and was still only issued twice a week. Outside we'd planted vegetables such as marrows, cucumbers, figs and other delights including sweet melons that turned to water in one's mouth. Beautiful flowers were also in abundance, and I felt at peace in our surroundings.

Often during breaks in the training periods, I'd sit with the officers in the rest rooms, drinking delicious black coffee, or my favourite, *shai-na'na*, which was tea with mint. We had several young officers amongst us and I got on well with all of them, but one in particular I clicked with was called Lieutenant Kamal Henoui. Some time earlier he'd had the ill luck of commanding a firing party at the execution of a soldier who'd been sentenced to death on a murder charge. Things had gone wrong, and Henoui had to administer the coup de grâce on this unfortunate soldier as he lay bleeding to death under the shadow of the Virgin's Breasts, two slender sand dunes behind the Abbassia Ranges. This had affected him, and almost overnight he went from a sparkling-eyed youngster to a morose outcast who shunned everyone's company. One morning he was arrested at the school. The secret police had found piles of communist papers in his room and he was accused of being a prime mover in Nasser's Free Officers' Movement. Henoui was posted to the frontier at Sallum and I never saw him again.

With so much going on in my life, I hadn't taken much notice of the different forms of punishment that prevailed in the Egyptian Army, but one day I was looking out of my office window and spotted a bayonet fighting dummy standing in the middle of the parade ground. This looked odd to me, as I always made sure any items that weren't in use were put away in the weapon stores. I asked Colonel Khalifa what it was all about.

'A soldier will be whipped in public at noon,' he said, casting me a hard stare. 'He will be strapped to the dummy to receive his punishment.'

'What on earth for?'

'For losing some army equipment.'

'And you think that justifies a flogging, do you?'

'Sorry, Paddy,' the colonel said with a shrug, 'but we still flog people here, as you did once in your army.'

'But that was over a century ago. Things have changed a little since then. We treat soldiers like human beings these days.'

The colonel threw me a look that made it clear there was no more to be said on the matter.

It was a scorching hot day in 1944 and the sun was approaching twelve o'clock. To the notes of a bugle ringing out the 'fall in', the squads, officers and even civil servants marched onto the parade ground and gathered around the dummy. The prisoner came next, escorted by soldiers with fixed bayonets. The commander and Colonel Khalifa followed behind them.

I recognized the prisoner as one of the school's mechanical transport drivers. He was only a little chap, and I saw him shudder as he glanced over to where the school sergeant major was standing, casually flicking his footwear with the cat o'nine tails. This was a stick approximately 16 inches long with twelve lengths of leather protruding from the handle, with many knots on each lash.

The little soldier was stripped to the waist as he stood between his escorts. A vehicle pulled up and out stepped a tall, well-groomed officer with a stethoscope resting on his breast. He waked towards the unfortunate prisoner and held the instrument lightly to his heart.

'*Tamam,*' he said in Arabic, which meant: 'okay'.

The prisoner was pushed forward and pinned to the makeshift whipping post. There was one instructor holding each foot; two others, his arms. They made sure to hold the man at arm's length to avoid receiving any impending blows themselves.

Colonel Khalifa read out the crime and the sentence, and then it began. The sergeant major raised the cat shoulder-high and commenced to bring it down onto the soldier's back. He administered thirty strokes in all, moving from one side to the other after every five. Each reverberating 'crack' made me feel sick to my stomach. With the exception of a groan after the first stroke, the prisoner made no sound. They say that after the first lash you don't feel the remainder. The parts of the little soldier's flesh that were usually hidden underneath his clothes were as white and soft as mine, apart from the red wheals that blossomed on the skin after each lash. At the end of the flogging his skin was broken, and a stream of blood ran down the middle of his back. The instructors released their grip on the man's weakened limbs, and his shirt was thrown back to him.

I was so upset by the whole debacle that I barged my way through the crowd to find my driver, and cleared off home for the rest of the day. My driver's eyes kept meeting mine through the rear-view mirror. He could tell I was upset.

'*La taqlaq effendi,*' he said. ('Don't worry about it, sir.')

I knew there was nothing I could have done. This was their own kind of justice, and it was one army practice I had no hope of reforming. No amount of training could change that.

Chapter 11

The Tiger of Faluja

Cairo had never seemed a friendly place to me. Though the Egyptian Armed Forces had accepted me as a friend, the civilians were not so welcoming. I had few friends outside the army, and one evening, feeling at a loose end, I decided to take a stroll through the city in the hope of stumbling across some excitement. A little further past the cinema I heard music playing, so I wandered over and found myself standing outside a club. Its name, 'The Heliopolis Sporting Club', was written in blue letters above the door, and on the wall a notice said 'private' in Arabic. I was just about to walk away when a smart young Egyptian stepped out of the doorway and greeted me.

'*Masaa el-kheer*,' he bid me, which meant 'good evening'. '*Hal beemkani mosa'adatuk?*' ('Can I help you at all?')

'I was just looking for somewhere I could buy a drink,' I explained.

'I am sorry but this is a private club and it is out of bounds to troops,' he told me.

I thanked the chap and continued on my way. I hadn't gone far when I was hailed by another tall, smartly dressed man about my age who was walking towards the club. He must have overheard my conversation because he kindly invited me for a drink as his guest. Upon entering, I was made most welcome by everyone I was introduced to. There was a gathering of men and women, both Egyptian and European, seated on the veranda of the clubhouse. Inside people were dancing to live music played by a resident jazz band and at the far end of the brightly lit room was a long, impressive looking bar, serving every kind of beverage imaginable.

I learned my host's name was Abdel Moneim Ragheb Bey and that he was on the Egyptian Council of Ministers. He introduced me to his good friend, the treasurer of the club and a lieutenant in the Egyptian Army. Like Abdel he was a tall and handsome chap with a quick, warm smile. I liked him on sight, for there was something indefinable about him that made him stand out from all the other Egyptian officers I'd met. He was introduced to me as Gamal Abdel Nasser, and he'd just returned to Cairo after serving in Mankabad and Sudan. I soon learned he was a bright and disciplined soldier, who became known within certain circles as the 'Tiger of Faluja', owing to his fearless heroism on the battlefield.

Nasser and I clicked at once. Over a few drinks we shared our life stories, and discovered we had much in common. He told me he was originally from Alexandria. His father, Abdu-Nasser Hussein, was a humble employee of the Egyptian Post Office, and upon promotion to sub-postmaster, moved his family to a small town called Khatatba, between Alexandria and Cairo. It was just a place of mud-baked sand. The houses were roofless and the inhabitants – who mostly comprised flies, cattle, dogs and urchins – all lived together in harmony. At night when the sun had gone down, the people of the town would come out of their homes and sit in the open air, smoking their hookah pipes and listening, enraptured, to the tales of the local storytellers. Few people in the village could read, so this was how they learned their information, however distorted the tale may have become.

Returning home from school one day, young Nasser fell foul of the local police and ended up in jail with a rather sore head. It was this incident that helped to secure a large chip on his little shoulders, which stayed with him as he grew into adulthood. Abdu-Nasser didn't want his son to end up on the slippery slope to self-destruction, so he packed his eldest child off to Cairo to stay with an uncle. The poor boy was passed around from pillar to post for pretty much the rest of his childhood, and never really had what one might call a stable upbringing.

'I spent many years living in Cairo,' he told me, 'and in that time my parents always kept their distance, never once sending for me, or coming to visit. I was lonely, so one day decided I should go home.' There was a brief pause as the flame that had been burning in his brown eyes throughout our conversation seemed to fade. 'When I arrived, it was too late. I learned my mother had died in childbirth a long time ago, and nobody had thought to tell me.'

Full of rage and despair, the youth plunged himself into his hate campaigns and joined the military. He felt it was here where he could meet other like-minded souls and stir up trouble for the authorities, in a conscious effort to put right all the wrongs in his land.

Nasser and his friends were cool and well organized. In fact, he was exactly the type of leader with whom the British should have negotiated to help establish a bright future for Egypt; but Nasser was from a poor family and was thus considered of little importance.

I was interested to learn that my new friend was residing not far from my flat in Heliopolis, with his charming wife and children whom I had the pleasure of getting to know. Though most of Nasser's spare time was taken up with his revolutionary writings, he invited me to return to the club to join him for a drink and a game of tennis. This I did, and from then on we met every week to play a few matches under the floodlights, and between us we'd put the world to rights. We shared long, deep discussions about the social issues in Egypt. Over time, as we got to know and respect one another, I learned all about the underground organizations that were dedicated to fighting against anything that kept the Egyptian *fellaheen*, like Nasser's own family, in poverty and ignorance. In many peoples' eyes, this was the fault of the British, for we were throwing money at the country but most, if not all, was landing in the wrong pockets.

I became a fully fledged member of the club and paid fifty piastres (about ten shillings) a month; it was well worth it, for it was here where I made many good friends. I'd already met a few members of the extended Nasser family, including Gamal's first cousins, Ali Sabri of the Royal Egyptian Air Force, and Captain Hassan Zulfiqar Sabri, who were colleagues of mine at the school. All three were quiet, unassuming types of men, but as the old proverb warns: still waters run deep.

The controversial Major General Aziz el-Masri Pasha had founded the Egyptian Army University Officer Training Corps where Nasser and his friends regularly gave lectures. Firearms were secretly stacked away and hidden, and I believe it was here where the whole structure of armed resistance in Egypt was formed. Some of the instructors at my school who were either jealous of the great Tiger's reputation, or were simply against his ideals, tipped me off about secret plans that the group was hatching. I tried informing the military authorities of this, but wasn't believed and was simply told to mind my own business. Not one to give in, I made another attempt one morning when I visited Mission HQ to let them know what was going on under their very noses. Captain Franklin listened to me quietly and intently until I'd finished.

'I'm not at all surprised by this,' he sighed, 'but there are people in high places in Cairo who … well, let's just say, I'd advise you not to get involved.'

Life was rather cushy for some in Cairo, and they wanted it to stay that way. However, with persistence I was allowed to voice my concerns to a higher-ranking officer who actually laughed at me.

'Don't talk such bollocks,' he said, lighting a cigarette and returning to his paperwork. 'Go back to your training school and get on with the job we're paying you to do.'

All too soon we began to witness the whole movement unfolding before us. Bombs were thrown into crowded streets; places of entertainment were destroyed, but still Britain closed her eyes, hoping it would all quieten down soon. I stood alone, believing that the sands of time were fast running out for the British in Egypt.

The year was 1944 and the war was nearing its end. News was coming through of great victories. Battles were being won. Rommel was finished; victory in Italy was in sight, and the whole picture was indicating triumph. I was in Colonel Khalifa's office having a cup of *qahwa* with him and some other officers when he told me he thought the Allies would soon attack with every means at their disposal. He pointed to a large map on his wall that he'd been keeping up to date with small coloured flags denoting the positions of the troops.

'Churchill will attack through the Normandy beaches,' he told me, quite casually, 'and nothing will stop him.'

It all happened just as the colonel had said. In June the Allies landed on the beaches and were once again fighting side by side on French soil. Victory was all but ours and our enemies were practically defeated.

'What do you think will happen in Egypt after the war?' I asked. I took a great deal of interest in this country and its people, but Colonel Khalifa studied me hard before answering.

'If you British are wise, you will leave Egypt,' he said. 'If you stay, it will be a mistake. Our people will go mad. We must be allowed to rule our own country, but it will be detrimental for both of us if we remove the British by force. We have a strong ally in you; the best we could ever have. A lot of my people think they wish to see the back of Britain, but Allah help us if the Russians ever get a foothold in this country.'

It was true that the Russian Embassy was working overtime in Cairo. Their lights blazed brightly throughout the night, and scores of people could be seen coming and going through its doors. During the many public disturbances that were a daily happening, it was sometimes said that Russian officials with wooden spoons could be seen mingling in the streets with the barefoot boys.

'It is about time Britain returned to Britain,' said a voice from the corner of the office. It was Hassan Sabri, who'd been listening intently to our conversation. 'Each and every man who dares to call himself Egyptian despises the very parchment the Treaty is written upon.'

'I'm not in a position to give an opinion on that,' I said, 'but I know there are people in this country who'll help in any way they can.'

'Oh yes,' he agreed, 'I know you are helping us – teaching us how to use our firearms – but there are other, more important ways in which we could be helped. We are quite capable of running our own show.'

Over another steaming mug of Arabic coffee, Hassan began opening up to me, and I was surprised when he revealed the 'truth' – or, at least, his version of it – behind the incident that led to the court-martial of him and his brother. He told me he was the duty officer at the aerodrome just outside Cairo. One evening in 1941 he received a message to say that 'a very important person' was to be flown away, and that further instructions would be given when the plane was airborne. He duly checked the aircraft before take-off and it appeared in good order, so he flicked the switch that started the petrol supply. He went inside the aerodrome to phone the gate and told them that when a certain car arrived, the occupants were to be taken straight to the waiting plane, and he was to be informed. The call came, and on returning to the plane, Hassan saw his brother, Ali, standing with another person who turned out to be none other than Major General el-Masri. Before he could question the men, Hassan was told to enter the aircraft as quickly as possible. Trusting his brother's judgement, he obeyed without hesitation.

Shortly after take-off, the plane began to splutter, and it wasn't long before two British fighter planes were on their tail. They had no chance of escape and were forced to make an emergency landing, when the trio were placed under arrest. It transpired that Ali, who was piloting the plane, had turned the petrol supply off by mistake. He'd not realized his brother had already turned it on, so he too had flicked the switch.

At the court martial it had come out that the major general was attempting to fly to Iraq to lead the uprising, and Hassan was sentenced to loss of seniority for five years and transferred to the army. Though Hassan had sworn on the Qur'an, nobody would believe his version of events, not even the British, in whom he'd always put his trust for fair play; but no longer.

At the Small Arms Training School, things were looking up. King Farouk paid a visit, and during an inspection of the weapon training stores he pointed to an open 2-inch mortar chest. Inside he'd spotted a cleaning brush, and as it was not in use, it was in two parts. The king asked the school commander what it was.

'I do not know, Your Majesty,' the commander replied, scratching his head and going rather red. 'I will ask my second-in-command.'

This officer in turn scratched his head and passed the query on to somebody else, who didn't have the faintest idea either, but decided to have a go at solving the mystery himself.

'They are drumsticks, Your Majesty.'

Being partial to a good ditty, the enthusiastic young monarch asked the commander to send for the embarrassed bandmaster, who was ordered to demonstrate. With sweat pouring from his brow and plenty of creative improvisation, he managed to drum out some sort of tune that was convincing enough for the king to believe the two halves of the dirty old cleaning brush were in fact army drumsticks.

This wasn't the only military cover-up. Shortly after the 2-inch mortar gun was introduced to the army, an Egyptian major received a report on the firing of the weapon. It was 100 per cent successful: all the bombs had been discharged without any trouble.

Several months later, some fishermen from Upper Egypt approached the major with a story that they'd seen some soldiers dumping unidentified black objects from a boat into the water. The major duly reported this to the army authorities, who in turn scoured the bottom of the lake and found the 2-inch mortar bombs that had, on paper, at least, been fired with great effect.

One afternoon I went out for a few drinks with one of the school instructors and was surprised to find he was in possession of a seemingly unlimited supply of Craven A cigarettes. I asked him why it was he had no difficulty in obtaining these when it was almost impossible for us British soldiers.

'Ah, Paddy Pasha,' he said, tapping the side of his nose, 'in Egypt we can find anything if we have money and know the right folk to ask.'

He revealed that a roaring trade of stolen NAAFI goods was being carried out down the alleyways and backstreets of Cairo. Abject poverty had made theft a common crime, and one of our military camps at the village of Tel el-Kebir had resorted to installing searchlights and barbed wire all around the perimeter. Things became so dire that sentries were ordered to shoot on sight. Many were the heartbreaking tales of the discovery of dead bodies, laden with the spoils of their crimes. This angered the local population, and by November bombs and bullets were again rattling through the streets, daubing the sandy coloured buildings blood red.

Lord Moyne, the British minister of state, was the next unfortunate target; he was shot down dead along with his driver, Corporal Fuller, of the Royal Army Service Corps. Incensed by Britain's unwanted interference in Palestine, members of the militant Jewish Zionist group, *Lehi*, stopped Lord Moyne's car. Fuller was given the chance to surrender, as the killers only wanted the life of Moyne, but Fuller was a loyal and faithful soldier, and refused to leave his commander's side. He gave his life in the old traditions of courage and duty.

The murderers were caught and sentenced to death. They were led to the gallows singing the Jewish freedom fighters' national anthem and were only silenced when their final breath was drawn.

The joint funeral of Lord Moyne and Corporal Fuller was a sombre affair. The streets and the cathedral were packed with people, and at 3.00 pm not a sound could be heard, except for the strains of Chopin's *Funeral March*, which floated over the hushed city. I took a special interest in the service as Lord Moyne was from Chapelizod. I remember as a young child admiring the beautiful Farmleigh House in Phoenix Park, the residence of the Guinness family, into which Lord Moyne was born.

Back at the school, as things were progressing so well, I suggested to Colonel Khalifa that we put on a five-day long shooting competition, open for all units of the Armed Forces to enter. He thought this was a splendid idea and permission was granted. King Farouk himself agreed to attend on the final day. The Egyptians were most excited and invited a huge number of teams to participate, including the elite Mohammed Ali Club – a society for the rich and famous – and the British Army, as well as teams from Switzerland, South Africa, New Zealand and America. Even the Royal Bodyguard decided to enter.

Life became busy for us at the Small Arms School, but the time flew by and soon the great day dawned. The Abbassia Ranges were transformed into a great fairground. Nobody could ever lay on bunting and frills like the Egyptians could. Among the officials in attendance were Colonel Nasser, the Sabri brothers, and a friend of mine from the army, Major Mohammed Naguib. He was an honest and sincere man who shared the Free Officers' ideals for Egypt, thus making him rather unpopular with the king.

The event got off to a good start and the final day in particular was a great success. Everybody was on tenterhooks with excitement as the band played and the teams lined up in ranks to await the arrival of the king. An air of anticipation rippled over the ranges when the royal car came into sight and drove across to where we were all assembled. As Farouk stepped out, I was taken aback by the sycophantic way he was received. The senior officers dashed to the spot where his feet touched the ground, fell on their knees and showered the back of his hand with kisses. It turned my stomach, and I was glad things were done with dignity back home.

The king fired the two opening shots of the day, and though they were marked as bulls, I had my doubts they got anywhere near the target. The Swiss Club ended up winning the competition, with the Royal Bodyguard and the American teams sharing second place. Next came the South Africans, followed by the Egyptian Army. I'm sad to say the British Army were much further down the list, but my disappointment was soon forgotten when the king invited us all for afternoon refreshments at the Royal Pavilion. Spotting my empty glass, King Farouk came over to where I was standing and asked me what I'd like to drink. He called the barman's attention and prompted him to fill my glass with whiskey as a gesture of thanks for my efforts in arranging the competition. I thanked him with a smile, relieved I wasn't required to kiss him.

As the day's events drew to a close, I was delighted to be told by Colonel Khalifa that my attendance was requested at a cocktail party that the Royal Bodyguards were throwing. Once everything at the ranges had been packed away, I dashed back to my flat, freshened up, and awaited the arrival of the car that was to take me to Abdin Palace. One or two of the other military advisers who lived in my building, and who hadn't received invitations, appeared irritated that I was going, but that didn't worry me one jot. I arrived at the palace feeling like an honoured guest, and was greeted by no less a person than the major general of the Royal Bodyguard. Until then he'd never shown the slightest hint of friendliness towards me, or any other British soldier, but that evening he shook me warmly by the hand.

'*Masaa el-kheer. Ahlan wa sahlan,*' he said, which meant: 'Good evening, my friend. You are very welcome.'

I entered the palace ballroom and my jaw dropped. It was more than I could have dreamed of. Great crystal chandeliers glittered high above our heads and there were gilt chairs all around for the elegant guests, dressed in their best attire. Soft Persian carpets adorned the floors and a large, well-stocked bar was situated at the far end of the room. The band members of the Royal Bodyguard, in colourful uniforms, were seated on the stage ready to play. A throng of exotic beauties in long, flowing gowns had been invited to dance with the guests. I grinned and thought to myself that this wasn't bad going for a company sergeant major of the British Army.

I was shown to Colonel Khalifa's table, where I was seated with Nasser and the usual crowd. Drinks were on tap, and a shooting range was set up in the corridor. I took a few shots and ended up winning a prize, in the form of a cloth-clad Egyptian belly dancer.

The dancing and floorshows went on until past midnight, and King Farouk, who'd honoured us with his company, retired at around 1.00 am. Up until then the Egyptian officers had been quietly enjoying themselves, but with the departure of the king, things livened up. After an hour or two the colonial troops were becoming rather too boisterous for my liking, so I thanked the major general for his hospitality, and took my leave.

I'd enjoyed myself that evening and was impressed by the efforts of the Egyptian Army. They really knew how to put on a show. Perhaps Egypt's luck was finally starting to change.

Chapter 12

In Old Cairene Society

Some of my happiest years were spent at the Small Arms Training School. My life until then had all seemed to pass me by in an uncontrollable blur. Somehow I'd wandered far across the desert, thousands of miles from a little village in Ireland, and had slotted comfortably into a new life with the people of Egypt. The Second World War was all but over now. Hitler's grand plans had turned to dust in a Berlin bunker, and his surviving deputies had been rounded up to face trial. The world breathed a sigh of relief, but for us, life in Egypt went on in much the same way as it always had done.

It was around this time when I made friends with a group of British Overseas Airways Corporation pilots, who were a grand set of chaps. After work we'd meet in the coolness of the evenings and sit on the veranda of a bar called the Amphitryon, opposite the Heliopolis House Hotel, where we'd drink and make merry. From there we'd go to my club where we could drink until the cows came home, although my pals always laid off the alcohol the day before they took to the air again.

One evening at the Amphitryon, we were introduced to four charming English girls. They were serving with the Women's Auxiliary Air Force and had only recently arrived in Egypt. The loveliest of the girls was called Marjorie Ragsdell. Soft brown locks framed her fair complexion and her smile was intoxicating. I'd been hit by Cupid's arrow. I made sure I got to sit next to this beautiful lady throughout the rest of the evening, and conversation flowed as freely as our drinks. I learned she was a humble farmer's daughter from a place called Long Sutton in Lincolnshire, the boundaries of which she'd never set foot beyond before the outbreak of war. Her father, George, had lost an arm in 1916 during the Battle of the Somme. Frustrated he couldn't return to the front line in the Second World War, he expressed his disappointment that his own two sons were just children, and too young to fight in his stead.

'I'll go, Father,' said Marjorie, the middle of five daughters; and with that, she packed her bags and went straight to Lincoln to enlist, without a backwards glance.

Egypt, February 1946: Paddy Rochford and Marjorie Ragsdell.

I felt so elated that night, I forgot to count my drinks and remember little more about the evening, except for squeezing into a crowded taxi when it was time to go home. I was so intoxicated I got a little friendlier with Marjorie than I should have. The next thing I knew, I found myself lying flat on my back on the road to Heliopolis, watching the taxi speed away.

I'd fallen in love with Marjorie at first sight, though as I picked myself up and dusted my jacket, I doubted the feeling was mutual. Aside from being some years older than she was, she'd clearly not taken kindly to the taxi incident and was equally unimpressed by the fact I'd let myself get into such a drunken state. She refused my subsequent requests for further dates, but fortunately my pal from the BOAC had begun courting Marjorie's best friend, and after persuading her that I was actually a jolly decent chap, despite first impressions, she agreed to meet me again.

As a foursome we went to all the best places in Cairo, and enjoyed many happy evenings together. I went to Zizinia to collect my suit of civilian clothes, so any 'out of bounds' notices became null and void; and after several months of walking out together, Marjorie and I became engaged. Everything was going well, until the tide inevitably began to change.

Cairo, 1946: Number Eight Company, GHQ. Paddy can be seen on the front row, fourth from the left.

It was a bright morning in 1945 when I was told my work with the Egyptian Army had come to an end. The British Military Mission had begun its slow withdrawal from Egypt and I was appointed to Number Eight Company, GHQ, as company sergeant major with immediate effect. It was with much regret I returned to the Small Arms School for the final time to gather my personal belongings and say farewell to Colonel Khalifa and all the other friends I'd made.

My new company was some 800 men strong, comprising warrant officers class I and II, staff sergeants, corporals and men. Almost everyone had been given a clerical position at the various departments that came under GHQ, and I was to oversee operations. I was taken aback at the size of the job I'd been given, but I knuckled down to pull the company around, as per the instructions of the commandant. Things were so busy for me that I was forced to put any ideas of marriage on the back burner for the time being. This didn't go down too well with my bride-to-be, but I had no other option.

Despite my initial dismay, I soon began to enjoy my new work, and the only bother I had was typing, which I could only do one finger at a time. As soon as I was settled in and began to get on top of things, I applied for leave to get married. To my surprise, I was granted permission to have twenty-eight days of leave all in one go, so Marjorie and I began planning our big day.

The anti-British groups were now well and truly stirring up the dust and it wasn't even safe to walk down the road anymore. Troops had been shot dead in the streets and curfews were on. We were fed up with being confined to barracks, listening to the bombs and bullets thumping and whining all around us. It was just as if the war had never ended.

Orders had gone out that no vehicles were to be out in the streets, and every morning our clerks had to be marched to work across the Qasr el-Nil Bridge, which crossed the river Nile. At about 9.00 am, just as everybody had arrived at GHQ, rebel guns opened up and swollen mobs of rag-clad Egyptians began scurrying along the streets. My company managed to reach the gates of our camp and halt a crowd of barefoot boys just before they caused any damage. They soon cleared off back into town when they saw us with weapons in our hands, and they no doubt helped with the looting that always followed these disturbances.

The sound of shooting carried on until noon that day, then started again after the sun went down. Rumours started circulating about what had been happening in the city, such as the ransacking of Cairo's beautiful cathedral. We also heard the shocking tale of two British vehicles that had been sent out against orders by some silly officer, and had run smack into the yelling crowds outside Qasr el-Nil Barracks. The crowd smashed the windows of the trucks and pulled the drivers out. They killed one and were in the act of ripping the other to pieces when a young sergeant, standing at the barrack gates, shouted orders at his men.

'Fix bayonets! Charge!'

They charged. No doubt there were many sore Egyptian bottoms that day.

Heliopolis was out of bounds that evening, so my BOAC pal and I had to sneak into town dressed as air force officers. Side by side we entered the Sporting Club and ordered our drinks. The bar was full of the usual Egyptian members, including Nasser and his family, and one Abdel Latif Boghdadi, a rich young man who owned many villages in Egypt. He was a wing commander in the Royal Egyptian Air Force, and a leading figure in the Free Officers' Movement.

Nobody spoke to us as we sipped our beers. We suspected everyone had been talking about the day's happenings prior to our arrival, and were probably not too pleased by the forceful retaliation of the British. The young wing commander soon began gloating about the damage inflicted upon the city's cathedral. On and on he went, until I could take no more.

'This atrocity seems to have pleased you, Abdel,' I remarked.

'*Aiwa*!' he cried, raising his glass in the air. Others followed suit, and the celebratory atmosphere sickened me.

'Now look here,' I said, walking over to face him. 'What would you be saying if the boot was on the other foot? What if our chaps had ransacked one of your mosques?'

'I would kill the dogs!' he retorted, his eyes flashing with fury at the mere suggestion.

I looked at him and felt nothing but disgust. How could somebody with so much power be so blinkered and hypocritical?

'Huh!' I said. 'You don't even have the will to swat a fly from your coat. You'd leave that to your servant.'

Boghdadi simply laughed at me and offered to buy me a drink, but the hour was getting late and I had to be back at Kubri Camp by midnight. Taxis and trams weren't running, so he offered to drive me back in his motorcar. I reluctantly accepted.

'But be careful I don't push you in the Nile on the way,' I added.

He didn't end up in the river that evening. Instead I woke the mess caterer when we arrived back at camp and bought my chauffeur a drink to show there were no hard feelings.

Over the next few months we were so busy at GHQ keeping Cairo under control that the time flew by, and the date of my wedding was upon us before I knew it. Marjorie and I had been invited to spend our honeymoon at the Shakour family's villa, but I was so rushed off my feet I had my doubts if we'd even get to Alexandria at all.

I'd arranged to have the ceremony in the beautiful basilica cathedral in Heliopolis on 27 April 1946. Marjorie was to spend the night before at the house of some friends, whilst I stayed with my pal from the BOAC. We had a rare bachelor's night, and I was first up the following morning.

The war had only just ended and everything was still rationed, so we'd planned to marry in uniform as we didn't have enough coupons to buy a wedding dress. Luck, however, was on our side. Marjorie and her three bridesmaids had gone to see a travelling show a few weeks earlier, and as they were involved in amateur dramatics themselves, they were invited backstage to meet the cast and crew. It was there they met a lady whose daughter had recently got married, and she kindly said that if her dress was the right size, then Marjorie could borrow it. It fitted like a glove. The bridesmaids were given the loan of three beautiful costumes that were being used in the show, complete with matching bonnets.

My bride looked radiant when she arrived at the church in her white lace gown. She had flowers in her hair that I'd been allowed to pick from King Farouk's garden.

Little had changed since the end of the war so it was impossible for our family and friends from back home to attend. It was particularly upsetting for Marjorie not to have her father by her side to walk her down the aisle, but I'm certain he would have been brimming with as much pride as I was.

After a glorious reception, we set off to Cairo Station with a couple of old boots dangling from the back of the car. Abdel Moneim Ragheb Bey, the first friend I'd made at the club, had arranged a private train carriage for us, and we travelled to Alexandria in style. During the long journey, with my wife asleep on my shoulder, I closed my eyes and allowed my thoughts to drift back over the past few months. Much had happened, and my mind was full of all the recent events.

My father had by now passed away. He'd died the year before, back home in Chapelizod. I'd never had the opportunity to say goodbye, but I'm convinced he came to me to say 'cheerio, son'. On the morning he died, I'd opened my eyes and I swear I saw him standing at the foot of my bed, watching me with that serene look on his face. He vanished after I'd blinked, but I knew I hadn't imagined him. Later that day a telegram came through from Mother, informing

Cairo, 27 April 1946: Paddy and Marjorie's wedding

me he'd tripped and fallen in the road some days earlier. He'd been taken to hospital but the fall had been too much of a shock, and his old heart had given way during the early hours that morning. Father was a gallant old soldier and it was a comfort to know he'd lived to see Britain, the country he'd loved and served so faithfully, emerge victorious. That in itself would have been enough to send him happily on his journey to the Pearly Gates.

I opened my eyes to find the sun was streaming in through the window of our carriage. The open country was flashing past our window and I noticed we were drawing close to Alexandria. I began to smell the pungent air and knew we were nearing Sidi Gaber Station, our stop. The old thrill of excitement I'd so often felt when alighting here, especially on my leaves from fighting in the desert, assailed me again.

Dashing forward to meet us as we stepped onto the platform came dear Yvonne, whom I loved as a sister, and faithful Joseph, who was like a brother. With much hugging and kissing we took our seats in the back of their car and headed to their beautiful house surrounded by palm trees, which I'd grown to love as my home from home. Standing at the door was Aunt Vanda and Uncle Charles. Their faces were full of warmth, and they loved Marjorie as soon as they saw her. After we'd unpacked and dined, we sat down together to have a long chat over refreshing drinks.

We were up and away bright and early next morning. The family owned a private beach cabin, so we spent the day bathing in the beautiful blue waters of the Mediterranean Sea and lazing on the soft, golden sands. We enjoyed our happy holiday to the full, and allowed our cares and burdens to ebb away with the waves. Marjorie came to love Alexandria and its friendly people just as I did. Unfortunately there were a few riots every now and again, but we escaped them by staying up in Zizinia, well out of harm's way.

All too soon our honeymoon was at an end, and the morning when we had to part and return to our respective units was a wrench. Marjorie was soon to be discharged now she was married, though as yet we had nowhere to live together. I reported for duty with Number Eight Company and was told the long-expected news that the British Army was scheduled to evacuate the Nile Delta and relocate to a new base at Fàyid. This was still many months away yet, so I tried to put it to the back of my mind. Until then, I was surplus to requirements, and was being reposted to the Egyptian Army and to my old job. This cheered me up no end, and the best part of it was that a flat in Heliopolis, where Marjorie and I could live, was being thrown in. Things couldn't have worked out any better.

Alexandria, May 1946: Marjorie Rochford relaxing on her honeymoon.

I duly reported back to Mission HQ and was pleased to see so many old faces. The Egyptian liaison officer, Major Shaheen, who was married to a Turkish princess, gave me a generous welcome, though he warned me that things weren't quite as I'd left them at the Small Arms School. Colonel Khalifa had gone and his replacement, I was told, was a complete arsehole. Unfortunately there was nothing the Mission could do about him, for he was well in at the top and couldn't be moved. Before returning to the school, however, there were some clerical duties I had to perform, so I was given a temporary desk at Mission HQ.

My wife and I moved into our lovely flat, and I found to my surprise that Abdel Moneim Ragheb Bey had arranged a 'welcome home' party for us at the Helmia Palace, a popular nightclub in Cairo, where we enjoyed a delicious dinner and watched the cabaret until early in the morning. We were introduced to a famous Egyptian singer called Mohammed Abdel Wahab, who was performing that evening. The Egyptians called him 'Abdel Crosby', and although I couldn't understand all the lyrics, he had a magnificent voice. He even taught me two Arabic love songs so I could serenade Marjorie, though I can't say she was terribly impressed.

We had some practical jokers at the Military Mission and one chap in particular had a strange sense of humour. He'd been out on a binge one evening and was walking home through the marketplace. Clasped tightly in his hands was a bag of eggs, which he intended to cook for a late night supper. On his way, he espied a sleeping native reclining in a chair outside one of the many coffee bars.

In the mood for a spot of 'fun', the soldier yelled at the top of his voice: '*Masaa el-kheer!*' which meant 'good evening'.

The previously slumbering man lifted his head with a start, and as he did so, the poor chap received the contents of the soldier's bag all over his face. With egg yolk dripping from his beard, the Egyptian rose to his feet and drew the longest knife from beneath his robes. He set off at top speed with an almighty roar, in hot pursuit of the now fleeing soldier.

Regrettably, this incident hadn't been enough to appease his mischievous spirit. Still feeling full of beans as he was undressing for bed, he woke his room-mate by sprinkling a bag full of insecticide powder all over him. With much sneezing, the unfortunate man leapt out of bed and lunged himself at the practical joker. In the commotion that followed, a mattress was thrown out of the window and it landed on the veranda of the flat below. The flat in question was occupied by an important Egyptian gentleman, who at the time was entertaining some VIPs. Clad in nothing but an army shirt and in his bare feet, the practical joker went to retrieve it. He must have looked a fright to the poor young serving girl who opened the door to him, for she fainted in shock. The semi-naked fool proceeded to march straight into the room, uninvited, and with a sweeping gesture to the horrified guests, he collected the mattress from the veranda and marched back to the flat from whence he'd come.

Thankfully for Marjorie and I, we lived a few floors up from this idiot so didn't have much to do with him. Our flat was small but pleasant. We had a little balcony outside our kitchen window that overlooked the open-air cinema. Sitting rapt in the evening light could often be spotted hundreds of male natives enjoying the latest Arabic film.

One of our chaps from a neighbouring balcony thought it would be funny one day to roar out: 'Hassan?'

A great roar came back: '*Aiwa effendi*?' (Yes, sir?) Hassan was a very popular name, bestowed upon almost every other baby boy.

One day, when the sun was hot and sensible people were having a siesta, a crowd of locals had gathered in the baking streets outside my office to watch some fire-eaters entertaining the people. Looking out of my window with some friends, we saw two young bints swinging lighted torches around their heads, whilst a *wallad* was lying on a bed of nails. A little further up the street, an Egyptian was putting his animals through their paces. Some monkeys were dancing and a goat was standing on a raised platform balancing a stool on its head. Still further up, another *wallad* was turning the handle of a street barrel organ and the jangled notes were grinding out *The Heliopolis Blues*.

The practical joker colleague of mine placed a coin, a ten-piastre piece, on a portable cooking range and lifted it off with a button stick as it became white hot.

'Here comes a *buckshee*!' he called to the crowd below, and with a grin that could sour milk, he dropped the coin out of the window.

One of the entertainers, grateful for the tip, roared back: '*Shukran jazeelan!*' (Many thanks.)

The young boy caught the coin in his outstretched palm, and screamed in pain as the hot metal blistered his skin. In a blind rage, out came his enormous knife and he was just about to fly up the stairs to my office when he was stopped in his tracks by an almighty thunder flash that smacked down into the narrow street. Black smoke filled the road from one end to the other, and when it cleared the street was completely empty. All that could be seen was the tail of a goat disappearing around the corner.

The police called round at our offices later that day, as it had been claimed that a live grenade had been thrown from one of the windows of our building. Everyone denied any knowledge of this, and in the end the whole sticky situation was resolved. The police had a sense of humour and they left our office building laughing their heads off, clutching a small gift in their hands.

We were truly living in a corrupt society where almost anyone could get away with anything. Dud money, for instance, was to be found all over the country and silver coins were a nightmare. In the army, the paying-out officer always had a slab of marble in front of his table on which he'd drop each piece. If it had a clear ring then all was well. If the ring was dull, he took it back to the bank, where they were happy to change it.

Street beggars of every age were found in their thousands, and they all had a hard luck story to tell. They roamed the streets with hands that couldn't be stilled, and they'd have the contents of a pocket out in a thrice without the wearer being any the wiser. Fountain pens, watches and wallets were the most sought after items. Outside the churches on Sunday mornings the beggars would crouch, with blood-stained bandages around their limbs and stumps held aloft, along with all the other horrors that could be thought up to win sympathy. The ones who made me angry were the women with babies held to their breasts.

'*Buckshees, effendi*. An English soldier gave me this baby and left me.'

This perpetual appeal irked me to my core. Everybody knew the babies had been hired. No respectable soldier would get himself mixed up with that sort of business; and even if he did, the girl's own people would have had her stoned to death instead of leaving her to beg on the streets, so I knew it couldn't have been true.

During my time in Egypt, a man was caught and arrested for putting children out into the streets to steal, and then, like Fagin's boys from the Charles Dickens novel, they'd hand their ill-gotten spoils to their master. During the subsequent trial it was found that this man had run a school where teaching the art of stealing was the only lesson. Among the many methods of instruction, the child had to frisk a dummy covered in collectables and small silver bells. If the bells rang, the child had failed.

In a desperate effort to deter any would-be lawbreakers, the local police started putting it around that they could solve any crime. There was, however, a spate of larceny that had them worried for a long time. Wallet after wallet went missing day after day, but the police couldn't work out who was doing it or where the items were going. All the usual suspects were ruled out. The months went by and still these crimes went unsolved.

One morning the police apprehended an old man for some petty offence or other, and they brought him into the police headquarters to await trial. The man begged that he be allowed to keep his pet monkey with him in the cells. After a long, heart-bleeding story about how he and the monkey were like father and son, the police gave in. The old chap was in possession of an old fiddle and was asked to play some music in return. As he was doing this, his monkey began going around everybody in the room with a hat, holding it up for alms and saluting at the same time. This had the policemen in stitches, and they all put their hands into their pockets and dropped a few coins into the hat. Suddenly, one of the police officers spotted the monkey stealing a wallet from another man's pocket and the whole story began to unfold. The elusive crack thief had been caught in the act, and at police HQ, no less. The man was sentenced to years behind bars and the monkey was shot, as he was old and there was little hope of teaching him the rights from wrongs.

After the First World War, drug trafficking and consumption in Egypt became widespread. *Hashish* was the most common substance, it being smoked by as many as 90 per cent of the native population, who'd all been raised on it. This caused such concern to the authorities that they called in the services of an expert. He became world famous and was known as Lewa (Police General) Thomas Wentworth Russell Pasha. This officer performed wonders in this country and despised the drug pedlar with a passion. Many were the tales of vast quantities being discovered, and it was learned that the most common method of drug smuggling was to sew the drugs inside the stomachs of camels, donkeys and horses. The suppliers would then cross the frontiers of Egypt, undetected, with their deadly loads. Great fortunes were made from this despicable trade. Lewa Russell Pasha had some job ahead of him, but there was no doubt he was getting results.

A senior Egyptian police officer, albeit a small-minded one, invited me many times to join him and his friends at *hashish* parties that were held at a place known as the City of the Dead, where inside and out of these desolate houses were the graves of late Egyptians. This was the haunting ground of drug addicts, crooks and a whole host of other miscreants. I wasn't in the slightest bit interested in joining in, but there would have been no use reporting the fellow, as much as I wanted to, as his father was a high-ranking official in Egypt who could have had me chucked out of the country in a heartbeat.

Cocaine, the most deadly of drugs, was beyond the slender resources of the average Egyptian native. It was a more common sight to see people smoking their hookah pipes. In fact, it was hard to miss them as they sat, trance-like, in the kerbside cafés. It was said this substance conjured up fitful imaginations in the mind of the smoker, and the drug was grown mostly in the poorest regions of Syria, Lebanon and Turkey, countries that depended on its revenue.

If caught, it was instant jail for a drug offender. Those of us who knew Egyptian jails understood to what lengths the crooks would resort to avoid detection. I've witnessed these poor fellows screaming and foaming at the mouth during strip searches before being dragged to their cells, thrashed all the way by a black-uniformed policeman, who most likely had a stash of the deadly drug secreted somewhere about his person for his own use. In those days rhino whips were issued to the Egyptian police, who'd lash out at anything that moved. This was just another part of daily life in Egypt, and one I detested with all my heart and soul.

I once took the opportunity of expressing my concerns to King Farouk during a small arms meeting on the Abbassia Ranges. We spoke about the fact that so few of the Egyptian soldiers were good rifle shots, and I told the king it was because of the way they were treated. They had no education and were cursed at and shouted at all day long. This crushed their spirits and destroyed their self-confidence. Much to everybody's surprise, King Farouk actually took note. He abolished flogging in the Armed Forces and took the rhino whips away from the police.

Despite these little changes, illegal substances were slowly sapping the life out of the people of Egypt, and are still doing so to this day. I feel it will take a long time, plenty of patience, and perhaps a miracle or two, before the war on drugs is finally won.

Chapter 13

The Three Cracks

Colonel Nasser once told me the Egyptians had never been more roused with anger than in February 1942, when Britain pressed Egypt's back to the wall and demanded a regime change. Farouk had given in, but his actions brought nothing but fury to the people. No matter what others said about them, the Egyptians were a proud race, and for another country to be allowed to interfere with their political leadership was just about the greatest insult possible.

This caused the first of three cracks to appear in Farouk's throne. Up until then he'd been popular with his subjects. He was young and eccentric, and had in recent years married the beautiful Queen Farida, whom the people worshipped and adored. The royal couple had two pretty little girls who were equally loved, and the family could often be spotted driving around the streets. The gathering crowds would cheer and wave like lunatics baying at the moon as the royal fleet of red Fiat cars passed by. The queen's radiant face never betrayed any sign that she was growing weary of her husband's sordid lifestyle of gluttony and debauchery, but behind the elegant façade the dynasty was crumbling.

One of the palace officials told me about a scandalous rumour that was circulating: Farouk was planning to divorce his lovely queen, who hadn't borne him a male heir.

'He'll rue the day he leaves her,' the official said with a trembling lip. 'The people of Egypt will be outraged.'

It was true that Farida was a hundred times more popular than her husband, who never seemed to understand what an asset she was. She had all the grace of a Hollywood starlet and the fact she was knee-tremblingly beautiful meant that she attracted interest wherever she went, particularly from the press. The second crack appeared when Farouk finally divorced his adorable queen after she gave birth to yet another girl, and just as predicted, the people were incensed. Rumour had it the king was looking for some fresh blood to inject some vitality into the Royal Family. He'd set his sights on a fair-skinned young maiden called Narriman, and she caused quite a stir among the nation, for many deemed her wholly unsuitable to be a royal bride. For a start she was just a commoner from a middle-class background, and worse, she was still only a schoolgirl, aged fourteen. When the news of their engagement was announced, with all the usual honeyed words, an angry silence descended. Though Narriman produced an heir, just eight months after the lavish wedding, public opinion remained unswayed.

The final crack appeared when the king fell out with the younger officers in both the army and the police force. It was now just a matter of time before the country's boot met with the king's very large backside. He must have feared his days were numbered, for he began trying anything he could to win the people's favour once more.

One day two English officers were leaving a club on the Pyramids Road at Giza. There was a transport strike underway and they couldn't find any means of returning home so they set off walking. During their journey, they were overtaken by a large, shiny car, driven by a young man of the *effendi* (upper) class. The driver pulled up just ahead of them.

'Would you care for a lift?' he asked, through a gap in his tinted window. 'I'm heading into Cairo. You're welcome to travel with me.'

The two officers gratefully accepted, for it was a long walk and the sun was cooking them. They clambered into the back of the darkened car and took their seats. Conversation was light during the journey, until it suddenly turned to the hot topic of the day: King Farouk.

'What do you two think about him?' the young driver asked.

Their reply was rather damning and the language choice, but their chauffer laughed gaily; and when they arrived in Cairo he dropped them off outside the Shepheard's Hotel, on the banks of the Nile.

'To whom do we owe this kindness?' one of the officers asked, turning to thank the driver.

The young chauffeur wound down his tinted window and the two Englishmen saw his face for the first time. 'King Farouk of Egypt,' he said.

With a hearty laugh he sped away into the distance, leaving the two mortified officers standing by the side of the road, mouths agape.

With the monarchy in disrepute, Colonel Nasser's Free Officers were beginning to fancy their chances. They were trotting around the place looking for other dejected officers to swell their ranks. The Misr al-Fatat Party, the Muslim Brotherhood and other similar movements became allied. Poised in the streets, and anywhere else that suited them, they were watching, waiting and preparing for action.

British troops were enjoying taking leave in Cairo and Alexandria, and this was when the troubles flared. Grenades were thrown into cafés and cinemas where the soldiers were sitting. Chaps were knifed in their backs; several service girls were killed, and many more were wounded. Nowhere was safe. A black Buick car regularly toured the streets looking for British soldiers, and whenever one was spotted, the occupants lobbed hand grenades at them as they passed. I had the misfortune to be in the way one evening as I was crossing Qasr el-Nil Street. Fortunately, I moved quicker than the black-hearted young passenger anticipated, and the grenade missed me by inches, hitting a wall behind me. Except for deaf ears for a couple of hours, I escaped unharmed. There were others less lucky than me, and the majority of them were just young lads.

It wasn't just the British who were targeted. The Egyptian prime minister, Ahmad Mahir Pasha, was assassinated in 1945. He'd only been installed as leader of the country four months earlier, following King Farouk's removal of his archenemy, Mustafa el-Nahas Pasha. The new prime minster was walking out of the council chambers when a young man approached him with an outstretched hand.

'*Mabrouk Sath el-Bey*,' he said, which meant 'congratulations Your Excellency', and pumped two bullets into the prime minister's stomach.

The executions didn't end there, and another prime minister, Mahmoud Fahmi an-Nukrashi Pasha, was shot dead by a member of the Muslim Brotherhood in revenge for his outlawing of the movement just days earlier. There'd been so many assassinations of prime ministers in recent years that a special mausoleum was erected in which to lay them all to rest. The wily old Nahas Pasha must have spent some sleepless nights, fearing he'd be next. He lived in Heliopolis, not far from this vault of death, and many were the attempts on his life. None were successful, however, and he lived well into his eighties.

Being privy to many conversations at the Sporting Club, I had a clear picture of everything that was going on. An Egyptian could never keep a secret; in fact, in my experience he couldn't share it quickly enough. As much as I continued trying to pass on these precious gems of knowledge to the British Army, nobody wanted to believe me. So, here we were in a simmering pot of hatred, and the British Army, who could have sorted everything out, refused to quench the flames. The Muslim Brotherhood had everyone running scared, so in the end I gave up trying and did my best not to get involved. It was best that way: you were nobody's enemy.

I'd enjoyed my short return to duty with the British Army but now I was required to return to my role training the Egyptians. I was eager to get back to work, for I felt there was much I could do to help encourage good relations between the two forces. As I entered the gate to the Small Arms Training School, I felt a chill run down my spine even though I was standing directly under the mid-morning sun. The school appeared empty and deserted. There wasn't even a sentry at the gate, and I wondered what on earth could have happened to the place since I was last there.

I made my way over to Colonel Khalifa's old office and stood outside his door. A plaque was engraved with a flamboyant inscription, and though I still wasn't fluent in reading the Arabic scripture, I could tell it didn't bear the name of my old friend. As I knocked and entered, I saw a new person sitting in the colonel's chair. He was a little man with a thin and sour-looking face. I smiled politely and introduced myself, but this new colonel didn't look the slightest bit pleased to see me.

'Have a seat,' he said, gesturing to the rickety old chair in front of his desk, 'but do excuse me for a moment while I attend to my important business.'

He fixed his gaze on a blank sheet of paper on his desk and commenced to write. I knew he wasn't really up to anything 'important', so I sat in complete silence and waited for him to finish toying with me. After a while he put down his pen, looked up at me and summoned the ghost of a smile.

'So, why have *you* been sent here, exactly?'

It was tempting to say something sarcastic in reply, but I'd been warned not to rub this chap up the wrong way.

'Your commander-in-chief personally requests that I continue the work I started here during the war.'

The colonel clearly hadn't been expecting that, for he looked as though he'd been smacked across the face with a wet dishcloth. He mumbled some apology about not being informed, and then showed me to my desk.

It didn't take me long to find out that this new chap, Colonel Fawzi, was clueless when it came to anything military related, but as has always been the case throughout history, it wasn't so much what you knew but who. This chap's sister was the country's chief Girl Guide, and as such, had the ear of the king, who held the rank of First Scout of Egypt. Colonel Fawzi took full advantage of this association whenever he found himself in trouble. This didn't go down too well with his fellow officers, who knew just how much of a slippery character he was. Try as I might, I found it impossible to get to like the chap. The feeling was clearly mutual, for he went out of his way to make my job as difficult as he could.

After several miserable weeks at the school, the British Military Mission sent out some new military advisers to join us, including an acting company sergeant major called Horace Robertshaw. He was a decent sort of chap but was fresh from England and lacked even a basic knowledge of Egypt. He had a quick temper and used to call the Egyptians 'wogs' to their faces, which wasn't liked. What was more, he hated Colonel Fawzi even more than I did, and every time he saw him he felt an overwhelming urge to punch him on the nose, so I had to keep a watchful eye on him at all times.

It was nearing the end of one particularly long and difficult day at the school. Colonel Fawzi, no doubt in the mood for some mischief, sent our truck out on a job just minutes before he knew we needed it to take us home. Upon discovering his dirty trick, Horace and I marched straight to his office and requested an explanation. The colonel simply looked at us as if we were dirt under his boots and blustered something about the truck having other purposes besides taking mere military advisers home.

I felt the blood beginning to simmer in my veins but remained as calm and collected as I could. 'Thank you, colonel,' I said. 'You'll be hearing more about this matter later.'

I turned to leave the office with all the dignity I could muster, and had to virtually drag Horace along with me. I think he'd have gladly stayed behind to have it out with the colonel.

'Don't be an idiot!' I hissed, closing the door behind us. 'That's just what our friend is wanting – a scene – and if that happens, he'll get rid of us both.'

I decided the best course of action was to call Fawzi's bluff, so I led my pal towards the school gates and we began to walk home across the desert. It was a long, blistering road but we soldiered onwards. After a while we heard a car approaching from behind us.

Honk, honk, went the hooter.

Turning around I saw Colonel Fawzi pulling up by the side of the road. He got out of his car and began jogging towards us, looking rather desperate, but we carried on walking despite his calls.

'Follow my lead,' I whispered to my pal. 'Let's see if we can get this nasty little chap hot under the collar.'

'Please get in the car, my friends,' said Fawzi, reaching our side. 'There has been a misunderstanding with the truck. I can run you both home. There is no need to make a fuss.'

'No thanks, colonel,' I said. 'We're enjoying the walk and the fresh air.'

Like hell we were.

'But I have a reputation to uphold!' he spluttered, almost dropping to his knees before us. 'If this gets out …'

'Be sure it will get out, colonel,' I said. 'I intend on telling every Egyptian and British officer I meet just how unaccommodating you've been towards my colleagues and me.'

We turned our backs on the snivelling colonel and continued our trek down the never-ending desert road. It was hard going, and after what seemed like hours, we finally reached Heliopolis. Though we were covered from head to toe in sand and sweat, our pride remained intact. As we passed by the cathedral, we were hailed from a window.

'Hey, Paddy!' a voice called out. I looked up and saw the friendly face of Father Morton, who'd conducted my marriage ceremony. 'What are you two doing walking so quickly on a hot day like this? Call in and I'll quench your thirst.'

The bottles of iced beer the father offered us were most welcome, and my companion was so surprised to be offered a beer by a Catholic priest he almost changed his religion.

Since that day Colonel Fawzi and I reached an unspoken understanding and found a way of rubbing along together tolerably, but soon after our ordeal in the desert I was struck down by sandfly fever. Horace was so incensed he had an almighty row with the colonel, whom he blamed for my misfortune. That was when he finally succumbed to that overwhelming urge of his and punched the little rat squarely on the nose, thus heralding the end of my pal's career. He was shipped off to Fâyid later that day, and I'm sad to say I never heard of him again.

Many a morning passed at the school and I would greet Colonel Fawzi with a salute and the word '*Sa'eeda*'.

Though it was all very reserved, one day he suddenly began taking his time in returning my salute and would respond in Arabic '*La, la, la*', which meant in English, 'No, no, no'.

I got fed up with this after a while, and before I could stop myself, I asked him if the sun was getting too hot for him.

'What do you mean?' he snapped, looking surprised that I'd dared to question him.

'What's all this *la, la, la* business?'

He flashed me one of those disgusted looks I'd grown so used to during my time in Egypt. 'My prime minister does not want the British in this country anymore,' he said, 'so we Egyptians have been instructed to refuse all Englishmen first thing in the morning in the hope they will finally get the message.'

It was a happy day when I learned Colonel Fawzi had finally been booted out of the school for being completely useless. The popular Major Ismail

Mohammed took his place, and I enjoyed spending many hours in his company. One weekend some of the advisers and I took him down to Ain Helwan, a place where bubbling Eastern waters used to flow out from the rocks, making one feel truly refreshed after a frolic in the pools. Our new colonel had a dry sense of humour, and tears of laughter used to stream from our eyes at the stories he used to tell.

Though the school was a happy place to work again, outside, in the wider country, a series of barbaric events were unfolding. Students crowded the streets of Cairo, yelling, setting fire to cars and overturning a couple of trams. They got their ears well and truly boxed by the Egyptian police, who pushed them back towards the Nile. As they were crossing the river, the police let up the bridge, and the students were plunged into the muddy waters.

Over in Alexandria, thousands of demonstrators were gathering for their usual 'hour of hate' against the British. The city was out of bounds, and the little Military Police Reporting Centre was manned by just one sergeant and three lieutenant corporals, who had two pistols between them. No doubt they'd been forgotten about by the authorities, for they should have been withdrawn from out of harm's way long before the trouble began. The iniquitous mobs congregated between the Cecil Hotel and this tiny outpost. The sergeant knew trouble was about to break so he telephoned the police headquarters at Kom el-Dik in Alexandria.

'Remain fast,' he was told, 'and only open fire if your lives are in acute danger. We'll send reinforcements soon.'

As the sergeant replaced the receiver, the mob attacked. Petrol bombs rained down all around and it wasn't long before the outpost was engulfed in flames. The only thing left for this little band of men to do was to make a dash for it. Across the road they fled with the savage multitude, armed with knives and butchers' hooks, in hot pursuit. Time had run out for the fleeing soldiers, and they were hacked down by the mob. Cut and bleeding, the four men pleaded for their lives, but the rebels showed no mercy and the British were beheaded. Their severed heads were pierced with long poles and paraded victoriously through the streets.

'English meat, free of charge!' the murderers cried in Arabic, much to the delight of the crowds.

The British reinforcements never arrived, for the Egyptian Army had stopped them as they tried to enter the city.

I began to wonder where all the trouble was going end.

Chapter 14

The Flight of the British

We'd all heard the tale of the Auxiliary Territorial Service girl who was stabbed in the back by a silent killer as she walked to meet her boyfriend in Gezira; then there was the WAAF girl who was shot dead as she walked hand-in-hand with her beau. There were countless stories of British men and women being butchered in Moascar Garrison at Ismailia; and lone soldiers who were slaughtered in the streets, their body parts thrown into the filthy waters. Day after day British corpses were fished out as they floated by, murdered by the same race of people whose liberties they'd fought to defend. I for one knew all too well what the Nazis would have done in retribution, had they succeeded in invading, but Britain was too soft; by doing nothing her sons and daughters continued to suffer at the hands of mad men.

Yet for Marjorie and I, all was well with the world. The doctor had just told us my wife was expecting our first child. In a few months I was to be a father, and I couldn't have been happier.

One day we were both invited by Abdel Moneim Ragheb Bey to join him and various other Egyptian, British and American dignitaries for a tour of one of the presidential buildings in the Garden City. We were taken to see the Egyptian printing press that was housed on the ground floor. As we wandered around, watching the men at work, I came across a large wooden table. On it I saw what looked like designs for postage stamps. I casually glimpsed down at them and noticed they were all to commemorate the evacuation of the British, not just from the Nile Delta, but the whole of Egypt and the Middle East. One showed a picture of dishevelled-looking British troops marching out of the Sudan, as a black cloud rose from over the land. Another depicted victorious Egyptian troops chasing the British out of the Canal area.

I glanced around me. The other members of my party were standing a few paces ahead, chatting to one of the workers as he pointed out a new, state-of-the-art printing machine.

'Taylor,' I hissed at my American friend, who was carrying a camera round his neck. 'Take a quick shot of these.'

I pointed at the designs and attempted to shield him from view, but that was when my luck ran out. One of the Egyptians spotted us and pushed the camera down, snatching the designs from sight. There was a heated exchange of words between the Egyptian officials, which I managed to catch a few words of.

'These are secret,' I heard one of them say in Arabic, 'and shouldn't have been seen by the English. Lock them away somewhere safe.'

I'd have loved to have got that photograph, and would have taken great delight in handing it over to the British Ambassador, who I felt was completely oblivious to what was really going on in this country.

Dark clouds were gathering all over the East, not least in Palestine, where Jewish and Arabic blood was being spilt in abundance as cultures clashed and violence escalated, all for the ownership of land. The *Haganah* groups, underground Jewish defence forces, were proving tough nuts for the Arabs to crack. Raid after raid, ambush after ambush; this was the order of the day, every single day. Explosions were erupting all over the place and the King David Hotel in Jerusalem was obliterated, taking many human lives with it. In Egypt, things fared little better, as riots rippled across the nation. This time, however, the protesters were directing their anger towards the Egyptian Government in a desperate plea for change. The American administration troops were fast pulling out of Cairo and I had a feeling it wouldn't be long before the British followed suit.

Christmas was approaching, but festive cheer was in short supply. It was at this time when it was finally announced, after some seventy years of occupation, that the familiar sight of the British soldier was to disappear forever from Cairo and Alexandria. Though our troops were withdrawing to the Canal Zone, the British Military Mission was staying behind, and I was instructed to remain in Cairo with the Egyptians and carry on my day-to-day work as normal.

For the countless thousands of Egyptian men who earned their daily bread by working for the British Army, the evacuation was a crushing misfortune. In some regions of these two major cities, more or less every other family was headed by a *dhobi* or similar employee, and the choice for them was grim: either follow the troops to the Canal Zone in the hope of finding work, or remain and starve. For many, that choice had already been made, as the British Army simply couldn't take all those citizens with them. The 40,000 or so workers who were lucky and found work at the new army base had a hard job finding accommodation. To those who did, it came at a high price. The army took a kindly interest and put some chaps up, for a small charge, but this didn't satisfy many and discontentment began to grow.

On the morning the British forces began to pull out, I went along to see them off with some other military advisers who were also staying behind. It was an abhorrent sight. Gangs of rag-clad youths were spitting and hurling stones at the departing troops. None of our lads did anything to stop them, for I think they all knew these urchins had been hired by the newly formed 'Nile Valley Liberation' gangs that were too cowardly to do their own dirty work.

As the last of the troops rolled away in their sand-coloured trucks, I walked down the main street of Cairo with my companions. I can't recall any other time in my life when I'd seen so many sad faces. The laughing, carefree Egyptian was no more. A deathly silence had descended over the cities that once lived off the troops. The shops and businesses that thrived not so long since, especially during the war days, were shuttered and silent. This once great city was dead.

That evening, the barefooted rabble was whipped up again as quickly as if somebody was handing out money by the bucket-load, so that the world would think the city was rejoicing. What did Nasser's middle-class friends know about the starvation and unemployment that was to follow? Little did they care, it seemed, as they congregated at the club and celebrated well into the night.

It was 3.00 am on a cool March morning in 1947. While the rest of Cairo was still sleeping, our taxi raced through the lamplit streets to the Anglo–American Hospital. We got there in good time, and I handed my heavily pregnant wife into the capable hands of the doctor. Being told there was nothing more required of me that morning, I made my way back home on foot, feeling anxious and exhausted. After snatching a few hours of sleep, I awoke at first light and telephoned the matron, who informed me I was the father of a healthy baby boy.

I was a father.

I dashed straight back to the hospital and blinked back the tears when I saw Terence Michael Rochford for the first time.

Nothing was too much trouble for the staff, who afforded Marjorie the same care and attention as even the British Ambassador's wife, Lady Lampson, had received when her baby was born.

That afternoon I went for a game of cricket in the hospital sports ground, and brought along Rex, the other new addition to our family. He was my faithful Alsatian Wolfhound, who'd been given to me by the Royal Military Police Dog School just before the pull-out from Cairo. Old Rex was almost the size of a small donkey. He was black with a lovely temperament, and enjoyed nothing more than chasing a ball across a cricket field. It was a beautiful afternoon, so

Marjorie was allowed outside to sit in the sun and watch the game for a little while.

The days that followed were pleasant and fruitful. Marjorie and Terence were discharged from hospital, and life at the Egyptian school went on much the same. Trouble was always flaring up, but my little family and I would take our usual trips to the native market and never ran into any harm; yet hatred lurked down every snicket, infiltrating the hearts of any man who embraced it. One afternoon, while meandering through the marketplace, I was hailed by our local butcher who'd spotted us passing by.

'Hey, Paddy Pasha!' he called. 'I need a word. Can you sell me a gun?'

'Whatever for?' I replied.

'I want to kill all the Jews!'

I hadn't expected that response. I told him exactly what I thought of his morbid fantasy, and advised it'd be better for him to keep his head down, sell his meat and stay out of other people's messy business.

Over in Palestine, trouble was reaching its peak and the British were pulling out in quick order. The whole area and its surroundings were fraught with danger. Neighbouring countries, including Syria, Iraq, Jordan, Saudi-Arabia and even Egypt, were gathering arms in an attempt to push the Jews from out of what is now Israel, but the Jews were fighting back. The powder keg was about to ignite.

One evening our friends from the BOAC invited Marjorie and me to the cinema in Heliopolis. There was a good film on so we told them we'd be delighted, but at the last minute we couldn't make it. Little Terence had developed a fever and wouldn't settle, so we had to stay at home to look after him. It was just as well. A crude homemade bomb had been planted in the row where we'd reserved our seats. It exploded, killing four people and wounding thirty-eight more. Our friends were unharmed, but their little girl was splashed with blood and a chap's severed arm hit her in the side of the head as it was torn from his body. The murderers were never caught, but it was well known which militant group was responsible. To inform meant instant death, so those who valued their lives held their tongues.

By this time, any collaboration between the Egyptians and English was over, and the military advisers were called to GHQ and informed by our chief, Major General Arbuthnott, that the days of the Mission were numbered. Our final date in Cairo was confirmed as New Year's Eve 1947, but the Egyptian Army authorities had asked for the advisers to be left behind so they could carry on their work with the Egyptian Government under contract. Unfortunately, the

War Office was not in agreement, and my colleagues were all to be withdrawn to the Canal Zone as soon as postings and married quarters could be found.

I, on the other hand, had been summoned to the hirings office in Cairo, the remaining building for British 'other details', the name given to the few personnel who were to remain in Cairo and Alexandria for clearing up and other such duties. Brigadier Hayes, the director of hirings and fixed assets, had heard about my good work with the Egyptians at the school and requested I was to be appointed hirings officer for the Cairo district. I was thrilled to be offered such a position: in spite of all the low points, I'd grown to love working in Cairo.

'We're very pleased to have you,' the brigadier said, shaking me warmly by the hand when I arrived for my first day.

He told me my job was to reconnoitre the old places the British forces had occupied and arrange to hand them back to their Egyptian owners. My first task was to arrange the dismantling of the Brew Up Café outside Cairo Station. After a last hot cup of char, I packed up the memorial stone, a sight so familiar to all the troops who passed by that way, and sent it to the new headquarters of British troops at Fâyid.

From there, I travelled to what used to be Qasr el-Nil Barracks, where I was stationed during the war, and couldn't believe my eyes. This once iconic fortress had been home to crack regiments of the British Army since 1885. Now it lay in ruins before my eyes, and looked as if it had been subjected to a long artillery barrage. All that remained were piles of rubble and roofless buildings. The woodwork, glass, doors and rafters had all been removed, and no doubt would have last been spotted fleeing the site on the back of a donkey. Looters had taken every single item of value away.

I recalled the melodious notes of the martial music and the calls of the bugle that used to drift around the barracks, as the tramping of heavy feet threatened to drown out the roars of the regimental sergeant major. All that was gone; it was just an echo from yesteryear. I closed my eyes that sunny morning, feeling a slight breeze on my cheeks, and saw what I'd once seen with open eyes: the little chapel where military weddings and subsequent christenings took place; the jolly tradesmen who'd grown up in the service of the army; the smart, well-groomed officers, and the snow-white gowns of the *dhobies* who'd sit by the gate and tell a soldier off if his uniform was soiled.

I opened my eyes. I was standing alone, finding it hard to believe that once upon a time these proud barracks were a landmark of Egypt. Even the church had been pulled down, and the altar site was being used as a parking place for buses. The barrack square and sports grounds were being used as public urinals. High up above the ground now flew the Egyptian flag, dirty and tattered.

When my job was done, I moved on to the next site: the general headquarters of the Signals Regiment, from where the so-called 'Monty trick', the greatest hoax of the war, was conducted, and I found it particularly emotional to hand this place back to the Egyptians. Back in 1942 the German secret agent Johannes Eppler and his companion, Peter Monkaster, were captured in Cairo while trying to ferret out the secrets of the Eighth Army, the Allied fighting force in the Western Desert. These two spies had been relaying their discoveries to Rommel using a secret code, which the British were trying to decipher. Our plan was to crack the code and send misleading information to Rommel, hence laying a false scent for the Fox's cold nose to follow, which would lead him straight into our snare. Eventually, our shrewd chaps of the Signals Regiment deciphered the mysterious enigma, after finding a copy of Daphne du Maurier's novel *Rebecca* in Eppler's possession, despite the agent not being able to read a word of English. This book was the key to unlocking the riddle, for the code had been secreted between the pages. A false message was thus sent to Rommel from the headquarters where I now stood. The Fox took the bait and became convinced the Eighth Army was to attack at a place called Alam Halfa, a spot in the middle of the desert just south of El Alamein. Rommel's greatest mistake was believing this falsehood, which ultimately led to his downfall. With the greatest artillery bombardment, our own fighting hero, Lieutenant General Bernard Montgomery, moved in at El Alamein and struck an almighty blow that sent the Huns staggering backwards.

All this ran through my mind as I finished my sad task and prepared to move on to the next location: the prison administration site, where I bumped into an old comrade of mine from the Small Arms School. Lewa Haidar Pasha had recently been appointed governor of Tura Prison, a maximum-security detention centre just outside Cairo, and he invited me there for a coffee at the end of the day. We made our way over to that soulless fortress and as I entered through the great archway, I felt a cold chill pass over me. Away to my left a chain gang was coming in from the stone quarries where they'd been toiling from the crack of dawn in the boiling hot conditions, under the watchful eyes of their guards who were armed to their teeth with whips and rifles. These, I was sure, were used all too freely on those wretched legions of the lost.

The interior of the jail was just as desolate as the outside. I drank my coffee in Haidar Pasha's office, where I was able to discern each and every cry and groan that drifted from the cells and down the long corridor.

'Do not be sorry for these barbarians,' said the governor, clearly spotting the look of unease in my eyes. 'Nobody forced them to commit their crimes. They came in of their own accord and will probably die in here.'

'What happens to them in here?' I asked.

He looked thoughtfully at me before answering. 'Well, they have fetters fitted to their limbs upon arrival. A heavy ball is attached for the first few years, but this is replaced by a lighter one as the sentence is served.'

There was a pause while I sipped my coffee and tried to blot out the screams that followed the lash of a rhino whip.

'After a while our prisoners just accept their lot,' Haidar continued, 'and, all things considered, they are reasonably happy here.'

I offered up a silent prayer of thanks on behalf of the prisons back home, where balls and chains, thumbscrews and whips weren't in use. I'd always found Haidar Pasha to be a compassionate sort of man, and wondered if he was simply kidding himself. Whether he was or not, I didn't enjoy my coffee that afternoon and was glad when it was time for me to leave.

My Egyptian friends at the club were in high spirits that evening, and they tried their best to coax me out of my dark mood.

'Do not be sad, Paddy,' Nasser said, buying another round of drinks for the room. 'Nobody is more surprised by the evacuation than we Egyptians. After all this time, the British finally took us seriously!'

'But now we've gone, it makes us no better than the vanquished Roman Empire,' I said. 'We're a spent force, confined to the pages of history. And none of you lot will rest until we're hurled out of Egypt completely.'

Nasser laughed and patted me on my shoulder. 'Do not worry, Paddy Pasha,' he said. 'You are a good man and our friend. We do not wish to see the back of you.'

By this time Marjorie, Terence and I had moved into a new flat in a less conspicuous area of Cairo, having handed back to the Egyptians the block of flats that once housed the British Military Mission families. However, we weren't destined to stay there long. While I was at work one day, a group of well-dressed young Egyptian men approached my wife and advised her to persuade me to move on, or else. They were most polite in manner and caused no trouble, but they knew an awful lot about me, including the fact I'd helped to train the Egyptian Army. Fearing for the safety of my family, I found us a new place to live and once again we began packing up our belongings.

With our entire home balanced on the back of a cart pulled by a donkey, and with Rex leading the way, we were off. We'd not gone far before the donkey 'decided' he was tired and sat down in the middle of the road, stubbornly refusing to get up again. With many eyes upon us from overhead windows, the wily Arab who was driving our cart demanded more money. As soon as I handed it over, the donkey miraculously rose to his feet and continued on his way.

It was a relief when we eventually reached our new home: a pleasant little villa near the racecourse. It was a decent part of town where we thought our troubles would finally be over, but I kept a loaded pistol underneath my pillow, just in case. I also kept a large cavalry sword, unsheathed, resting against my bedside, and with old Rex keen and ready at all times to savage anybody who wasn't known to him, I had every faith all would be well. The fly in the ointment turned out to be my new houseboy, smiling little Ali, who was barely more than thirteen years of age. I'd acquired his services through a friend, and after much training and encouragement had finally got Rex to accept him.

Returning from a party one night and feeling a bit squiffy, I failed to notice Rex was off colour, having no doubt been slipped something objectionable in a titbit. It was a stifling hot night so I opened the bedroom window before climbing into bed and falling straight to sleep. Some hours later I awoke with a start, sensing someone was around. I jumped to my feet and groped in the darkness for my sword.

'Get him, Rex!' I shouted, but the poor dog was no use at all that night.

Our bedroom was on the ground floor so I leapt through the open window into the garden, but lost my footing and fell. I heard rustling noises coming from the bushes but was too busy fumbling around on the lawn to get there in time. With no chance of catching up with the culprit, and having no clue in which direction he'd fled, I went back inside to see if anything had been taken. Alas, my black box had gone, which contained some fifty Egyptian pounds, hundreds of cigarettes and several other items of value. My wife's wrap and fur coat were also missing.

I went out into the street and hailed a passing policeman. I tried to explain what had just happened but unfortunately the fellow was rather dim, as policemen were uneducated in those days.

'I did see a small boy running down the road, in that direction, with a black box under his arm,' the policeman said, after much scratching of his head.

I was more than a bit exasperated by this time. 'Well, don't you think you should have stopped the *wallad* and found out what he was up to? Especially at this time of the night! Isn't that what you're paid to do?'

'*Effendi*,' the policeman began, shaking his head, 'all the money in Abdin Palace would not entice me to chase a robber across the racecourse at this time of night.'

Maybe he was smarter than I gave him credit for. He told me the racecourse was a notorious hiding place for all the vagabonds of Egypt, who wouldn't think twice about thrusting a knife deep into anybody stupid enough to encroach on their sanctuary in the dead of night. Anyway, I never saw Ali or my black box again.

I'm sure whenever a person has had the misfortune of being burgled, they feel they can never again be truly happy in their home. It was exactly so for my wife and me. We'd grown to hate our little villa so decided to move into a private hotel for a while until we could find suitable housing. It was a select little place, owned and managed by a Frenchman called Mario who'd served as an officer with the Free French Forces during the war. We were given comfortable rooms and it made a pleasant change for my wife not to have to do any housework.

Some few days after we'd moved in, Mario received a call from the American Embassy. They were trying to find accommodation for four families who were working for the Naval Research Hospital, and Mario was more than obliging. The American guests duly arrived at the hotel, and over time, as we got to know each other, we became close. Their work sounded most interesting: they were engaged in a complete study of tropical sicknesses in the hope of finding vaccines.

One of the chaps was from Texas, and he always carried a gun strapped below his armpit. I often went with him and his friend, Rusty, for a drink at the Shufti Inn and they always ordered a double whiskey rye. It was downed in one swift gulp as a handful of money was placed on the counter for the barman to help himself to, which he did with pleasure. These new companions of ours always had money to burn. Their allowances had been trebled since coming to Egypt, no doubt to show the world that America wasn't short of the ready.

When I was with the Egyptian Army, I'd enjoyed the privilege of purchasing scotch and gin at the knockdown price of 3s. 6d. a bottle. I still had a sizeable stash in my possession, so I invited my American friends to a drinking party in my rooms one evening. Their eyes popped when they saw the display of spirits.

'Damn, Paddy,' the Texan declared. 'Back in the States, the only time we get to enjoy a bottle of gin is Christmas Day or Thanksgiving!'

Being thick-skinned and used to drink, it took a little time to get them all into the party spirit, but once they did, they were the life and soul. I was surprised by their unusual custom of throwing the empty bottles either over their heads or out of the window. Thankfully, the street below was fairly empty and they didn't cause too much damage. At one point in the evening, after a few choruses of *Molly Malone* and *Danny Boy*, I remember singing *There'll Always be an England* but my rendition was met by a stony silence. I quickly substituted the word 'England' for 'America', which delighted everyone.

My new friends were called Rusty, Wayne and Ed. They soon became fully paid-up members of my club, though all three were shocking at driving so I insisted on catching a taxi whenever we went out together. They were somewhat of a novelty in Egypt, with their strong accents and brash ways, and unfortunately made mistakes that were socially unacceptable, so it took time for the locals to get accustomed to them. Despite this, I found them pleasant enough and we spent many happy hours in each other's company. On Sunday mornings, after church, we played golf at the Mena House Hotel. It seemed like an age since the days when I used to pass this lovely clubhouse, never daring to enter because of the 'out of bounds to other ranks' sign that was hanging outside in bold red letters. Now, of course, there were no British officers around anymore, so the notice had long since been taken down. The Americans were quite good at golf. I had only a little knowledge of the sport, but thoroughly enjoyed my Sunday mornings nonetheless. We'd leave our wives on the veranda of the clubhouse to sip long iced drinks and enjoy the sunshine, while we'd go round the course having the time of our lives.

All good things come to an end, and this happened all too soon in our case, when the dreaded gang of well-dressed Egyptian youths turned up at the hotel one afternoon. They manhandled the owner's wife and threatened to cut me to pieces on my return. Fortunately, I was late coming home from work, and by the time I arrived they seemed to have long gone. Not wanting to take any chances, we found ourselves on the move once again.

During my last few months in Egypt, trouble was the order of the day. Houses and buildings were blown skywards, mob rule took over and life was unhappy for many. Egypt was a frightened land and people were always looking over their shoulders. I soon began to notice that many of my once good friends were cooling off towards me. The welcome they afforded me at my club was restricted to a quick smile at best, and then I was treated to a view of their backs for the rest of the evening as they continued to whisper amongst each other. This rudeness stirred my Irish blood, so one evening I decided to have it out with them.

'Why are you all avoiding me?' I directed to the room, slamming my glass onto the table. 'Have I suddenly grown the head of a sphinx or something?'

Everything fell quiet. I was ushered to the bar and found a large whiskey and soda had been placed in my hand.

'Do not be such a fool,' my friend hissed. 'Nothing has changed, but these days we have to be careful who we are seen talking to, if we know what is good for us. There are those in high places who are telling us to beware of the English who are left behind. This includes you, Paddy Pasha.'

Though the Second World War was over, another war was hotting up. Under a Labour government at Westminster, the British troops had been withdrawn to the garrison towns at Moascar and Fâyid. The British Army was busy building new barracks, offices, married quarters and sports grounds on the virgin sands that had only ever seen tents before. The Royal Air Force was doing likewise, and constructed some splendid looking aerodromes. GHQ relocated to the Fâyid area and everybody thought that'd be enough to please the Egyptians, but it wasn't. Spurred on by the easy evacuation from Cairo, the underground factions became bolder. Brimming with confidence and with a promised victory in sight, the Egyptian forces marched to Palestine on a gamble that didn't pay off.

Civil war had descended across this nation, as Jew clashed with Arab, Arab clashed with Jew, and both despised the British in equal measure. Bombs and bullets roared across the barren Sinai Desert wastes, and for the first time since the nineteenth-century Sudanese revolt, the Egyptians found themselves facing the wrong end of a gun. Thanks to their king, their illiterate army was ill-equipped, scantily supplied and commanded by officers who had little idea of what they were doing. One story went around that the boots of the Egyptian soldiers parted company with their wearers long before they reached the borders of Palestine. Morale was at an all-time low, for this motley force had crossed the blazing desert only to be met by a wall of steel when they finally arrived. Behind every gun was a well-trained soldier. The Jews were determined their new home under the Star of David wasn't going to be taken away from them so easily, and were well prepared for an Egyptian incursion.

Meanwhile, the streets of Cairo were going wild with delight for the great 'victories' that were being won; or, at least, so the papers and radio sets were telling everyone. The *Rose al-Yūsuf*, the *Akhbar el-Yom*, and the many other newspapers that once told the Arab world that the British were committing the worst crimes imaginable were now stoking the fires of hell. The rural storyteller was in his element as he spun his web of lies to his spellbound audience. Though there were no Jewish planes over Egypt, anti-aircraft guns in the Egyptian towns and cities were spitting out red-hot lead high into the air, blowing off the tops of houses. Their aim was really rotten. Night after night from dawn until dusk the gunners performed their pantomime, aiming for nothing but the stars, while the air raid sirens wailed through the streets. The Jews were never more hated for crimes they weren't committing.

Back on the battlefields, the Egyptians must have been wondering what had gone wrong. They'd been told so long and often that the Jews could be beaten with a stick, but now they were learning the hard way that the truth was quite different. Most of the leaders of the Egyptian forces fled, leaving their troops to be killed or chased back across the desert. A group of Jewish women actually captured a band of soldiers and ordered them to remove their trousers and footwear, before making them walk all the way back to Egypt. On their way home, they ran into a spot of trouble when they met a posse of local Bedouin tribesmen, who scoffed at and attacked the degraded troops.

Still out fighting in the deserts, littered with the dead, were the last remains of an Egyptian Infantry Brigade. Its commander had long since fled, and the officer who assumed control was none other than Lieutenant Colonel Gamal Abdel Nasser. He set such a high example that his battle-hungry troops remained fighting until the bitter end. Short of ammunition, food and water, they held on, and received full honours of war from the Palestinians, who allowed them to march past their commanding officer at Faluja Gap and return to Egypt, defeated but alive. Colonel Nasser covered himself in glory that day, earning the nickname 'the Tiger of Faluja'. At the head of his troops, he arrived back in Cairo. Though their heads were held high, hatred still burned deep in their hearts, and Nasser vowed he'd live to see the day when he'd get another crack of the whip.

I stood on the balcony of my office overlooking the crowded city and watched the victory procession pass by. There was no doubting the Egyptians were labouring under a delusion. They'd turned their defeat into a triumph and even began to believe they'd been victorious. Lorry after lorry rolled past, as legions of infantry troops marched by with their rifles held at a position that would have made a Guards' instructor want to blow his brains out. Fireworks rocketed high overhead, lighting up the evening sky. Over at the palace, the king was preparing to honour the Tiger, but I had to wonder why. Nasser wasn't by any means what I'd term an efficient soldier, but he was undoubtedly a brave, determined and ambitious soul, with a burning patriotism that couldn't be quenched.

Despite all the bravado, I was especially pleased to hear that some of my old comrades from the Small Arms Training School were also to be honoured. Colonel Khalifa was given command of the Egyptian Armed Forces in the Sinai

Desert, and Captain Hassan Zulfiqar Sabri was promoted to colonel and took up an appointment as Egyptian Ambassador to the Sudan.

The war in Israel had ended with the utter defeat of the Egyptian Army, but the Egyptians followed the old – and some might say sensible – proverb: He who lives to run away, lives to fight another day.

Chapter 15

My Final Post in Egypt

I was one of the last remaining British soldiers left in Cairo. The others had been withdrawn to the Canal Zone, and, at last, the time had come for me to follow. My role as hirings officer had ended and I was preparing to leave the capital city after six long years. I felt as though I'd spent all that time balancing on the sharp edge of a sword, never knowing if or when I'd fall; but despite the perils I'd learned much, and was quite the authority on Egypt by now. I spoke its language, had helped to train its armed forces, and knew the full strengths and weaknesses of its army. I was known by its citizens across the class divide, from the shoeshine boys on the ramshackle streets to the leaders of the Free Officers' Movement, all the way up to the king himself. I could have been a great asset to the British authorities if they'd allowed me to stay in Cairo, but it wasn't to be.

In some ways I was pleased to be leaving. I'd seen enough blood spilt and there was so much hatred in the air it would have been folly to remain. I had a wife and small son to think about now, and couldn't risk putting their lives in danger too.

I left Rex in the custody of my old pal, Rusty, who was returning home to America. My faithful four-legged friend had a heart of gold and it was a wrench when I had to let him go, but he couldn't come with me. For a long time afterwards I received regular letters from Maryland, informing me he was fit and well, and as fat as a butterball.

On our final evening in Cairo, the Sabri brothers came round to our flat to wish us well.

'Goodbye, Paddy Pasha,' Hassan said, shaking me warmly by the hand. 'Come back to Cairo one day in the future, and you will be surprised at what you see.'

'I'm only going to Moascar,' I chuckled, 'not the other side of the world.'

'We will be taking over Moascar and Fâyid very soon,' Ali promised, with a glint of malice in his eyes.

I laughed off his remark but couldn't get the veiled threat out of my mind as I bid my friends farewell and finished packing up my belongings. I dwelt on

Cairo, circa 1947: Rex the dog on the balcony of Paddy and Marjorie's flat.

Ali's words for a long time afterwards, and recalled he hadn't been the only one to voice such omens.

'When the British have built Fâyid, we will take it from them,' I'd overheard the Egyptian chief of police boasting at the club one evening.

Why would nobody at the Mission take my concerns seriously? I sat up long into the night at my writing desk, trying to put into words everything I'd gleaned: all the overheard plots and schemes, and the little niggles and suspicions that ate away at me, keeping me awake night after night. I didn't know what I was trying to achieve, for I knew my efforts would be thankless. The hours ticked by and I knew I had to try to get some rest. I crept under my mosquito net and closed my eyes. I lay there with the heavy smell of the East in my nostrils, but sleep refused to come. So many things were running through my mind. Each time I thought of offering myself as a spy, a vision of Marjorie and Terence flashed into my mind. What would happen to them if I was discovered? Eventually I resolved to forget the idea and accept my fate; and I drifted off into a dreamless sleep.

Bright and early the following morning, a car arrived to take us to Ismailia, and before I knew it we were speeding away on a clear, sunny day to start our new lives. The driver dropped us off at the transit camp on the side of Lake Timsah, a picturesque spot on the Nile Delta.

I'd been appointed regimental sergeant major at Moascar, the last garrison of the British Army in Egypt. We were to live in one of the married quarters, and though it was small and unsuitable for a growing family, we made the best of it. We had a lovely garden with a dozen or so banana trees that bore plenty of fruit. I used to spend many an evening and weekend picking and wrapping this delicious bounty in brown paper, and then putting them away in the cupboard until they were ripe.

We enrolled Terence at a Roman Catholic nursery school. Though it was quite a distance from the garrison, he seemed to settle in well, enjoying his time with the other military children and the friendly nuns who ran the establishment.

Before my arrival at Moascar, the general officer commanding had returned home to prepare for posting to Germany. His replacement, General Sir George Erskine, was a kindly Scot who filled the position with style, commanding admiration and respect from every rank. He was an authoritative figure, yet there was a benevolent twinkle in his eyes, which reminded me so fondly of my father's.

As was usually the case at headquarters, the warrant officers were also the chief clerks, spending most of their time behind desks. As a result they had little idea about the regimental side of soldiering. Drill and weapons were far removed

Moascar, circa 1950: Paddy (crossed) in the officers' mess.

Moascar, circa 1950: Paddy and General Erskine (centre) enjoying a drink in the officers' mess.

Moascar, 1951: RSM Rochford participating in the garrison swimming gala.

from their minds, so I took it upon myself to correct this. In fact, it soon became clear there was much that needed putting right. I arranged physical training for all ranks living in the barracks, and after breakfast there was a turn of drill. I wasn't very popular over this, but that didn't worry me. There is no worse sight in the world than a sloppy soldier.

My wife was extremely helpful during our time at Moascar and formed a ladies' club that met weekly on the lawns of our new quarters. She accrued some ninety members in total, including Lady Erskine, and together they played a fundamental role in life at the garrison, throwing fetes, tea dances and charity events, which helped to take everyone's minds off the darker side of being in the army.

Smith, Golbey and Heinzmann were the names of three notorious gunners from the Royal Artillery's 41 Field Regiment, who between them had left a trail of crime from Cairo all the way to Ismailia. Their iniquitous ways came to a head in 1950 with the murder of an Egyptian taxi driver who'd agreed to take these chaps back to their desert camp one evening. Some miles from their destination, one of the three blew a hole into the back of the taxi driver's head.

Moascar, circa 1950: Marjorie (centre) and her ladies' club.

There was no apparent motive, apart from pure evilness, and perhaps a touch of insanity. In the act of dumping the body in a nearby ditch and covering it with sand, a car drove past and disturbed them, but the three soldiers managed to escape into the darkness.

I was at a party that evening in the Arab quarter of Ismailia. On hearing a babble of angry voices outside, my host and I went to find out what was happening. A crowd of locals had gathered in the street, all wailing and beating their breasts. The body had been discovered, and it didn't take long before all the gory details of the crime began creeping along the grapevine. The RSM of the Special Investigation Branch was told through an informer where the murderers were hiding, so he took a band of men to their lair and flushed them out. All three came quietly.

Egyptian blood was boiling over this and the death sentence was passed, though the rumourmongers doubted an execution would actually take place. Everyone assumed the British were bluffing in an attempt to appease the Egyptians, and it was widely expected that the men would be released as soon as the uproar died down. The scaffold was erected and the nooses were hanging, but still no one believed the stools would be kicked away.

The celebrated British hangman, Albert Pierrepoint, was sent for. He stayed at our garrison the night before and showed some of the officers in the mess the bag he put over the faces of the condemned. He always carried this around in the top pocket of his suit, like a handkerchief.

The mothers of the three murderers came out from England and were allowed to spend a few final hours with their sons. Then, early in the morning on 31 August 1950, Pierrepoint took Smith and Golbey from their cells, and side by side the two men went to meet their maker. Heinzmann, the more vicious of the three, was led out last, dressed in physical training shorts and a matching vest. He spat in the face of the provost marshal as he walked up the steps that led to the rope, where he passed from this life without a flinch.

The bodies were buried in a row at the far end of the garrison cemetery, well away from the graves of the heroes who'd died in the service of their country. Since the start of the war hundreds upon hundreds of headstones had sprung up like daisies in this once desolate spot. Yet with so much evil still in the world, I often wondered what their sacrifice was for.

By now, the Egyptian Government was screaming its head off for the complete evacuation of the British forces. The fact we hadn't returned to Cairo or Alexandria affirmed the impression that Britain was a spent force, defeated and beaten as a global supremacy. The Egyptians saw this as their chance to remove us from their country once and for all, and consequently life became hectic in the Canal Zone. Coffin after coffin passed by my door as British soldiers were cut down by the ruthless foe. The authorities were even contemplating the withdrawal of all troops to the safety of the barracks and camps, and sending their families home to the United Kingdom, well out of harm's way.

The Egyptians soon began cutting off our supplies from the larger towns. Beer and other such luxuries were running out fast, and our stock of Stella had long since been drunk. The local NAAFIs had all closed, so my wife and her ladies offered to open one and run it themselves. This was met with cheers from the troops, who flocked to the homespun NAAFI every night, where they passed away their free time with singsongs around the piano.

Egyptian employees were slowly being enticed to stop working for the British forces. The country's government had set up offices where these chaps could report and receive the same amount of wages in cash. We still had about 400 native staff members at Moascar Garrison, so one day I sat them all down on the grass outside my office and told them not be intimidated by the terrorists, and to hold fast. I could tell they were all frightened, though. I'd received a tip-off that agents from the terror gangs had visited these men at their homes at night, informing them to collect their money and then clear off as far away from the Canal Zone as possible.

The next day I was detailed to go to the bank in Ismailia and collect the cash for the employees' payment. I was a little nervous about the journey, for there'd been a spate of bombings in recent weeks on the roads leading from the garrison into town. Homemade devices were being slipped into British trucks as they pulled up at crossings, and the culprits had so far eluded capture. With Sergeant John Boyd of the Royal Inniskilling Fusiliers as my escort, we moved off at a quarter to eight in the morning. John thought I was off my rocker wanting to go so early, as the bank didn't open until 9.00 am, but I had a feeling something bad was going to happen and I wanted to get there in good time. We followed the track that ran parallel between the Arab Town Road and the Sweet Water Canal, where mutilated body parts were often fished out. Our road had been nicknamed Snipers' Alley due to the number of bullets that flew over from the nearby mud houses, but we arrived safely without incident, and were the only people in town. Being so early we were first in and first out again, and though it was a relief to be heading back, I kept my Sten gun at the ready the whole time.

'You know, sir, I would never have believed you could be scared,' John said as he drove our truck back towards Moascar.

I ignored his remark and continued scanning the roadside for any signs of an ambush. Ahead of us, a little further along past the bridge that crossed the canal, I spotted a large group of Egyptians running in our direction, and they didn't look happy in the slightest.

'Turn across the water, now!' I roared at John, grabbing the wheel of the truck.

The vehicle swerved as we passed over the bridge, reaching the other side just in time to see the mob speeding down the road towards Ismailia. I felt much happier with the river between us: I knew dirty people didn't care much for water. Looking over my shoulder, I saw the swelling crowd weren't all that interested in us, anyway, and continued on their way without so much as an insult yelled in our direction. I wondered what they were up to, so upon our return I sent a convoy of troops into Ismailia to find out.

By lunchtime, everything became clear. From the garrison we could see a great pall of smoke hanging over the town of Ismailia. Scouts reported back to say the mob had grown bigger and had begun roaming the streets, breaking into stores and setting alight every parked car they could find. They'd cleaned out the shops from top to bottom but, perhaps on Nasser's orders, they didn't interfere with any of the ladies who were buying at the counter. With burst after burst of fire, our troops began to drive the mob back, and by the end of the afternoon they'd managed to restore order to the town.

In 1951 Iran nationalized the Anglo-Iranian Oil Company and expelled Britain from the city's refineries. This undoubtedly pleased some authorities, but Britain was enraged. We on the canal really thought the British Government would bare its teeth and do something about it. Armed and ready, we awaited the order to act, but it never came. This was just the tonic the Egyptians were waiting for, and the lack of military retaliation confirmed that Britain was a wounded, elderly lion that had lost all its teeth.

Weekend after weekend, terrorists came up to Moascar from Cairo and snuck around the camps, shooting and stabbing any Briton they came across. Nightfall would herald volleys of shots from the darkness, mingled with the barking of nearby dogs. Orders went out that we were all to carry arms inside the garrison as well as outside. Though she was heavily pregnant with our second child, Marjorie began running a shooting group for her ladies, and I was amazed at the progress they made.

One evening, a British military police officer and one of his NCO escorts were shot dead as they passed by the Egyptian police barracks on their way to Ismailia. If that wasn't bad enough, it was discovered that the shots had been fired from inside the barracks. Shockwaves rippled through our garrison when the truth of the matter began sinking in: it was a police officer who was responsible. That was the last straw. We'd had enough, and weren't prepared to take any more. General Erskine sent an ultimatum to the police force, ordering them to hand over all of their weapons, or else. This, of course, was ignored, so within two hours the general and some 7,000 of his men began pounding the barracks with heavy artillery. It was an almighty conflict. Messages flooded into my garrison that the Lancashire Fusiliers had gone in with the old cold steel – their bayonets – and had stirred up the 700 Egyptian policemen, who refused to surrender. After several hours the result was a resounding victory for the British, who'd killed about 10 per cent of the armed police. The rest we sent packing to Cairo by train, minus their armaments.

The Egyptians had fought with courage. This surprised even me, as they never struck me as a force to be concerned about. One of their officers, a captain, covered himself in glory. He showed great bravery that day and stuck it out until the last moment even though he'd had the chance to surrender.

Covered in blood, he appeared at an open window during the shelling and asked for a ceasefire so he could clear away some of his dead and tend to the wounded. He also asked the British for medical supplies for his comrades. This was all granted, and when the ceasefire was over, he was asked through a loud speaker if he was ready to surrender his men.

'Fight on!' he cried.

The captain was captured when the barracks fell.

Though 1951 had been tainted by so much savagery, from out of the ashes some good had been born. I'd become a father again. My first daughter had been delivered into the world safe and sound, although the birth was not without its complications. My poor dear wife had been rushed to a medical tent where it was discovered the baby was breech. The medical officer was in rather a state, as he'd never encountered this condition before. As brave and as selfless as ever, Marjorie was more concerned about the welfare of the poor doctor than she was for herself. Fearing he was going to pass out, she kept showering him with praise and encouragement the whole way through.

My family was blessed with a few months of bliss, and it was Christmas Eve 1951 when our peace was shattered once again. A figure, lurking in the shadows, made an attempt on my life as I stood at the gate of my quarters, bidding my guests goodnight. Bursts of Sten gunfire tore into my garden gate, inches from

Moascar, Christmas Day 1951: Christmas dinner in the garrison.

Moascar, 1951: General Erskine (centre) inspecting the diners with Paddy and other colleagues.

where I was standing. I dropped to the ground like a sack of potatoes and managed to crawl to safety as the bullets ripped into the walls of my quarters. I was terrified: my wife and children were inside. Terence was upstairs in bed, watching on as 'shooting stars', as he called them, whizzed through his bedroom window and over his head. Mercifully, nobody was hurt. The mystery of who should do such a thing, and why, was never explained. The only thing that was clear, however, was that the Sten was a British weapon.

After Christmas, Sister Anthony, one of the nuns from the convent on the fringe of the Arab town of Arashiya, began making regular trips up to the garrison with her basket of eggs and fresh fruit for the troops. I knew her well, as she was Terence's favourite teacher at school, and a close personal friend of Lady Erskine. It was quite a walk from the convent and she had to pass along the dangerous Snipers' Alley. Naturally, I was concerned for her safety.

'You're not a martyr yet,' I said, 'but you may be one of these days if you're not careful. I should think it would be best if you stayed in your convent for now, at least until the troubles have died down.'

Sister Anthony chuckled. 'Ah, but you see, I'm collecting British and Egyptian bullets,' she jested in that soft, American accent of hers. 'They do tend to whiz over our convent, and I can find lots of them on the road to the garrison.'

Moascar, circa 1950: the military children at play.

The following Sunday, the nuns were busy entertaining the military children prior to serving their usual afternoon tea. Across the road was a patrol of British troops, sitting around, enjoying a cigarette or two in the warm weather. A little further down the lane came an Egyptian barrow boy, pushing his barrow full of fresh fruit and vegetables. He stopped in front of the troops and flashed them a toothless grin.

'A present from me to you,' he said, gesturing towards his little wooden barrow. With another smile, he turned on his heels and skipped off, leaving his offering in front of the puzzled patrol.

No sooner had the chaps stood up to examine their unexpected gift when an explosion crashed through the air, taking the Trojan barrow and the troops with it; blown to pieces by the device concealed among the fruit. Before the survivors could regain their senses, a machine gun opened up from a small copse of trees. Behind the weapon were Egyptian terrorists, sniping at the injured soldiers and any other target that presented itself.

The nuns and the children at the convent began fleeing into their courtyard, taking refuge in their air raid shelter. The mother superior dashed to the telephone to raise the alarm, but just then she heard Egyptian voices coming from outside.

'Cut the telephone wire!'

She managed to get through to Moascar Garrison just before the line went dead. All she could do was hope and pray that reinforcements would make it in time. She joined the others in the air raid shelter, where together they waited for something to happen.

After what must have seemed like forever, Sister Anthony, aware the children were in some distress, decided to risk going back into the convent so she could bring them some water. She was a completely fearless woman. The minutes passed and the nuns, who were still below in the air raid shelter, heard more guns and tank fire from above: the British had arrived.

As soon as things began to quieten down the mother superior went outside to make sure the coast was finally clear. To her horror, she found Sister Anthony lying dead on the porch steps. A bullet had passed straight through the left side of her heart, travelling down into her right arm, breaking the bone completely in two. To the left of the convent was the position the Egyptian terrorists had held, and to the right was where the British soldiers stood; yet nobody knew whether the sister had been shot as she was leaving the convent, or as she'd turned to go back inside. Some of our lads claimed to have heard the Egyptians cry: 'We've killed the daughter of a dog!' so it seemed undeniable that the rebels were responsible for her murder.

With five warrant officers, I drove through the chastened streets past Arashiya towards the convent. Sister Anthony was to have a military funeral, making her the first non-military personnel to be granted the honour, and we six were to be the coffin bearers. As we passed the police barracks, I wondered if we might get sniped at, as tensions were still fraught since the infamous battle, dubbed by Egyptians as 'the Ismailia murders'. I'd always been one to obey an order down to the last letter, but this was a day when I chose to think for myself. We'd been told no firearms were to be carried by my bearer party, but I wasn't prepared to take any chances, so I placed a Luger pistol under a handkerchief on the seat beside me, and would have gladly used it had we come under fire.

As we entered the convent, we were led to the chapel where the coffin was waiting. The little room was packed with nuns and children of all nationalities whose lives had been touched by this brave and compassionate woman. Some began to cry as we placed the white rosewood coffin on our shoulders and carried it gently to the vehicle. I felt my own eyes filling with tears. This woman was an innocent victim of a war that should never have been fought.

We drove her remains to the nearby Roman Catholic Church and laid her in the chapel of rest. I'd arranged for a grave to be dug at the military cemetery at the rear of Moascar Garrison, but just as we were leaving the church, one of the warrant officers remarked how wide the coffin shoulders were, and how it might not fit into the grave. It was quite late in the day by that time and the funeral was due to take place the following morning, so I hurried back to the little chapel and, as people were silently praying, I began measuring the shoulders. I didn't have a tape measure on me so had to improvise with my pace stick. To my horror, I found the warrant officer was quite correct: the grave was far too small for the coffin. We dashed back to the garrison as fast as we could, and I sent hurried orders to Sam Reeves, my provost sergeant, who hastily corrected the error just in the nick of time.

The funeral was a most impressive affair, more like a state funeral. Hundreds of people had turned up to pay their last respects at the graveside, including the American Ambassador. I'd managed to 'borrow' a Stars and Stripes pendant from the front of his car, which I placed on top of the sister's coffin. Afterwards, when the time came to return it, the chaplain calmly informed me it must have accidentally been buried with her, for nobody had seen it since. My heart began to race as panic set in. I knew I'd be in hot water over this. Thankfully, it turned out one of my quick-thinking corporals had taken the pendant from the coffin just before it had been lowered into the earth, and had slipped it under his bush jacket. Taking it from him, I raced over to the general officer's residence, where the ambassador was being entertained. I placed it back on his car without being seen, and not a moment too soon, for just then the door opened and out came the general officer, closely followed by the ambassador. I stepped back and saluted as he walked towards his vehicle. As he drove away, I breathed a heavy sigh of relief. I made my way straight to the mess, where I had a large glass of beer.

An inquiry into the murder of Sister Anthony was held, and the proceedings were treated as top secret and sent on to the United Kingdom. Though a British doctor had examined the body, we never heard the result of the findings, and so we never knew who was to blame for the death of this kind and gentle lady.

It was 26 January 1952, a date many of us would never forget. It was the day an army of barbarous civilians marched into Cairo, hell bent on utter destruction. These weren't mindless mobs but organized squads, armed and prepared with all the implements required for arson, looting and murder. So well prepared were these hundreds, if not thousands, of anti-British protesters that the authorities were too afraid to intervene. Even the police kept off the streets, no doubt in sympathy for their fallen comrades.

The prime minister, who at that time was the Wafdist Mustafa el-Nahas Pasha, begged the chief of the Egyptian Army to send his men to defend the city, but the chief was an honest man and was forced to admit his army was in a state of mutiny, with many of the troops and officers siding with the rioters. He was powerless to assist.

That was the day the great city of Cairo lay down to be ravished by a bloodthirsty, half-crazed army of students and barefoot natives. Shopkeepers lowered their shutters, but they offered no protection. They were prised open by the rioters, and the premises looted then set alight. Hundreds upon hundreds of buildings were targeted, and in no time at all, the entire city was ablaze. Nothing was spared, from the brothels and backstreet bars all the way up to city landmarks such as the Shepheard's Hotel and Barclay's Bank. All were completely destroyed.

Those trapped inside suffered horrific deaths. Limbs were sliced off with scythes; shopkeepers had their throats slit, whilst others were disembowelled and then set on fire. The screams of terrified victims filled the dilapidated streets, mingled with the explosions from petrol bombs and the maniacal laughter of the mobs.

The exclusive Turf Club had been holding a lunch party that day, despite several warnings of what might happen, but British people often act strangely, especially when they're abroad. With no police guard outside, the approaching mob battered the doors down as easily as if they were made of cardboard. They doused the entire building with petrol and set it alight. Those who tried to escape were hacked at with cleaving knives and pushed back into the flames.

We on the Canal Zone were waiting with baited breath to be called into action. General Erskine even received a telegram from King Farouk, begging for British assistance.

'Send British troops back to Cairo: foreign lives and property in danger,' it read, but a follow-up telegram from the British Ambassador called a halt to any desires the general may have had about moving. That was Britain's last chance to go in and put an end to the trouble, and we didn't take it.

I was appalled when I read in the newspapers that Colonel Nasser had said it would be difficult to know where to lay the blame for this massacre, insisting – rather too keenly, for my liking – it had nothing whatsoever to do with the Free Officers. Be that as it may, somebody knew who was to blame, and they remained silent to their dying day.

Moascar, 1951: Paddy, the Deputy Provincial Grand Primo (second from the front), and other members of the RAOB marking the first birthday of their Prince Charles Lodge.

26 January 1952 became known as Black Saturday. Even though it was the blackest day, it led to the fall of the Wafd government, which I believe was a small mercy. A new prime minister was appointed, General Hussein Sirri Pasha, but he resigned after just three weeks. All eyes fell upon Major General Naguib, a prominent Free Officer, who was now regarded by many as the best man to lead Egypt. This, of course, wasn't popular at the top, so the king, fearing for his own position, had him posted to the Frontier Brigade, well out of the way. That was the spark that lit the blue touchpaper. An enraged Nasser and his followers soon became extremely busy, shutting themselves away and conspiring long into the night, until the Free Officers were at last ready to make their move.

Chapter 16

A New Beginning

With the help of his Free Officers, Colonel Nasser had spent the past few years building up a guerrilla campaign against the British on the Canal Zone. This was all part of his long game, and I often wondered if he'd ever dare chance his arm against us in a real battle. If he had, our forces would have cut his men down, one by one; but Nasser was clever, astute and above all, stealthy. He wasn't going to risk an open war, not after all his efforts. He had bigger plans to focus on: Nasser was committed to dissolving the monarchy and establishing a fair republic, and now the perfect opportunity had presented itself. Farouk and his government had gone to Alexandria for the summer, and Nasser knew he had to get cracking otherwise his grand scheme would be upset, and he'd receive a bullet in the back of his head for his part in the plot.

Events were moving quickly, and timing was key. On 20 July 1952, yet another weak Egyptian government stepped down, after just eighteen days in power. It was now or never. Colonel Nasser summoned a secret meeting between the seven hardcore members of his revolution command council and informed them it was time to act. He stressed, however, that if they succeeded, Farouk was not to be harmed; instead he was to be allowed to abdicate with full military honours, and sent into exile. Some of the group were opposed to this, and would have liked nothing better than to blow the king's head clean off, but Nasser was a patriot and didn't want a drop of Egyptian blood to be spilt unnecessarily.

His main concern was that the British Army might intervene, marching back on Cairo from Fâyid and Moascar. There were only 300 Free Officers in Cairo he could summon for assistance, but it'd be too risky to call on them all lest it aroused suspicion. Speed and planning were the officers' main tactics now, so on 22 July Nasser and his military associate, Abdel Hakim Amer, sped away in the colonel's trusty old Austin motor car to collect some troops from Abbassia Barracks, which was halfway between Cairo and Heliopolis; but they were too late. The barracks had been tipped off and the gates were sealed by the military police.

It looked as though Nasser's plan was finished before it had even begun. The pair turned around and as a last resort began making their way to Almaza Barracks, on the outskirts of Cairo. As they travelled down the dark, unlit road, they ran into a company of Egyptian troops. They were surrounded and dragged from their car, fully convinced this was the end, but just in the nick of time one of the Free Officers, a lieutenant colonel named Yusuf Sadiq, appeared on the scene and ordered his men to stand down. Joining forces with the lieutenant colonel and his troops, the company marched on Abbassia Barracks. After a brief struggle outside, where two soldiers were killed, Colonel Nasser and Hakim Amer entered the conference room with pistols drawn. There they found the chief of staff, Lieutenant General Hussein Farid, at the head of the table, where he'd been busy making plans to foil the Free Officers. Farid and the other members of staff put up no resistance and were marched away with their lives.

By some miracle Nasser had pulled it off. Allah must have been on his side that night.

In the early hours of the morning, seven prominent Free Officers met in the same conference room. Nasser wanted to be certain there'd be no counter-attack from Britain or America, so he telephoned both embassies from the very room where the chief of staff had been plotting Nasser's downfall just hours earlier.

'The Free Officers have taken control,' he declared. 'Providing there is no intervention, the whole takeover will be completed in good order, and the lives and property of all aliens will be safeguarded.'

Though the embassies must have been staggered by this proclamation, they stood by, allowing Nasser to grasp Egypt's reigns with both hands.

At 7.00 am, just as Egypt was waking, it was broadcasted across the nation that a new era had dawned. The bleary-eyed Egyptian population cried with joy; but it was a different story over in Ras el-Tin Palace. Upon hearing the news, the king was said to have descended into an inconsolable rage. He went running up and down the long corridors, his crown on his head and his medals pinned to his chest.

'I am still the king of Egypt!' he screamed, over and over again.

An armoured column set off from Cairo to surround Farouk's summer palace at Alexandria. The American Ambassador telephoned the quaking monarch to tell him his life would be spared, providing he signed the abdication document that had already been prepared. The hysterical king read the document twice before signing with a shaking hand.

Egypt's last sovereign was granted the dignity of leaving aboard his royal yacht, bound for exile. Naguib and Nasser had afforded him the final courtesy of packing wherever he liked for his journey. Farouk took full advantage of this, and sailed away with 273 bags and suitcases. The vessel was barely out of sight when a great crowd surged towards the palace, swarming inside to feast their eyes on the treasures within. The whole place was stacked with treasures beyond the wildest dreams of avarice. For the first time in history, the private and most intimate details of the ex-king's sordid life were exposed to his once loyal subjects.

Shortly after the abdication, teams of Egyptian Army officers visited the British camps at the Canal Zone, keen to learn how long it would take us to pull out. I recognized some of the officers from my time training them and their army. Not so long ago they were little more than incompetent novices, clueless about anything soldierly, and now here they were, issuing demands and telling us we had twelve months to clear out.

A new British commanding officer had recently arrived at Moascar. This was his first time on foreign soil, and he'd expected everything to be just as the book said. He hadn't witnessed the bloodshed and heartache that had shaped this land, and his refusal to show any understanding towards the Egyptians only served to aggravate the situation.

General Sir George Erskine had returned to England, his job done, and a magnificent job it was too. We gave him a tremendous send-off. Together with the warrant officers and sergeants from my mess, we pulled his car with towropes and marched behind the band of the Lancashire Fusiliers who were playing stirring martial music. We marched all the way down the mall, which was lined with troops, Boy Scouts, Girl Guides and sad-faced Egyptian tradesmen. At the gate, a guard of honour of the Royal Air Force presented arms. A crowd of locals from the nearby Arashiya had even gathered to see him off. We were taken aback when they broke into applause, cheering and waving as the general shook hands with his officers.

'Thank you, sergeant major, for your loyalty and help during my time of command,' he said when he reached me. 'I'll never forget it, and I wish you all the luck in the world.'

I would have died for this man, as I know many others would have done; but I was sick of death and had made up my mind to return home by the end of the year. In the meantime, I decided to take a long overdue holiday with my family.

Moascar, 1952: the farewell to General Erskine parade, with Paddy at the front, leading the car pullers.

It was a blistering hot day as we reached the boat to Cyprus, but just before we boarded, Marjorie realized she'd mislaid her passport. After a frantic and unfruitful search through our bags, we were granted special permission to board, and settled down with some friends of ours for our three-day journey at sea, bound for a few days of rest and relaxation high up in the Troodos Mountains.

Arriving at Limassol, one of the largest cities on the island, I was impressed by the warm welcome we received from the Cypriots, and we undertook our long but pleasant drive into the clouds. It was one of the most exciting journeys of my life. Up and up the road we went, passing lines of fruit trees that were ripe for the picking. Union Flags were flying from almost every window, and the olive-skinned people waved and threw fruit into our hands as we passed. As we drew into our holiday camp, which was run by the NAAFI, we found ourselves surrounded by a strong smell of pine trees. It was a wonderful tonic. Just when I thought life couldn't get any better, Marjorie informed me we were expecting our third child.

Our fun was cut short some days later when the holidaying troops and I were summoned to the camp office, where we were told various scuffles were breaking out in Egypt. The country was once again in a state of political unrest as Nasser's government negotiated a bumpy take-off, and we were ordered to return with urgency. Leaving our families behind, we departed by road to the dockside, where we caught a return boat to Port Said.

Before I knew it I was back in the thick of things at Moascar, and the next few weeks were miserable ones without my family by my side. The powers that be had decided it was safer for them to stay where they were. I would have moved heaven and earth to get them back, but whatever I tried and whomever I approached, the answer was always the same.

'There are currently no plans to return the military families to Moascar. They will stay at our Cypriot base for the foreseeable future.'

I was starting to feel blue, so one day I went to Fâyid to talk to some friends in the Royal Air Force. Over a few drinks in their mess they introduced me to a pilot who was going over to Cyprus on a training flight, and was due to return in several days' time. After several more drinks he agreed to try to smuggle my family back with him.

After some anxious days of waiting, the phone call came from my RAF pals who told me the plane was due to arrive back that evening. I made my excuses to the officers in the mess and set off in one of our trucks; and as the sun began its descent, I raced across the desert road to Fâyid, where I spotted a plane circling above my head. I said a hurried prayer and dashed across the tarmac, ignoring the call of angry voices telling me to get back. The plane landed some way ahead, and as I drew closer, I saw my wife and two children climbing down the steps. All three looked tired after their long journey and Terence was still clutching the little paper bag he'd been sick in.

I embraced my wife, and as the four of us drove happily back to Moascar, Marjorie began telling me her story of how we came to be reunited. She'd been sitting alone in her room at the holiday camp, feeling lonely and fed up, when a senior officer came round and told her she was to gather up the children and pack as quickly as she could. After a mad dash down the mountain roads to the airport, she was just about to board the plane when a corporal of the Royal Air Force stopped her.

'I'm afraid you're not on the passenger list,' he told her, double-checking his documents. 'And in any case, you can't leave the country as you're not in possession of a passport.'

The whole plan looked as though it was doomed already, but just as she turned to head off back into the mountains, a young army captain handed her some papers.

'I know this lady's husband well and can vouch for her identity,' he told the corporal. 'I'm sorry for the confusion, Mrs Brooks,' he said, turning to Marjorie. 'You are boarding this flight.'

As the plane touched down at Fâyid Airport, a voice called: 'Mrs Brooks and children,' and my wife was escorted off first. It turned out she'd been 'mistaken' for the wife of a senior officer of the RAF.

The sun was setting on 1952, and as the year drew to a close, so too did my time in the Middle East. I was due to leave for England after fifteen long years. During that time my life had changed beyond my wildest imagination. I'd experienced war, murder and despair, but I'd also met and married the most beautiful lady I could have wished to meet. I'd been blessed with two wonderful children, and knew our family would continue to grow in the years to come. I'd also become close to the second president of Egypt, Gamal Abdel Nasser, and members of his extended family had been good friends of mine, enriching my life in ways I'd never thought possible. They'd been kind to me when I was nothing but a stranger in a foreign land; and now those very same people were clamouring to see our backs. After seventy-five years of administration, Britain was friendless in the East, and all the barracks, married quarters and other installations we'd built with our own sweat and blood were falling into Egyptian hands.

After many sad farewells, my family and I packed up our belongings and made our way to the point of departure. There were several busloads of personnel leaving for home that day, and I managed to wangle some seats in one of the buses. Sitting close to us was a friendly major who was returning to the United Kingdom with his family. We had one or two things in common and made pleasant conversation as we made our way to Port Said, where a boat was waiting.

As the bus tore along the winding road at a breakneck speed, it broke down just as we arrived at the bridge that would lead us to the port. We'd only been stationary a matter of moments when a gathering of armed natives began approaching us, and they didn't look friendly. On the other side of the water dozens more were making their way over, all with the same hard looks on their faces.

The major and I managed to sneak off the back of the bus and found a telephone box a little further down the road. I tried to call the military police but couldn't get through, as they, along with all other British units, had already pulled out of the town. In the end I managed to get through to the British consular offices and was told we should never have gone to Port Said, for it was too dangerous, but due to some outlying emergency at the original port, we'd been left with no other option.

'I'll get in touch with the military authorities straight away,' the consular reassured me. 'In the meantime, be careful. The natives from the outskirts of

Moascar, circa 1952: Paddy, Marjorie and their young children outside the married quarters at Moascar Garrison.

Said are very hostile, and the spot where you've broken down is where a British officer and his men were murdered just the other week.'

Not feeling at all comforted by that, I replaced the handset, and the major and I stood anxiously at the side of the road, waiting for some backup to arrive. We had no firearms and were responsible for some fifteen families aboard our vehicle. It was a boiling hot day and there was no shade. The gathering mob hadn't gained access to the vehicle just yet, so under the circumstances we felt the passengers were safer where they were. After several more minutes the natives began surrounding the bus. Though they didn't draw their weapons, they did their best to try to intimidate the passengers by banging on the sides and windows, and yelling insults in Arabic. It wasn't long before some Sudanese chaps who were working in a nearby factory heard the commotion and came outside to see what was going on.

'The Egyptians from this part of the country are very nasty,' they warned the major and I. 'They cannot be trusted.'

As the minutes passed, the hostile mobs became more and more aggressive, and I was starting to worry. Even with our friends from the Sudan, we wouldn't have lasted long against this savage bunch. Some of the rebels had begun boarding the bus, threatening to kill all British citizens on board. Luckily most of the passengers could speak a sufficient amount of Arabic, and began trying to convince the hoodlums there were no Britons among them.

Just then an Egyptian Army car came by and I was able to hail the driver. From out of the vehicle stepped an Egyptian major whom I knew from my days at the Small Arms Training School. He shouted to the angry crowd, telling them exactly what he'd do to them if any harm came to us. As if by magic the mob dispersed. I thanked my old comrade and he continued on his way.

After what seemed like an eternity, the welcome sight of a three-ton British Army lorry came trundling along the road. It came to a halt next to the bus, and out stepped a sergeant in civilian clothes, holding a tow rope. In no time at all, he got the bus going again and away we roared towards the port. We made it with little time to spare.

At last our troubles were over; we were about to set foot on the gangplank and leave all our worries behind in this battle-scarred land. What could possibly go wrong now?

'*Effendi!*' I heard a voice calling behind me.

Turning around I saw, to my surprise, our Egyptian cook, who'd lived with us at the garrison, dashing towards me. He was a nice chap, and I felt touched that he'd come to see us off. He shook Terence and me by the hand, and patted my little blue-eyed daughter on her head as she slept peacefully in the arms of her mother. The cook turned to say farewell to Marjorie, and just as we were all distracted by his kind words, he snatched my little girl and made a run for it. My wife screamed as I gave chase across the crowded port. He ran for what felt like forever, weaving in and out of the would-be passengers who were waiting to board the ship, but I caught up with him before he'd managed to slip into the shadows of the city's backstreets. Channelling the skills I'd learned during my boxing days, I whipped him a beauty right across his face. I grabbed hold of my daughter before he hit the ground, and as I carried her away to safety, I heard him calling out to me.

'The golden-haired child is an idol!' he yelled. 'I can sell her for much money!'

I called him an unfavourable name in Arabic and returned to the dockside.

At long last we stepped aboard the *Lancashire*, the ship that was to carry us back to Britain. I felt the relief flow through my body like a warming tonic. We were bound for a little thatched farmhouse in Long Sutton, close to the Wash in rural Lincolnshire, where Marjorie's family lived. I for one was looking forward to a bit of peace and quiet.

The red shores of Egypt soon began to fade away into the blue, and as I stood on deck, I found myself wondering what the country's future would hold. It looked so insignificant from far away, but colossal events had happened there. Though I'd grown incredibly fond of the land and its people, I wasn't sorry to be leaving.

It was 1 October 1952 when we first saw the distant lights of Liverpool. As dawn came and the vessel drew closer, I was surprised to spot so many shipwrecks from the war days. My war had been overseas, so it hadn't really crossed my mind how scarred England would be.

After several happy months with Marjorie's family, the time had come to take my wife and children to Dublin to meet the Rochford clan. Standing by the port at Dunleary, I helped my heavily pregnant wife into our train carriage, and advised her and the children to wait for me there while I went to collect our luggage. A short while later I returned with half a dozen cases in tow, only to find the platform completely empty. I blinked in surprise, assuming I must have been dreaming. Where had my train gone? I was sure it hadn't been due to leave for another few minutes. Feeling slightly panicked, I looked around for some assistance and noticed two Irish-looking gentlemen some yards away, propping up the platform wall.

'What's the matter, there?' one of them called over to me.

'I've just lost my wife and children,' I said, still reeling over the apparent disappearance of an entire passenger train.

'Ah, to be shure,' the other one said, puffing on a pipe, 'nobody gets lost in Oirland, let alone a loving wife. Now, if she's a queer one, well, thank your lucky stars she's gone.'

Finding that remark not at all helpful, I hopped on the next train to Westland Row Station near the centre of Dublin, and as it pulled in, I spotted a flustered-looking Marjorie who, I was relieved to see, had been picked up by my two sisters. They'd recognized her from a photograph I'd sent home to Mother. It turned out I'd been mistaken about the train times; and though I was in bother for a while afterwards, we did laugh over it in the end.

Arriving in my beloved village that had changed so much, we were welcomed home by my family in true Irish style. My mother was waiting for me on the doorstep of her home. For all her years, she still looked the same. I felt a lump in my throat as we embraced for the first time in fifteen long years. Now, of course, she was a widow, and had learned to live without her fine, upright husband by her side. Father had always strived to set such a high example to us all, and his death had left a hole in all our hearts that couldn't be filled.

That evening we enjoyed a splendid feast, and stayed up long into the night, singing, playing music and catching up on lost years. The following morning, my younger brothers, Jack and Charles, took me to the Grangegorman Military Cemetery to visit our father's grave, which had found its place alongside the other heroes of the Emerald Isle. I felt my stomach turn as I entered the cemetery. Here before me lay a sea of brave warriors without even proper headstones, save for those whose families could afford to pay for one. My father's grave had been marked with a simple wooden cross. I was ashamed and angry that the British Legion couldn't provide their former soldiers with this one final honour. When I wrote to them about this later, their sickening response was simply: 'Your father didn't die in battle, so he's not entitled to a military headstone.'

As I hadn't been able to visit on Armistice Day, I planted a belated poppy beside Father's cross, clutching his polished medals as I did so. He would always be a hero to me, even if the legion didn't agree. The three of us stood with tears in our eyes, holding our own two minutes of silence.

I'd been told that at the conclusion of the local church service, held in the cemetery every 11 November, the crowds were always instructed to disperse without singing the British National Anthem, as this would offend many of the mourners. This was no good to me, so at the conclusion of our private vigil I broke into song, and to my surprise, my brothers joined in.

God save our gracious queen,
Long live our noble queen,
God save our queen.

I imagined our voices floating across the river Liffey to the old Royal Hibernian School in Phoenix Park, where the white granite memorial cross had been erected in honour of the brave ex-boys of the school who'd laid down their lives in the First and Second World Wars. Countless thousands of Ireland's sons had died on foreign battlefields. None had wanted to die, but went forward to face danger nevertheless, never knowing if they'd live to see their loved ones' faces again. That's why I feel so strongly that those whose lives were spared should never forget their brothers who fell.

'We shall remember them.' Whenever I hear those words at the end of the annual armistice ceremonies, I wonder if those who speak them truly understand what they say.

As much as I wanted to stay in Chapelizod, there was no work for me in Ireland, so I returned to England and was posted to the military education

The Officers' Training Corps at the University of London, England, 1953: Paddy (crossed) and his trainees.

committee at the Officers' Training Corps at the University of London, where I completed two years' service as the regimental sergeant major. I became the proud father of two more children: a son, in March 1953, and a daughter, who arrived the following year, making our family unit complete.

One day I decided to take my wife and children to visit to my old regimental headquarters on Birdcage Walk. To my sorrow, I saw before me the ruins of the lovely Guards' Chapel, which had been bombed by the Germans in 1944. Across the road was Buckingham Palace, where I'd once proudly served my king, father of George VI, who'd led this country through her darkest days. The late monarch had left his crown to his eldest daughter; and as I walked past the palace, I wished the young queen a long and glorious reign.

I was posted to the Royal Military School of Music at Kneller Hall in Twickenham, Middlesex, and though I was kept busy, my mind often wandered back to my years spent under the Egyptian sun. I had high hopes for the country under President Nasser's leadership, but the occasional damning headline made me cringe with despair.

'CRACKS IN CAIRO REGIME WIDEN', the national papers screamed.

Startling declarations such as 'SHOTS FIRED AT COLONEL NASSER' and 'NASSER JAILS A CRITIC' were splashed everywhere; but no story was more condemning than the Cairo 'spy trial', which hit the news in 1957.

James Albert Zarb, a Maltese businessman, and James Swinburn, a British business manager in Cairo, had been arrested the previous year on suspicion of spying, and were waiting in the grimmest of Egyptian jails to learn their fate. Some of their alleged accomplices had already been executed. A huge show trial had taken place and British MPs were calling for the release of the two men, who had the threat of the noose hanging over their heads. In the end the pair were sentenced to fifteen years between them, but in my opinion, that was just as bad a fate.

I took a keen interest in the story and, from my small housing estate in London, wondered if there was any way I could help. I decided to write to my old friend, urging him to show pity on these prisoners by releasing them, thus proving to millions of people, not just in Britain but around the world, that he was a merciful leader.

'I would like to inform you,' Nasser replied in a letter dated ten days later, 'that the Egyptian authorities, in an attempt to foster better relations with Britain, have treated Swinburn and Zarb with the utmost generosity. Such a fact is evident from the light sentences compared to the magnitude of the crime, which, I must remind you, is spying in a foreign country, the punishment for which is universally known. Furthermore, they are receiving every humane treatment while serving their sentences. I hope you will appreciate that it is impossible for me to release them at any earlier date.'

This, I felt, was less than satisfactory, and over the next couple of years I entered into regular correspondence with Nasser on behalf of the two prisoners. His replies were curt, and simply assured me that both men were healthy and being treated well; and that, he made clear, was the end of the matter.

In 1959 I received an unexpected telephone call from Mrs Elda Zarb, the wife of James, who'd read about my efforts in the national press and invited me to call round to her house in Southall so she could thank me in person. She and her four children were all grateful for my help, and after a long discussion over tea and cakes, I promised I'd continue doing everything in my power to get the head of their family home safely.

After appealing once again to Nasser, Swinburn was released. This was a great victory for my cause, though the battle was only half won. I wrote again and again to the president of Egypt, telephoning Mrs Zarb on a regular basis to offer her hope and comfort. Weeks later, I received an encouraging letter from Nasser's private secretary.

'The president sends his good wishes, and has decided as a mark of goodwill to you to further remit the sentence of Convict Zarb by one fourth.'

In early 1960 the United Arab Republic sent a diplomat to London in an attempt to reopen diplomatic relations with Britain. I remembered this man from my Cairo days, and was invited to meet him at the former Egyptian Embassy in Mayfair. Over several cups of coffee, we discussed the entire predicament from every angle imaginable. I couldn't stress enough that by releasing this unfortunate Briton, who had the support of the British public, the West would look upon Egypt in a favourable light; and as we were leaving, my friend promised to write to Cairo to see what could be done.

In February that year, I was invited to attend the first reception of the Diplomatic Corps at the Egyptian Embassy. I was humbled by the request, but also nervous. What would officialdom think of an ordinary chap like me mixing with the Egyptians after the recent Suez Crisis? This terrible conflict in 1956 had brought about the end of British supremacy in Egypt once and for all, and feelings between our two nations were still incredibly bitter.

My former commanding officer, Sir Guy Salisbury-Jones, had by now been appointed marshal of the Diplomatic Corps at Buckingham Palace, so the first thing I did was call on him for advice.

'You must come,' he enthused. 'You're absolutely the right chap to help, as you know the Egyptians better than many. You served them well and they'll remember you for that.'

The following evening, dressed as smartly as my meagre wages would allow, I arrived to meet Sir Guy outside the embassy. He greeted me like an old friend and introduced me to an array of diplomats. I was pleased to meet the Egyptian chargé d'affaires, Mr Kamal Khalil, and was soon in full flow explaining to the room what I was hoping to achieve. The Egyptian officials had read the recent articles in the *Daily Express* and *Sunday Graphic* concerning my attempt to obtain Zarb's release, and had appreciated the sensitive tone in which they'd been written.

The chargé d'affaires listened intently to what I had to say, and invited me to call on him the following Wednesday. This I did, and during our meeting Mr Khalil agreed to meet with Mrs Zarb. As soon as I returned home, I telephoned to give her the good news. She was delighted and kept the appointment with Mr Khalil, who granted her permission to visit her husband in Cairo.

The months dragged on and I received no further communication from Nasser. As the year drew to a close, I decided to send one final plea to the president, and really laid into my old friend.

'How can you sleep at night?' I asked. 'How can you expect any empathy or understanding from this country while Mr Zarb is allowed to rot in one of your filthy jails? Do yourself and your country a favour and let him go.'

I hesitated for a long time by the post box, knowing that if I dropped the letter into its mouth, I'd be calling time on our many years of friendship. I did post it, and as I walked home through the dusting of snow, I felt satisfied I'd done all I could. I learned the news a short while later that President Nasser had, at long last, decided to grant Zarb his freedom.

I returned to work the following day expecting to find a renewed spring in my step, but somehow the life of a soldier had become dull to me. After a full and exciting life, my role in the United Kingdom had gone stale, so I decided to hang up my hat and try my luck as a civilian. I'd given my best in duty and in sacrifice, and knew the time had come to pass on my pace stick to the next generation. Besides, I'd started to realize I was never born to be a soldier. Knowing what I know now, I'd never have chosen such a life for myself; but then, I never had any choice in the matter. For years I'd been taking my work home with me, putting an immense strain on my marriage and my family. Vowing to become a better husband and father, I took the decision to find somewhere where we could make a fresh start, far from the soulless suburbs of smoky London.

I was offered a new position with the Sutton Dwellings Trust, an organization providing the working classes with affordable housing. A post had become available in a pretty little part of Leeds in the West Riding of Yorkshire, and I became the superintendent of a housing estate off the York Road. My family and I were housed a three-bedroomed property, and we all settled in well. What struck me most was how friendly and welcoming the Yorkshire folk were, particularly in comparison to Londoners, who were often surly and aloof as they hurried along to attend to their own businesses, without even a sideways glance at their fellow men.

I've lived here in Leeds ever since, and I still receive letters and Christmas cards from President Nasser. I treasure the happy hours we spent together in dear old Heliopolis, playing many a game of tennis. Over long iced drinks we'd chat about Egypt, her people, her ambitions, her future and her dreams to become a great nation once more.

My own great wish would be to see Ireland united together as one nation, and on the strongest possible terms of friendship with England. I believe our great country has much to offer the world, and if we and our allies all work together, there's still a chance we can make it a happy place to live in.

As my old friend Nasser once wisely said: 'Humanity does not deserve the honour of life if it does not strive with all its heart in the cause of peace.'

Afterword

The Sutton Estate where Paddy Rochford lived and worked stands adjacent to a main road leading to the centre of Leeds; a road that grew busier and busier as the city developed in the 1960s and '70s. As the years rolled by, and it became commonplace for families to drive their own cars, the road became an accident black spot, earning the nickname 'the Mad Mile'. Fearful for the safety of his tenants, Paddy contacted the local authorities, requesting the installation of a pedestrian crossing. The council responded with a courteous reply, thanking Mr Rochford for expressing his concern and assuring him his comments had been duly noted. No action was taken, however, and Paddy devoted the best part of the next fifteen years chiselling away at the council's thick red tape, in the hope of one day making York Road safe for pedestrians.

This was just one of the many ventures Paddy involved himself in during his spare time. To keep his mind off the horrors of army life, he tried to stay busy, and was always on the lookout for new challenges that would keep him occupied. However, it was during his spell in London when the ex-RSM began his most ambitious project of all: he decided to put his entire life story to paper. For years he'd been reliving his harrowing experiences and couldn't escape the tormenting images of his past. He sought advice from an old military friend, who suggested that turning his hand to writing might prove a therapeutic way of getting the army days out of his system. Paddy duly signed up for a course on creative writing, and though he wasn't a skilled typist, he invested in a typewriter in order to record his amazing adventures, one finger at a time. His words tumbled onto the pages with overwhelming enthusiasm, and his first draft, which began as a few scribbles on the backs of envelopes, soon turned into a tottering pile of inked paper. He continued writing long after his move up north, and his manuscript even made headline news in the *Yorkshire Post*, the reporter explaining how Paddy hoped to see his book in print one day.

Despite the decades spent sitting at his typewriter, he never finished telling his story. Joseph Patrick Rochford died of a coronary thrombosis on 1 May 1977, exactly one month after he'd retired from his role as superintendent of

Leeds, Yorkshire, circa 1960s: Paddy, who championed road safety during his retirement from the army.

the Sutton Estate. He passed away just after learning the news that the council had finally approved the construction of a pelican crossing over York Road's notorious Mad Mile.

Councillor Alan Pedley led the opening ceremony the following year, and together he and Marjorie took the inaugural steps over the crossing, as dozens of Paddy's former tenants watched on, surrounded by reporters and photographers. It was marked by the unveiling of a plaque beside the busy road,

The *Yorkshire Post*, 1977:
Paddy's obituary in the
local press.

Mr. Joseph Rochford

Leeds man who knew Nasser dies

A former soldier who became a confidant of the late President Nasser of Egypt has died shortly after retiring as the estates superintendent of the old people's Sutton Housing Trust, York Road, Killingbeck, Leeds.

A trumpeter with the Coldstream Guards will sound the "last post" at the funeral on Thursday of Mr. Joseph Patrick Rochford (65), of York Road, Leeds, who died on Sunday.

Today, an official at the Sutton Housing Trust's regional office at York paid tribute to Mr. Rochford.

He said: "Mr. Rochford was a very popular figure on the Sutton Trust estate, always ready to give a helping hand and held in considerable affection by tenants.

"A military send off has been arranged for him with serving members of his former regiment attending the funeral."

Mr. Rochford, who retired in March after being in charge of the estate since

1960, joined the Coldstream Guards as a drummer in 1927.

Many of his Army years were spent in the Middle East and by his retirement in 1953 he was a regimental sergeant major.

He came into contact with many Egyptians who subsequently became important political figures, including the late President Nasser.

Mr. Rochford was a tireless campaigner for road safety and was instrumental in mounting a successful campaign to get a pedestrian crossing across the busy York Road.

Pelican crossing at last

A 20-YEAR road safety campaign culminated in the official opening of a pelican crossing at the Sutton Estate, York Road, on Tuesday.

Cr Alan S. Pedley, chairman of the County Road Safety Committee, inaugurated the crossing over York Road's notorious Mad Mile and spoke of the efforts of residents and councillors to make the road safer for pedestrians.

"We have tried to persuade the authorities for more than 20 years to change their criteria for pelican crossings and allow one to be put up here," he said.

Cr Pedley also paid tribute to the efforts of Mr Joseph Patrick Rochford, the late superintendent of the Sutton housing estate, who died last May after more than 15 years fighting for the crossing.

The pelican had been named "Paddy's Crossing" in memory of Mr Rochford.

Then Cr Pedley pressed the button and crossed York Road with Mrs Marjorie Rochford, the superintendent's widow.

Mr Fred Goodall, a committee member of the Tenants' Association also spoke of Mr Rochford's work and thanked the councillors and officials who had backed the Sutton residents' campaign.

Paddy's Crossing then became one of the few dedicated road crossings when it was blessed and dedicated by Father Tom

Maudslay, of Our Lady of Perpetual Succour, Seacroft.

Also present at the opening were Mr R. G. Poulter, general manager of the Sutton Housing Trust, Mrs M. French, representing the Trust's north-eastern regional manager; Mr Ernest Jackson, superintendent of the York Road estate; Mr A. J. Mitchell, superintendent of the Selby Road estate, and Mr G. Carline, County Road Safety Officer.

After the ceremony, one of the estate's oldest residents, Mr John Snowdon, a pensioner of Collin Road, recalled the days, over 40 years ago, when there was a zebra crossing over York Road at the bottom of Sutton Approach.

"Forty years ago, some idiot decided we did not need a crossing and they pulled it up. We have been fighting for some kind of crossing ever since," he said.

Another one

After the opening of the Sutton Estate crossing, County Cr John Sully (Labour, Osmondthorpe) inaugurated another crossing over York Road, this time outside the Highways flats.

Present were Mr George Coultate and Mr Harry Thompson secretary and treasurer respectively of the Highways Community Welfare Association, which, in conjunction with the Sutton residents, has endeavoured to get the two crossings along the Mad Mile.

Cr Sully said the two crossing would take away the fear of crossing York Road.

First across! Cr Alan Pedley and Mrs M. Rochford lead the way, after the opening of the pelican crossing over York Road.

The *Yorkshire Post*, 1978: a feature about the opening of Paddy's Crossing, after many years
of campaigning.

and was eponymously named 'Paddy's Crossing' to commemorate the untiring efforts of the late superintendent, making it the only crossing in the county to have an official title.

Phyllis, Paddy's youngest sister, is the last surviving Rochford sibling. She still lives in the village of Chapelizod, just a short walk from the street where her parents, Joseph and Annie, began their lives together all those years ago. Their little house has long since been demolished and a shop now stands on the site of the old family home. Phyllis has six grown-up children, who now have children and grandchildren of their own. They still talk about their brave Uncle Joey, who used to enthrall them with stories about his adventures whenever he visited home.

Paddy's son, Terry, went on to run a family business in Wakefield, West Yorkshire, selling paper-testing equipment. He still remembers his time in Egypt, and when his own son, Michael, was little, he filled his young mind with fantastical stories of his childhood in the East. Michael took a keen interest in his grandfather's life, and developed a passion for his own family's history, soon disproving Paddy's grand theories of their Rochford ancestral origins. After much study he became a professional genealogist, prompting his grandmother, Marjorie, to gift him stashes of Paddy's notes, letters and military related documents. She also gave him the unfinished manuscript, in the hope of one day seeing the story in print.

Crossing name honours road safety campaigner

The *Yorkshire Post*, 1978: a photograph taken for the newspaper, showing Marjorie unveiling the York Road memorial.

It was only by a stroke of luck that the manuscript still survived, for it was stolen not long after Paddy's death. Two youths from a nearby estate broke into Marjorie's house, causing untold damage and making away with a whole host of items including photograph albums, bottles of whiskey, the family war medals and all of Paddy's paperwork. Though the culprits were eventually caught and some items returned, the manuscript still hadn't been found. Many of the photographs were never recovered, but some days later a policewoman spotted a cascade of typewriter paper floating down the local beck. It was Paddy's story. She managed to fish the sheets out and dry them off before returning them to their rightful owner.

Marjorie passed away on a cold October morning in 2011, surrounded by her family. It was her eighty-eighth birthday. She'd lived a full and happy life, always cherishing the years she shared with Paddy; and it's hoped that this book will prove a lasting legacy to the memory of them both.

Index